Son
The Un

Somalia – The Untold Story

The War Through the Eyes of Somali Women

Edited by
Judith Gardner and Judy El Bushra

CIIR and
Pluto Press
LONDON • STERLING, VIRGINIA

First published 2004 by
Pluto Press
345 Archway Road, London N6 5AA
and 22883 Quicksilver Drive, Sterling, VA 20166–2012, USA

www.plutobooks.com

British Library Cataloguing in Publication Data
A catalogue record for this book is available from the British Library

ISBN 0 7453 2209 3 hardback
ISBN 0 7453 2208 5 paperback

Library of Congress Cataloging-in-Publication Data
Somalia—the untold story : the war through the eyes of Somali women / edited by Judith Gardner and Judy El Bushra.
p. cm.
ISBN 0–7453–2209–3 — ISBN 0–7453–2208–5 (pbk.)
1. Women—Somalia. 2. Women refugees—Somalia. 3. Women and war—Somalia. 4. Women—Crimes against—Somalia. 5. Somalia—History—1991– 6. Somalia—Social conditions—1960– I. Title: War through the eyes of Somali women. II. Gardner, Judith. III. El-Bushra, Judy.
HQ1795.S66 2004
305.4'096773--dc22

2003020195

10 9 8 7 6 5 4 3 2 1

Designed and produced for Pluto Press by
Chase Publishing Services, Fortescue, Sidmouth, EX10 9QG, England
Typeset from disk by Stanford DTP Services, Northampton, England
Printed and bound in the European Union by
Antony Rowe Ltd, Chippenham and Eastbourne, England

Contents

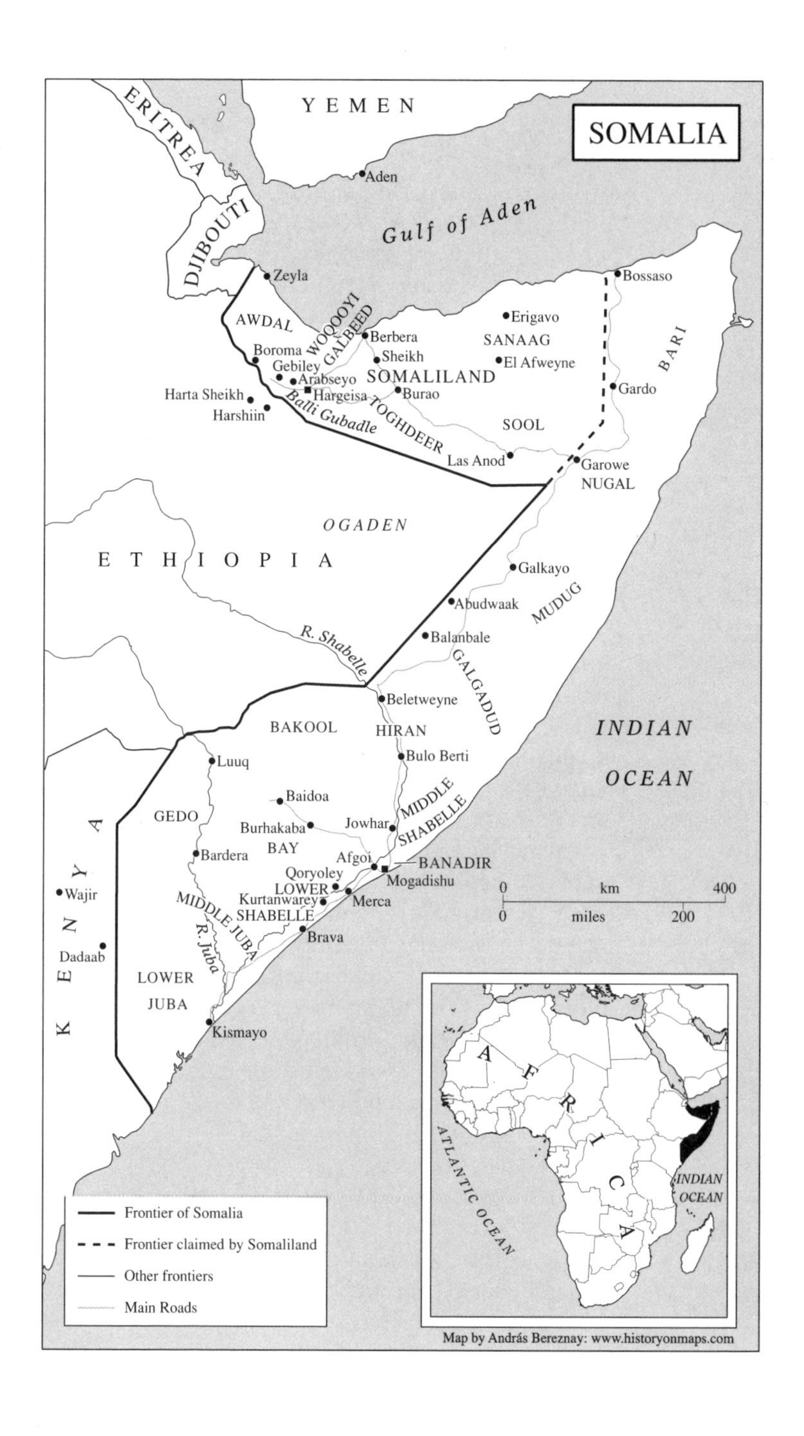
SOMALIA
YEMEN
ERITREA
DJIBOUTI
Aden
Gulf of Aden
Zeyla
Bossaso
AWDAL
WOQOOYI GALBEED
Berbera
Erigavo
SANAAG
BARI
Boroma
Sheikh
El Afweyne
Gebiley
Arabseyo
SOMALILAND
Harta Sheikh
Hargeisa
Burao
Gardo
Harshiin
Balli Gubadle
TOGHDEER
SOOL
Las Anod
Garowe
NUGAL
OGADEN
ETHIOPIA
Galkayo
Abudwaak
MUDUG
Balanbale
R. Shabelle
GALGADUD
Beletweyne
BAKOOL
HIRAN
INDIAN OCEAN
Luuq
Bulo Berti
Baidoa
MIDDLE SHABELLE
GEDO
Burhakaba
Jowhar
BAY
Bardera
Afgoi
BANADIR
Qoryoley
Mogadishu
Wajir
LOWER SHABELLE
Kurtanwarey
Merca
0 km 400
0 miles 200
MIDDLE JUBA
R. Juba
Brava
Dadaab
KENYA
LOWER JUBA
Kismayo
AFRICA
ATLANTIC OCEAN
INDIAN OCEAN
Frontier of Somalia
Frontier claimed by Somaliland
Other frontiers
Main Roads
Map by András Bereznay: www.historyonmaps.com

Abbreviations

BBC	British Broadcasting Corporation
CCS	Committee of Concerned Somalis
CIIR	Catholic Institute for International Relations
COGWO	Coalition for Grassroots Women's Organisations
COSONGO	Committee for Somaliland NGOs
FGM	Female genital mutilation
FIDA	Federation of Women Lawyers
ICRC	International Committee of the Red Cross
IGAD	Inter-Governmental Agency on Development
NGO	Non-governmental organisation
NSS	National Security Service
PENHA	Pastoral and Environmental Network for the Horn of Africa
RRA	Rahanweyne Resistance Army
SNM	Somali National Movement
SNRP	Somalia National Reconciliation Process
SOLWO	Somaliland Women's Organisation
SOWDA	Somaliland Women's Development Association
SOWRAG	Somaliland Women's Research and Action Group
SPM	Somali Patriotic Movement
SSDF	Somali Salvation Democratic Front
SWA	Somaliland Women's Association
SWDO	Somali Women's Democratic Organisation
SWM	Somali Women's Movement
TNA	Transitional National Assembly
TNG	Transitional National Government
UNDP	United Nations Development Programme
UNHCR	United Nations High Commission for Refugees
UNICEF	United Nations Children's Fund
UNIFEM	United Nations Development Fund for Women
UNOSOM	United Nations Operation in Somalia
USC	United Somali Congress
WADA	Women's Advocacy and Development Association
WAPO	Women's Advocacy and Progressive Organisation
WPDC	Wajir Peace and Development Committee
WPF	Women's Political Forum
WSP	War Torn Societies Project
WWP	Wajir Women for Peace

Acknowledgements

Our biggest thanks go to the women whose words are published here, for allowing their experiences and topics of study to be shared through this book and for their patience while the text was being finalised. We were in contact with many more women than are represented in this final version, and we would like to thank all those who showed an interest in the book and who helped along the way. These include Zamzam Abdi, Faiza Jama, Sara Haid, Faisa Loyaan, Sacda Abdi, Amina Adan, Qamar Ibrahim, Safia Giama, Faduma Mohamed Omer 'Halane' plus Anab Ali Jama and the other women of Sheffield Somali Women's Association and Welfare Group.

Thanks too to all those who shared their expertise and helped to shape the final manuscript: Amina M. Warsame, Dr Adan Abokor, Faiza Warsame, Mark Bradbury, Adam Bradbury, Judith Large, Pippa Hoyland, Ruth Jacobson and Dr David Keen; and to Joy Lawley for her invaluable commitment to the project over six years.

Among those whose voices are missing is Zeynab Aideed, whose oral account of her experience as an internally displaced person was one of the inspirations behind the book.

This book was made possible through the generous funding support of the Department for International Development, Comic Relief, NOVIB, Christian Aid, CAFOD, UNICEF Hargeisa, and ActionAid Somaliland.

Preface

The idea for this book came about during a conversation I had in 1993 with a Somali refugee who had formed a London-based Somali organisation. On the day in question this normally calm man was clearly preoccupied. It emerged that he had recently learnt that his wife, who had stayed in Somalia when he fled the country, had been captured by militia, imprisoned in a villa with many other women and girls, and repeatedly raped and sexually violated for months during some of the worst violence in Mogadishu in 1992.

Recently reunited with his wife after two years he had found her greatly changed. She had been unable to tell him about her ordeal but had eventually confided in a female friend.

This woman's experience pointed to a side of the Somali conflict that the outside world, and many Somalis themselves, were largely unaware of – the extent to which gender-based violence, most notably rape, had been used to prosecute the war.

It was this story that led CIIR to begin research for a book with the aim of ensuring that women's experiences of gender-based violence in the war would not be forgotten. Early on in the research for the book, however, it became obvious that there was much more to tell about the impact of the war on women's lives. It was also clear that one of the most powerful ways to document such history was for Somali women themselves to tell it. The result is this book, which seeks to contribute to understanding about the war's impact on women as seen through the eyes of women themselves. Here women write and talk about the war, their experiences, and the difficult choices, changes and even opportunities the war has brought. In the process they describe the position of women in Somali society, both before and since the war.

The contributors come from different parts of Somalia, including the towns of Brava, Mogadishu and Baidoa in the South, the region of Puntland in the north east, and Somaliland in the north west. Also represented is the Somali-speaking region of Kenya's north east, and Somali women refugees from the vast Somali diaspora in Yemen, Canada and Britain. That the book contains more contributions from women of northern Somalia and pastoral cultures than from the south and non-pastoral ones is the result of difficulties in collecting contributions rather than of intentional bias. Together the individuals represented here give an insight into most sides of Somalia's clan divisions. They met as a group for the first time at a workshop in the UK in 1997 to share their views and develop the book's themes.

Some of the contributors are academics and researchers, some are health professionals, social and community workers, teachers, artists. As educated, professional women they represent a tiny minority among women in Somalia where female literacy is around 12 per cent. But what they speak of is relevant to the majority of Somali women. The war has rocked, and in places cracked, the foundations of society – the family – and in Somalia women, whatever their relative wealth or poverty, gain their social value from their role as wives, mothers and sisters.

All of the contributors have been forcibly displaced by the war; many have become refugees or asylum seekers; some still are unable to return home and remain refugees. Others have built new lives for themselves in parts of the country where they may have had no previous experience but where, because of their clan identity, they are relatively safe. Almost all have endured agonies of separation and loss. For most, their nuclear family – mother, father and children – has been riven by the conflict between clans, forcing them to make heart-breaking decisions in order to save themselves and their children. For many this has meant separation from partners and children as each sought refuge in their own clan territories or outside the country.

The contributors have in common their experience as war-affected women. But most also share a resolve to overcome their adversity and help others by whatever means they can. 'I lost everything and witnessed killings and saw dead people lying in the street', says one. 'I became traumatised and suffered from stress and deep depression yet somehow I developed an inner strength and have not given up hope.'

Some of the stories in this book are painful to read and some material will upset many Somalis who may believe it shames their culture. Many contributors struggled with the rights and wrongs of talking about certain events but concluded that it is more important to tell the truth than protect cultural sensitivities. The accounts in this book are part of a wider collective memory of the war. It is a memory still being built more than 10 years on: as the United Nations Development Programme (UNDP)'s 2001 *Human Development Report* for Somalia notes, sexual violence remains a critical issue in many parts of Somalia. On the positive side, there are Somali human rights organisations in Somalia today where none existed before the war and some are trying to tackle the issue of sexual violence. The Dr Ismail Juma'ale Human Rights Centre in Mogadishu, for example, monitors and records incidents of sexual violence. Hopefully the work of such organisations will help prevent a recurrence of the kind of atrocities that happened in the early years of the war.

Judith Gardner

Editors' note

Because we have attempted to preserve each author's personal approach, the style and structure of the material varies between chapters. For example, some include notes and bibliographies, others don't.

On the assumption that Somali spellings might present difficulties for non-Somali readers all the contributors spontaneously chose the most frequently-used spellings of Somali places and names, many of which differ from the spellings according to the 1972 Somali orthography. (In 1972 the Somali language became a unified written language; before that it was oral although there were some written versions in English and some in Arabic.) For example, Baidoa is used instead of Baydhaba, Asha instead of Casha. We have respected the authors' decision and tried to maintain common spellings throughout.

A note on Somali poetry

We have included a number of poems composed by Somali women (and translated from Somali) to illustrate certain points of concern to the authors. Where the poets and translators are known, we have given their names.

In a society without a written common language until 1972 oral poetry has a special place in Somali life. The eminent Somali language scholar, the late Professor B.W. Andrezejewski noted in his introduction to *An Anthology of Somali Poetry*:

> When Sir Richard Burton visited Somalia in 1854 he found that a most striking characteristic of its inhabitants was their love of poetry ... so that the phrase 'a nation of poets' became current among people acquainted with the Horn of Africa.[1]

The 'Somali devotion to poetry' is more than an appreciation of an art form described by Andrezejewski as 'reminiscent of Classical Greek' (Andrezejewski 1993):

> Before the Second World War oral poetry was used in inter-clan and national politics as a weapon of propaganda and to bring peace where there was conflict; it was used in forging new alliances and reviving old ones; it was used to praise or criticise friends and opponents. Poetry also provided entertainment ... By custom, opinions expressed in verse could be much sharper in tone than anything said in ordinary language.[2]

The Somali dictator Siad Barre acknowledged the potency of oral poetry early in his reign when he tried and failed to stamp out anti-government poetry by imprisoning poets such as Hadraawi and Abdi Aden Gays. Women in this book (see Chapter 6 for example) refer to the way certain poems helped end outbreaks of violence during the civil war. Women have used verse to build support for women's empowerment and human rights (see Chapter 9).

Scansion, alliteration, imagery and message are all qualities by which a poem is judged in Somalia. Whilst there are no cultural restrictions on who can be a poet, they have tended to be spokespersons for their group. There are, however, poetic forms for women and poetic forms for men. The *buraanbur*, examples of which are included in this book, is the highest poetic form in women's literature and has sub-categories which include the *hobeeyo* (lullaby), the *hoyal* (work songs) and the *sitaat* (religious songs). The Somali scholars, Dahabo Farah Hassan, Amina Adan and Amina Warsame, point out that '*Gabay*, the highest of all poetic forms, is considered male territory and women are discouraged to participate in its composition'.[3]

Andrezejewski (1993) noted in *An Anthology of Somali Poetry* that 'although there have been many women poets, their poetry seldom reached the public forum; in the traditional Somali society it would have been recited within a limited circle of family and friends'. Hassan *et al* go further:

> ... you will never hear of a great woman poet in Somali history, while there have been a great many celebrated male poets, whose poems have been documented and memorised by a large number of people. ... This, of course, does not mean there were no women poets; but the reality is that nobody, neither foreigners nor the Somalis themselves, bothered to view women's literature and the themes they talked about as important enough to be recorded. Even the women themselves did not see their importance because they had internalised the idea that their culture was of less significance than men's. (Hassan *et al* 1995)

NOTES

1. B.W. & Sheila Andrezejewski (1993) *An Anthology of Somali Poetry* (Indiana: Indiana University Press).
2. Cited in Faraax Cawl (1982) *Ignorance is the Enemy of Love* (London: Zed Press).
3. Dahabo Farah Hassan *et al* (1995) 'Somalia: Poetry as Resistance Against Colonialism and Patriarchy', in Saskia Wieringa (ed.) *Subversive Women: Historical Experiences of Gender and Resistance* (London: Zed Books).

Introduction

Judith Gardner and Judy El Bushra

Why were you born?
Why did you arrive at dusk?
In your place a boy
Would have been welcome
Sweet dates would have
Been my reward.
The clan would be rejoicing
A lamb would have
Been slaughtered
For the occasion,
And I would have
Been glorified.[1]

Somalia grabbed international attention in 1992 as the world's media broadcast images of a people dying from hunger in the midst of a terrifyingly violent conflict between competing warlords and their drug-crazed fighters vying for control of a collapsed state. Later that year television cameras followed American troops as they landed on the beaches of the capital Mogadishu to lead what turned out to be a disastrous United Nations intervention intended to end hunger and restore peace.

The Somali state had collapsed in 1991 as civil war engulfed Mogadishu and the corrupt and oppressive military regime of President Mohamed Siad Barre was forced from power. After 30 years of independence Somalia had ceased to function as a single state. In May 1991 the north west regions seceded from the rest of Somalia to form the independent Republic of Somaliland.[2] Here a fragile peace was quickly established and fledgling governmental and non-governmental organisations emerged to take responsibility for governance, security and reconstruction. Elsewhere, notably in Mogadishu and further south, Siad Barre's fall gave way to clan-based militia warfare that brought terror to hundreds of thousands of people.

Described by a US diplomat in 1992 as 'the worst humanitarian crisis faced by any people in the world', Somalia had by the end of that year seen an estimated 500,000 people – 300,000 of them children – die in the war and subsequent famine.[3] Some 1.5 million Somalis had fled to neighbouring countries and beyond.

But the world's attention soon switched to the atrocities of the Rwandan genocide in 1994, followed later by the crisis in Kosovo. Only as a result of the post-11 September war on terrorism has Somalia again touched the headlines in the West, this time as a suspected haven for Islamic terrorist groups.

Historical background

The Somali state was created by the partition of the Horn of Africa by Britain, Italy and France, and the Abyssinian empire, during the scramble for Africa in the nineteenth century. Formed by colonial treaties, Somalia's borders today bear no resemblance to the distribution of the ethnic Somali people who, as well as predominating in Somalia itself, inhabit lands within neighbouring Kenya, Ethiopia and Djibouti.[4] During the colonial period Somalia itself did not exist as a single state, divided as it was between a northern British Somaliland and a southern Italian Somaliland. On 26 June 1960 Britain granted independence to the north and four days later the Italian-administered UN Trusteeship Territory of Somalia achieved independence. On 1 July 1960 the people of the former British and Italian territories united to form the Somali Republic.

Since May 1991 Somalia has again been two countries. To the north is the self-proclaimed Republic of Somaliland where amid the physical wreckage left by conflict, the population is rebuilding and rehabilitating the country. Although its secession is unrecognised internationally – and is contested by many Somalis – Somaliland has its own government and constitution, police force and judicial system, and has enjoyed stability and peace since 1997. The situation is very different in most of the rest of Somalia. A Transitional National Government formed in 2000 struggles to control even the area of Mogadishu in which it is based. Even though the scale of warfare has diminished much of central and southern Somalia remains volatile as warlords compete for resources.[5] Kidnappings, rape, banditry and extortion are a constant threat to security.

The civil war

Somalia's civil war of 1978–91 has commonly been analysed as a conflict between competing clan-based groups. Identity-based conflicts are not unique to Somalia. A tendency to interpret the war in clan terms emerges in several of the testimonies in this book, in which women describe how life or death could hinge on a person's claims to clan membership. And as Dahabo Isse's testimony illustrates, a clan-based interpretation of the war influenced the UN's controversial peace-keeping operation in Somalia. (Bradbury 1997)

The clan certainly is the basis of social organisation among ethnic Somalis, as detailed in Chapter 7; and clan loyalty was used by warlords to mobilise support for the war. Yet the clan system was not a cause of the Somali civil war. The causes lie in a complex set of issues relating to distribution of resources and power, Somalia's economic marginalisation in the world economy, long-term corruption and exploitation, oppression and uneven development.[6]

General Mohamed Siad Barre's military coup in October 1969 overthrew a democratically elected but corrupt civilian government, suspended the constitution and banned political parties. In their place Siad Barre set up a Supreme Revolutionary Council of military and police officials and declared 'war on ignorance, hunger and tribalism as enemies of the people'. Exploiting the Cold War superpower politics of the time, he declared Somalia a socialist state in 1970 and introduced Soviet-backed 'Scientific Socialism' as the ideological framework for the country's future development.

Although Scientific Socialism was progressive in some areas – for example improving literacy and women's status – its prevailing impact was a high degree of centralised state control. This found expression in many aspects of daily life, press censorship, the banning of trade unions and (as described in Part 2, Section 3: 'Women's rights, leadership and political empowerment') the Party's manipulation of civil organisations such as the Somali women and youth associations. The regime's priority was to maintain political control at all costs.

In 1977 Siad Barre invaded the Ogaden region of Ethiopia in an attempt to regain lands and people separated from the Somali state by colonial treaty. Somalia was heavily defeated when the Soviet Union switched sides and backed Ethiopia in the war. Defeat in the Ogaden was soon followed by the emergence of armed opposition groups within Somalia – first the Somali Salvation Democratic Front (SSDF) formed in 1978 by military officers from the Majeerteen clan in the north east, and then in 1980 the Somali National Movement (SNM) drawing support mainly from the Isaq clan in the north-west. But it took another decade to overthrow Siad Barre. During this period, the government prosecuted a scorched-earth policy against the Majeerteen and increasingly repressive policies and human rights abuses against the Isaq. Barre increasingly concentrated power and resources within his own clan and sub-clan family, manipulating Somalia's clan system to his own ends.

By the early 1980s the country's economy was starting to collapse, with gross national product (GNP) per capita just US$280 per year and an estimated 70 per cent of the rural population living in absolute poverty. Security expenditure accounted for nearly three quarters of government spending, and consumed more than half as much again as was earned from exports.[7]

In May 1988 the SNM attacked and briefly captured Burao and Hargeisa, the two main towns in the north west. The government's response was savage: relentless aerial bombardments destroyed most of the buildings in both towns and forced thousands to flee. Shukri Hariir's testimony is an eye-witness account of what happened. By March 1989 an estimated 50,000 people in the north west had been killed by their own government.[8] This massacre eventually prompted the international community to cut most development aid to the country, which was by now bankrupt.

Siad Barre's downfall came three years later when an alliance between three armed opposition groups led to an attack on Mogadishu by the United Somali Congress (USC)[9] headed by General Mohamed Farah Aideed, in December 1990. This is considered the start of the civil war in the south, a war that has yet to be laid to rest.

Somalia since 1991

Siad Barre's downfall did not bring an end to injustice and misery for the people in Somalia. The loose coalition of forces that had defeated the dictator disintegrated with the sudden collapse of government institutions. The country fragmented into areas controlled by warlords and their heavily armed clan-based militias. The USC split into two power blocs headed by General Mohamed Farah Aideed and Ali Mahdi.

For some 16 months, from December 1990 to March 1992, when the United Nations eventually brokered a ceasefire, there was almost continuous warfare in the south as clans fought for control of resources, especially land and water.[10] As many as 25,000 civilians died in the first four months of fighting in Mogadishu alone. The coastal towns of Merca, Brava and Kismayo and the inland town of Baidoa, in the country's most fertile zone, suffered waves of invasions by fighters of the different clan-based opposition militia groups. Widespread rape of women, mass executions, destruction and expropriation of agricultural land, looting of grain stores and livestock, and destruction of water supplies and homes led to massive displacement of people into other parts of Somalia, Kenya, Ethiopia and Yemen. By the time the United Nations took action at the end of 1992, several hundred thousand people had died of starvation and hunger-related diseases. Testimonies by Halimo Elmi, Habiba Osman, Amina Sayid and Dahabo Isse provide first-hand accounts of this period of the war.

The governance of Somalia since 1991

The formation of the Republic of Somaliland, May 1991

The Act of Union which had united former Italian and British territories in 1960 into the Republic of Somalia was broken in May 1991 when the people of the north west regions of Somalia announced the secession of the Republic of Somaliland, a territory demarcated by the former colonial boundaries separating British and Italian rule. This act was the decision of a clan conference in Burao at which the Isaq and non-Isaq clans (Darod and Dir) living in Somaliland reconciled after a long period of animosity and civil war. It was a decision taken in response to the pre-emptive formation in February 1991 of an interim government in Mogadishu by the USC. The people of the north west, particularly the Isaq, feared that further rule from Mogadishu would lead to a repeat of the persecution they had suffered under Siad Barre, when more than 50,000 people in the north west had been killed and more than 600,000 forcibly displaced. Secession was also a pragmatic move to distance the north from the factional fighting in the south; it signalled that northerners had no territorial claims on the south. The decision to declare independence from the rest of Somalia was made without consulting Somalia's numerous other political factions. Somaliland, although functioning since secession as a separate state, remains unrecognised by the international community.

The formation of the Puntland administration, 1998

On 23 July 1998 the political and traditional leaders of Somalia's north eastern regions declared the autonomous Puntland State of Somalia under the presidency of former SSDF chairman, Colonel Abdullahi Yusuf. A nine-member cabinet was appointed and a 69-member parliament, including five seats reserved for women. According to its founding charter Puntland is a first step towards rebuilding a future united but federal Somalia.[11] Even though it lacked the infrastructure and potential revenue sources of Somaliland, the administration's first term did see the establishment of a police force and integration of former militia members into a new security force. In June 2001, however, the administration's three-year term expired and failure to agree a transfer of power led to a constitutional crisis which has now threatened the region's security.

Transitional National Government for Somalia, 2000

The formation of the Transitional National Government (TNG) in August 2000 was the most significant development in the politics of Somalia for a decade. The TNG was the outcome of a lengthy process of public dialogue and negotiation that placed more emphasis on civil society involvement rather than factional representation. In contrast to other Somali peace conferences it formally included women and minor clans among the voting delegates. Although the conference attracted participants from most of Somalia's regions, some prominent Mogadishu-based faction leaders chose not to participate, as did the Somaliland authorities and the formal Puntland representatives. The politico-military leadership of the Rahanweyne groups of clans, the Rahanweyne Resistance Army (RRA) took part but withdrew support once the conference was ended.

Established in Mogadishu in October 2000, the TNG has a 245-member Transitional National Assembly (of which 25 seats are reserved for women – see Chapter 9) and a president and prime minister supported by a 25-member cabinet selected from the 75 ministerial posts. It enjoyed international acceptance in the UN General Assembly, the Arab League and the African Union, which gave Somalia formal representation in these bodies for the first time in a decade. However, it was slow to win support within Somalia. In October 2002, with conflict increasing, the Inter-Governmental Agency on Development (IGAD) launched a 14th internationally sponsored peace process, held in Kenya. At the time of writing, April 2003, this process was still ongoing.

People and livelihoods

Somalia is often misrepresented as a country with a homogeneous population, culture and language. Its total population in 2001 was estimated to be 6.3 million. (UNDP 2001) The vast majority are ethnic Somalis (of Hamitic origin) which comprise two distinct groups associated with one of two livelihood systems: nomadic pastoralists, who are the majority, and agro-pastoralists.[12] In addition, there are also significant populations of non-ethnic Somalis in the southern part of the country.

Much of Somalia is semi-desert with few seasonal water sources and therefore suitable only for nomadic pastoralism – practised by about 59 per cent of the population. (UNDP 2001) Agriculture is confined to the areas of the fertile Shabelle and Juba river valleys (see map), and the valleys of the northern escarpments. The clan basis of the social organisation of pastoral society is explained in detail in Chapter 7, 'Women, clan identity and peace-building'.

Somalis from the clan lineages of the Darod, Isaq, Hawiye and Dir are by tradition nomadic-pastoralists and the pastoral culture has become the dominant political culture in Somalia. Their language, *af-Somali*, was made the official and unifying language of Somalia after independence. They include the 'outcast' groups such as the Tumal, Midgan, Eyle, Yahar and Yibr. Historically politically marginalised, Somalis from the clan lineages of the Digil and Mirifle clans, known collectively as the Rahanweyne, are traditionally agro-pastoralists. Their language, *mai* or *af-maimai*, comes from the same Cushitic root as *af-Somali* but the two languages are not mutually intelligible.

There has been tragedy and loss for all groups in the civil war but some groups have suffered more than others. The Rahanweyne agro-pastoralists, inhabitants of the fertile lands between the Juba and Shabelle rivers which were the epicentre of the war and the 1992 famine, experienced some of the worst of the war's horror, as Habiba Osman's testimony describes.

Somalia's non-ethnic Somali populations, sometimes termed 'minority groups', include the riverine semi-subsistence farming communities of the Juba and Shabelle valleys – also referred to as the people of the *Gosha* (meaning 'dense forest'). These people do not constitute a single ethnic or political group but since colonial times have been classified as a group by outsiders. The majority are descended from slaves brought to Somalia from East Africa. Considered inferior to ethnic Somalis by the colonial and post-independence powers alike, their history has been one of subjugation. Besteman sums up the stigma attached to the people of the *Gosha* who 'speak Somali, practice Islam, share Somali cultural values, are legally Somali citizens and most consider themselves members of Somali clans[13] ... however, many look different, and so are considered different by Somalis'. (Besteman, 1995) The people of the *Gosha* inhabit an area of fertile arable land in a country that is predominantly semi-desert; in so far as the civil was has been a war over land and wealth, the *Gosha* peoples have been one of the main victims.[14]

The other major non-ethnic Somali people are the Benadari – including Hamari, Barawanese and Bajuni. These groups populate the urban coastal settlements, historically important trading centres linking Somalia with the Gulf and Asia as well East African ports to the south. Rich in cultural heritage, and claiming descent from Arab, Persian, Pakistani, Portuguese and Somali ancestors who came as early migrant settlers to the Somali coastline,[15] these groups are important artisans and traders. The skills they are renowned for include fishing,[16] leatherwork and weaving. The Barawans of Brava have their own language, Jimini, which is related to Swahili, the language spoken by the Bajuni fishing community. They traditionally practice endogamous marriage, that is marrying within the extended family; this is in contrast to the exogamous marriage practice of pastoral groups. Amina Sayid's testimony includes more detail on the culture of the Barawanese.

Being outside of the Somali clan system, these unarmed groups had no protection during the war and were killed in great numbers by militias and looters. One analyst has concluded that 'the civil war may represent the last stage of the[ir] extermination'.[17]

With its predominantly rural population, more than 70 per cent, Somalia is often portrayed as a country of nomads; however, by the 1980s Somalia had one of the fastest growing urban populations in Africa (UNDP 2001) and a growing urban and educated middle class. Migration to urban areas, which is once again on the increase, did reverse during the war as people moved back to their clan territories to find safety from the conflict. The war has thus led to a redistribution of Somalia's educated, urban elite. Formerly concentrated in the cities of Mogadishu and Hargeisa where they were employed as civil servants, commercial and private sector workers, and public sector employees, they are now scattered throughout the country in the small regional towns and villages where they had rural clan relatives.[18]

These regional settlements, such as Bossaso in the north east and Beletweyne in the west, have experienced rapid population growth over the past decade. The population of Bossaso for example is estimated to have increased from 10,000 to 60,000 since 1991.

(UNDP 2001) Lacking the infrastructure and services to cope with such influxes, these new urban magnets also lack ready employment opportunities. As discussed in Part 2, a high proportion of male urban dwellers are unemployed and depend on income from relatives, usually female, who in turn depend on informal employment, petty trading and remittances from relatives in the diaspora.

Several chapters in this book refer to the significance of the remittance economy. This has grown in importance during the war as the diaspora has expanded. Studies indicate that the main beneficiaries are urban households with educated and skilled members in the diaspora. (UNDP 2002)

Gender relations[19]

In Somali culture all children are considered a blessing from God. However, it is a patriarchal society and greater symbolic value is placed on a male than a female child. Generally, the birth of a boy child is celebrated with the slaughter of two animals, while for a girl only one is slaughtered, if any. Male homicide requires twice the compensation a female homicide demands and revenge killings, obligatory for men, are rare for women. For both women and men, having children is key to one's place in the clan structure (see Chapter 7). Children, particularly boys, are the continuation of the clan and boys will continue their fathers' lineage. A childless woman or man is called *goblan*, meaning barren and unproductive – 'the worst curse that may be wished on someone'.[20]

Living in a highly structured patrilineal society women and girls in Somalia are traditionally assigned a status inferior to men, who take the dominant roles in society, religion and politics. However, in the words of three Somali women scholars, 'Somali women, whether nomadic or urban, have never been submissive, either to natural calamities or to social oppression.' (Hassan *et al* 1995)

Strict division of labour makes women responsible for dealing with domestic tasks from finding and preparing food to child-rearing and water and firewood collection. Having to do domestic chores leaves little or no time for involvement in community decisions or education.[21] And although within most groups women have always played a significant role in the economy, traditionally their sphere of influence and decision-making was, publicly at least, confined to the home (see Chapter 9). As described in Chapter 6, the exception is during conflict when a woman may be expected to play the role of peace envoy or messenger between her husband's clan and her father's clan. Unlike men whose status in the community increases with age, a woman's status diminishes when her child-bearing years come to an end. (Warsame 2001)

With the exception of some cultures, such as the Bravanese, women are traditionally allowed to work outside the home, especially when it is in the family's interests, as in agro-pastoral and nomadic pastoralist families. According to gender researcher Amina Warsame, whilst men are traditionally the family provider women have always sought some degree of economic independence, whether through their own labours or by saving some of the household budget provided by their husband. Within the pastoral community livestock represents a family's wealth and was traditionally the property of men. A pastoral woman could not own livestock except those she could claim as *meher* (bride price) on her husband's death (see Chapter 2). However, women had full control over the sale and exchange of livestock products such as milk and ghee and used these resources to provide for both the household needs and their, and her own future economic security.

As described elsewhere in this book, one impact of the war is that women are increasingly replacing men as the breadwinners of the family. This is a major change in gender relations and the household economy. Before the war, as one Somali woman commented, 'whatever a woman earned was for her and it was shameful for others, especially men, to be dependent on her'.

Progressive reforms were made to Family Law in 1975 assuring women equal rights with men and making discrimination against women illegal. However, little was done to educate the general population about women's equality, or to enforce the provisions of the law. Hence the reforms made no impact outside the urban areas and elites. Nothing really changed for the vast majority of women who are rural and uneducated. Currently, in the parts of Somalia where administration and governance is restored, the reforms to the Family Law play no part in contemporary legal practice, discredited completely by their association with Siad Barre's regime. Custom, tradition and lack of education have ensured that few women have ever reached senior positions in government or the civil service. Publicly influential women have been the exception rather than the rule.

A woman's or girl's life will be determined by: how rich or poor her family is; whether she is literate or illiterate, urban or rural based; and, if rural, whether she is part of a pastoralist, agro-pastoralist or sedentary agricultural social group. In the pastoral society described in Chapter 1 women are valued for the role they play in the economy and for the livestock they bring to the family on marriage. Life is perhaps hardest for a girl born into a landless agricultural family.[22] The same is probably true for boys.

Even before the war Somalia had among the lowest literacy rates in the world for both women and men. (See Appendix 2 – 'Somalia in facts and figures'). The decade-long conflict has severely affected all children's chances of accessing education. The war has made families more dependent on girls to substitute for or help their working mothers. This has diminished still further their chances of entering, let alone completing, even primary level education.

Lacking education, and especially Arabic comprehension, Somali women tend not to be well-versed in Islam and Islamic *shari'a* law. In communities where there has been a rise in Islamic fundamentalism since the war it is increasingly common for religious references to be used by members of the community to exert control over women.

In Somali society men too lack education and are brought up to fulfil traditionally ascribed roles and expectations. Generally assumed to have a social status superior to women, and free from everyday domestic responsibilities, men are assigned the dominant roles in religion, economics and politics. Society holds them responsible for most of the decision-making from the household upwards. According to oral tradition, in times of conflict 'a man who was engaged in killing and looting was usually admired and praised, while a peace advocate was scorned and dismissed as weak and worthless'.[23, 24]

Able to take up to four wives through polygamous marriage, a source of great misery to women, men are expected to be responsible for the maintenance of the family as provider and protector. Men are expected to act in prescribed ways to promote the family's survival. In the nomadic pastoral context, as Chapter 1 describes, this may mean separating from the family in hard times in order to maximise remaining family members' access to whatever resources are available. As protectors men are expected to take part in wars or build alliances for peace, and if necessary die for the sake of the family and clan.

Somalia – the untold story

This book consists of nine authored papers and seven testimonies, all but one by Somali women. Four of the testimonies were tape-recorded in English and transcribed; three were given verbally in English and then submitted as written testimonies in Somali, and then translated. Edited versions of the testimonies were checked by their authors. The vivid detail of the testimonies is characteristic of Somalia's tradition of oral culture, and will form part of a collective memory.

Of the papers three relate to research the authors had conducted before the war; the other six derive from the authors' or contributors' experience of the war period. Three chapters, 'Women and peace-making in Somaliland', 'Women, clan identity and peace-building', and 'Post-war recovery and political participation', were compiled by the editors from written texts and interviews with the authors and other women.

The book is divided into two parts – 'Women's experiences of the war' and 'Women's responses to the war'. Part 1, looking at women's experiences, includes two chapters setting out the normative situation for women pastoralists, Chapter 1, by Rhoda Ibrahim, and marriage in Somali society, Chapter 2 by Sadia Ahmed. In contrast Chapter 3, by Fowzia Musse, records the profound violation of social norms by the extensive use of rape and sexual violence against women as a weapon of war. Part 1 also includes personal testimonies of three women, Habiba Osman, Amina Sayid and Shukri Hariir. These women are from three different cultural groups in Somalia.

Key themes in Part 1 include the slaughter and loss of men and boys which occurred in the first year of the war. This echoes a caution from the organisation Justice Africa that, 'the idea of men, somehow "escaping" from famine or conflict zones, abandoning women to suffer, is not generally borne out by the facts. We need to be cautious in assuming that men somehow "benefit" from conflict: most of them do not.'[25]

Part 2, looking at the impact of the war on women and their responses, is divided into three sections: 'Changing roles and responsibilities in the family', 'Women mobilise for peace', and 'Women's rights, leadership and political empowerment'. The first section, looking at changes in the roles and responsibilities of women and men at the family level, includes Chapter 5 by Amina Warsame describing women's involvement in trade. Ladan Affi's report in Chapter 4 looks at female-headed households among Somali diaspora communities in Canada. Shedding light on family upheaval and changing roles, but from the point of view of an internally displaced woman, Halimo Elmi's testimony deals with the impact of the war on her and her extended family, which represented three of the opposing clan groups in the war.

The second section of Part 2 ('Women mobilise for peace') consists of three chapters: two detail the role women have played in peace-building processes. The third is a gendered analysis of the clan system and women's position at the centre of both suffering and peace-building. The final section of the book – 'Women's rights, leadership and political empowerment' – looks at the important leadership and organisational roles women have taken on in the community as a result of the war. It also highlights the fact that although women are playing more significant roles than ever before in terms of the economy and decision-making at family and community level, this has not yet led to equal inclusion of women at the political level. Chapter 9 ('Post-war recovery and political participation') documents women's collective response to emergency and post-war recovery needs in their communities through the formation of civil society organisations. It also charts the struggle of women throughout Somalia and Somaliland to translate their aspirations for equal political rights into reality. This section includes personal testimonies by two women who, like numerous others, demonstrated leadership and bravery within their communities: Dahabo Isse who worked with the International Committee of the Red Cross feeding programme which saved the lives of over 1 million people displaced by the war and famine in the south; and Noreen Michael Mariano, a significant figure in the establishment of peace and rebuilding of Hargeisa before her death in May 2000. The book closes with a tribute to Somalia's best-known female leader to emerge from the war, the late Starlin Abdi Arush of Merca who was killed in October 2002.

Women and conflict

The book aims to reflect the experiences and perceptions of Somali women in and about war. It seeks to contribute to our understanding of the conflict in Somalia, and hence of conflict as a phenomenon. Describing war entirely through the eyes of women, the commentaries and testimonies show just how cataclysmic the Somalia conflict was for men, women and children, and for Somali society in general. The experiences of war described in this book are often shocking, but they appear to have been similar in different regions of Somalia, and for different clans and other social groups, despite the differing political and social contexts. Compare, for example, Habiba Osman's account of the fighting around Baidoa and during the fall of Mogadishu with that of Shukri Hariir in Hargeisa in 1988.

Conflict has not been the only factor driving change in Somalia in significant ways. Urbanisation was already having an impact on Somali society prior to war breaking out. Rhoda Ibrahim shows how Somali pastoralists have always needed to be able to adapt to drought and sedentarisation, while Amina Warsame describes livelihood diversification as the main risk-avoidance strategy of Somali society whatever mode of livelihood was practised. The violence, insecurity and penury that accompany war have accelerated changes in social relations, and increased the importance of emergency coping strategies such as petty trade; they have also made the economy dependent on remittances.

The connections between conflict and gender have been the subject of a growing interest, over the last two decades in particular, in academic, policy, and humanitarian and development circles. The material in this book contributes to this debate by presenting women's own descriptions of their experiences of conflict and their responses to it. Their evidence throws light on three broad areas: women's experiences of conflict, the impact of conflict on gender relations, and women's participation in the political arena and in particular in peace initiatives.

Writers in this book have few illusions about women's peace-loving nature, since several describe how both women and men took part in or encouraged violence, often turning against neighbours. Dahabo Isse, for example, describing her attempts to set up secure feeding centres for malnourished adults and children in Mogadishu, shows how threatened the clan structures were by this strategy, and how both male and female clan members resented her for undermining their interests. Halimo Elmi describes scenes from Mogadishu of women mobilising their menfolk to take up arms and fight. The extent of women's involvement as war activists through, for example, financial backing for certain warlords, paid for through remittances and the sale of personal possessions, is an under-researched aspect of the war. Speaking to women at a peace conference in 1997, Fadumo Jibril summarised the situation: 'Let us not pretend innocence ... Women have empowered and encouraged their husbands, their leaders and their militia to victimise their fellow countrymen.'[26] Even less is known about the small minority of women who took up arms alongside men both in the civil war and as part of the armed liberation struggle of the 1980s.

However, the testimonies in this book also show time and again that women's response to violence and misfortune is often to provide assistance, whatever the cost to themselves. Women like Halimo Elmi, a midwife who after settling in eastern Somaliland provided the only medical services for miles around, or Noreen Mariano, who helped restore Hargeisa maternity hospital and organised women to take part in community rebuilding, have ensured the provision of basic medical and social services at a time when all else was destroyed. Their work has been critical in preserving life and in facilitating the huge task of social reconstruction facing Somalia and Somaliland.

Many women have become involved in trade and commerce, as Amina Warsame describes. They are meeting their obligations to ensure food security for their families, but in ways that require new skills and a new spirit of entrepreneurialism and independence. Moreover, women's trading activities are providing retail and financial services throughout the country, and hence supporting food security at a national level.

Women and political participation

What impact does conflict have on women's perception of their social position and hence on their potential for social activism, either as individuals or groups? If their experiences of conflict lead them to develop their role as carers, does their record of achievement create space for them to be accepted into the political arena? Do women as a group have interests that transcend the divisions which split a society in conflict? The chapters in this book on women and leadership and on women and peace provide rich insights into these questions, and describe how women's organising evolved from the height of the war in the late 1980s up to a period of consolidation in the mid 1990s and beyond.

The book presents two descriptions of women-initiated peace processes, one in Somaliland described by Zeynab Mohamed Hassan and others in Chapter 6, and the other in a region of north east Kenya affected by Somalia's civil war, described by Dekha Ibrahim in Chapter 8. These provide empirical evidence about what motivates women to work for peace, and how they do it. In both cases the women had had enough of the violence; they believed it was sapping the society's strength. In the Somaliland case women used the methods of anti-war protest traditionally open to women in the region, such as interposing themselves between the fighting forces, wearing white head-scarves, holding prayer-meetings and composing poems. In the Kenyan example women travelled around the country in teams offering to mediate, organising cultural festivals, and dispensing grants (from funding they had raised) to rehabilitation projects.

In both cases women have helped to prevent violence and registered the legitimacy of women's activism in this area. A number of the accounts in this book suggest that women's success in peace-building owes much to their particular position in the clan system. Chapter 7, on 'Women, clan identity and peace-building', spells out the analysis made by a group of contributors to this book. According to this view women lack an exclusive clan identity which stems from their exclusion from the system of *diya*-paying groups. (This is in contrast to men, whose sense of identity is intimately bound up with their clan membership.) Women are thus able to move with relative ease between clans and see beyond clan interests. Dekha Ibrahim, a Somali Kenyan, identifies a number of other practices that have traditionally enabled women to be peace-builders, such as their role in providing hospitality in negotiations and the respect given to women's opinions. Yet the women's successes to date have been limited, hard-won and generally unrecognised, and the book suggests that part of the reason for this lies in Somali society's failure generally to accept women as equal to men in the political arena.

Section 3 of Part 2 (on women in leadership) notes that before the war increasing numbers of women were joining the professional classes. These women, including most of the contributors to this book, tended to work in the education, health, social and community development fields, and included both practitioners and researchers. When war broke out many were keen to contribute their skills in the absence of organised services. Numerous Somali women's organisations in both north and south and in the diaspora were founded by such women.

Women's organisations not only supported women struggling to meet their domestic roles, but they also provided a platform through which women could contribute to reconciliation and reconstruction processes. Interviews with Noreen Mariano, Shukri Hariir and Zeynab Mohamed Hassan describe how women, building on their experience of the women's movement in the 1950s and 1960s, re-organised Hargeisa Hospital, managed funds for the re-integration of demobilised ex-fighters, and supported the re-establishment of the police force.

Women's organisations then lobbied for female participation in political fora. When it came to the process of forming the Transitional National Government, where representation was based strictly on clan lines, they argued that women represented their 'own clan' (see interview with Zakia Alin, Chapter 9). In other words they transcended clan politics and their objective was the welfare of the country as a whole. In fact it was this very detachment from clan politics that prevented male politicians from fully accepting them into the political arena (and which discouraged other women from supporting them, as Zakia Alin suggests). Although they were welcomed and respected as informal contributors to political debates (much like the meetings under the tree described by Dekha Ibrahim in the Somali areas of north east Kenya), their inability to represent clans excluded them from political decision-making.

Changing gender relations

Does war change gender relations? Does it provide opportunities for improvements in women's status? There have been both setbacks and gains for women. They have borne the brunt of the stress on marriage and the family that the Somalia conflict has engendered. Exploring how conflict has affected the institution of marriage, Halimo Elmi points out that in a social system based on exogamous marriage, war has broken families apart, severing relations between husband and wife and between mothers and their children and grandchildren. She suggests that conflict has reduced marriage to a matter of pursuing personal interests rather than being a genuine partnership of equals.

Rhoda Ibrahim shows how in pastoral communities, increases in the proportion of female-headed households have led to changes in herd management practices and to women's greater involvement in livestock trade. Amina Warsame describes how women, able to travel more safely than men, have used their position in the clan system to create new economic niches for themselves. Ladan Affi traces these changes into the diaspora, and suggests that women have responded more positively than men have to the opportunities offered them in exile.

But does this mean that gender relations are changing fundamentally, or are women simply finding more ingenious ways of discharging their traditional roles? Sadia Ahmed points out that although Somali marriage practices reflect a patriarchal society, they also enshrine areas of choice for women, and offer them support and protection from their natal family. Dekha Ibrahim likewise suggests that conflict has enabled some women to find new and more fulfilling roles albeit without shaking the pillars of a patriarchal society. As Ladan Affi points out, despite the increased respect women have acquired as a result of their increasing economic responsibility, most men and women still believe women are fundamentally inferior to men. Gender roles may have been rearranged and adapted but women have generally not acquired access to decision-making fora.

In a separate study in Somaliland Amina Warsame points to the added work burdens for women which their new roles have demanded. (Warsame 2001) She points to the possibility of a male backlash against women, while there have been no corresponding changes in women's social status or legal rights. She concludes that

> the challenge facing women in Somaliland today is how can the gains that they made be consolidated and built on and how can the negative tendencies be done away with. Unless some meaningful workable strategies are worked out fast, whatever benefits that Somaliland women gained so far will be thrown into the dustbins of history.

NOTES

1. A poem by a Somali woman, name unknown, voicing a mother's frustration at the attitude of society regarding the worth of female children and regretting the birth of her daughter (Hassan *et al* 1995). The Somali original of this poem was at one time held on audio cassette in the Somali Academy of Arts and Culture but has been lost in the destruction of Mogadishu.
2. 'Somaliland' refers to the north west region; otherwise 'Somalia' will be used to describe the country defined by the borders with Kenya, Djibouti and Ethiopia including Somaliland.
3. John Prendergast, quoted in Mark Bradbury (1997) *Somaliland Country Report* (London: CIIR).
4. Although the human and structural devastation of Somalia's civil war has been felt mainly within its borders, Kenya, Ethiopia and Djibouti bore the brunt of the massive displacement in the early years of the war.
5. UNDP (2001) *Somalia Human Development Report 2001* (Nairobi: UNDP).
6. See for example C. Besteman & L. Cassanelli (eds) (2000) *The Struggle for Land in Southern Somalia: The War Behind the War* (London: Haan).
7. Ahmed I. Samatar (1985) 'Underdevelopment in Somalia: Dictatorship without Hegemony', *Africa Today*, 32, No.3, pp 23–40.

8. For details of this period in Somalia's history see Africa Watch (1990) *Somalia. A Government at War with its Own People. Testimonies About the Killings and the Conflict in the North.* (New York: Human Rights Watch).
9. The battle to oust Siad Barre lasted almost two months. He fled Mogadishu on 26 January 1991, twice attempting to recapture it before fleeing into Kenya in April 1992, leaving devastation in his wake.
10. Mohamed Haji Mukhtar (1996) 'The Plight of the Agro-pastoral Society of Somalia', *Review of African Political Economy* No.70: 543–53.
11. Ahmed Farah (2001) in *Rebuilding Somalia: Issues and Possibilities for Puntland* (London: War Torn Societies Programme/Haan Associates).
12. According to tradition these two clan-based groups are descended from the two sons, Samaale and Sab, of a common legendary ancestor.
13. Catherine Besteman notes that 'the ties of affiliation Gosha individuals felt to their Somali clans may very well be overridden by the lack of protection these clans provided Gosha villagers during the years of pillage and violence'. C. Besteman (1995) 'The Invention of Gosha: Slavery, Colonialism, and Stigma in Somali History', in Ali Jimale Ahmed (ed.) *The Invention of Somalia* (Trenton NJ: Red Sea Press).
14. For information on the impact of Siad Barre's government and the war on the people of the *Gosha* see Ken Menkhaus, 'From Feast to Famine: Land and the State in Somalia's Lower Jubba Valley' in Besteman & Cassanelli 2000.
15. Many have an affinity with other East African coastal communities of Swahili origin, such as in Mombasa.
16. Despite having the longest coastline in Africa, Somalia's fish stocks remain an underdeveloped resource. During the 1980s fishing contributed about 2 per cent to gross national product with an artisan fishing community employing more than 30,000 people.
17. Ken Menkhaus, Special Political Advisor to the UN Operation in Somalia, quoted in Minority Rights (1997) *War: The Impact on Minority and Indigenous Children* (London: MRG).
18. In Somaliland peace and security are vastly better than other parts of Somalia; the capital city, Hargeisa, is re-establishing itself as a magnet for displaced middle-class Somalis.
19. Christine Choi Ahmed notes that 'in current significant histories written about Somalia, women and gender dynamics are excluded'; Christine Choi Ahmed (1995) 'Finely Etched Chattel: The Invention of the Somali Woman', Ali Jimale (ed.) *The Invention of Somalia* (Trenton NJ: Red Sea Press). The same point is made by Hassan *et al* 1995. Oral data and unpublished material collected before the war by the Somali women researchers with the Women's Documentation Unit of the Somali Academy of Arts and Culture have been destroyed or are missing as a result of the war.
20. Safia Giama (2000) *Caring for Our Children. The Somali Tradition* (New York: UNICEF).
21. Amina M. Warsame (2001) *Queens Without Crowns: Somaliland Women's Changing Roles and Peace Building*, Horn of Africa Series 4 (Kenya: Life & Peace Institute/Somaliland Women's Research and Action Group).

22. UNICEF (1998) *Somalia. Situation of Women and Children Report 1997/8* (Nairobi: UNICEF Somalia).
23. Somalia Delegation of the International Committee of the Red Cross (1997) *Spared from the Spear: Traditional Somali Behaviour in Warfare* (Nairobi: ICRC/SRCS).
24. Nuruddin Farah reports how a similar situation prevailed among the *muuryaan*, or gang members, fighting and looting in Mogadishu in the early years of the civil war when to refuse to commit a rape was met with suspicion and punishment from gang leaders. Nuruddin Farah (2000) *Yesterday, Tomorrow. Voices from the Somali Diaspora 2000* (London: Cassell) p 23.
25. Alex de Waal (ed.) (2002) *Demilitarizing the Mind: African Agendas for Peace and Security* (Trenton NJ: Justice Africa/Africa World Press) p 103.
26. Cited in UNIFEM (1998) *Somalia Between Peace and War: Somali Women on the Eve of the 21st Century*, African Women for Peace Series (Nairobi: UNIFEM). A rare interview with a woman gunfighter, recorded in August 1996 in Merca, is given in the same book

Part 1

Women's Experiences of the War

Editors' introduction

> *'Colka ninka soo arkay iyo kan loogo warama si ugama wada cararaan.'* Somali proverb, which translates as 'the one who experiences conflict and the one who hears about it will have different fears'.[1]

During a workshop in 1997 which brought together the contributors of this book, women from various regions of Somalia shared their experiences of the war. Many had witnessed people being killed, mostly men, including their closest relatives. Some had been present when women and girls were being raped. Many had lost everything, their homes looted and destroyed. Some described how they had to act as a 'shield' for the men and children in their families, lying about their clan identity, paying bribes and helping families cross from one side of Mogadishu to the other. Some had moved many times within Mogadishu to escape danger, and all had eventually left the city for other parts of Somalia or neighbouring countries. These experiences were not exceptional; hundreds of thousands of women and men and children across Somalia have been through similar ordeals.

Part 1 presents first-hand accounts of women's experiences (others appear later in the book). How war has affected women, individually and collectively, economically, socially and politically, is examined in Part 2. But as essential background for understanding the impact of the war on women, Part 1 also includes two chapters that locate women's experiences in the context of women's social position in Somali society. The first is an ethnographic description of the life of women in nomadic pastoral society, and the second is an examination of marriage within this society. These 'normative' descriptions are in stark contrast to the personal testimonies and Chapter 3, an account of war-crimes committed against women.

Women's experiences of conflict

Do women experience conflict differently from men? Are women the unnoticed victims of war? Both questions have been hotly debated and contested. A recent World Bank conference presented a strong case for viewing women as targets of male abuse during conflict, and an equally cogent case for emphasising women's active participation in conflict, their resilience in the face of violence and upheaval, and the view that both men and women are victimised by war.[2] UNIFEM's recent review of the global evidence on women and war drew in sharp relief the horrors experienced by women in war:

> knowing all this did not prepare us for the horrors women described. ... We heard accounts of gang rapes, rape camps and mutilation. Of murder and sexual slavery. We saw the scars of brutality so extreme that survival seemed for some a worse fate than death.[3]

Proponents of all these arguments will find evidence to support or oppose their views in the pages of this book. There can be no doubting the terror experienced by ordinary Somalis nor the devastating consequences for women. Unusually, this book presents the experiences of professional women, reflecting both their personal experiences and their professional observations. Habiba Osman, Amina Sayid and Shukri Hariir present harrowing pictures of the mass exodus of families from major towns, fleeing in the face of extreme violence yet risking their lives to keep together and assure each others' protection (see also Halimo Elmi's testimony in Part 2). A common feature of these accounts is the need to be always on the move to be safe. Midwives Habiba and Halimo describe the consequences of flight for pregnant women, with stress-induced labour often taking place in the absence of facilities or even elementary security and privacy. They note the lack of medicines and treatment facilities, the health problems caused by lack of access to water, and the secondary consequences of these in terms of general ill-health, as well as the direct impact of violence.

The proposition that in wars women become targets for abuse centres on rape as a weapon of warfare. In Somalia rape is at once abhorred by clan values (as described by Rhoda Ibrahim in her chapter on Somali pastoral society, Chapter 1) and yet integrally linked to behaviour that the clan system can engender in its most destructive form. Amina Sayid's testimony reveals the vulnerability of the relatively powerless non-clan based groups such as her own community in Brava, reflected in the extent of sexual violence endured by women in that community. Fowzia Musse's description of the rape epidemic in Kenyan refugee camps reinforces testimony from other writers in the book about the viciousness with which rapes were carried out. She also shows how both the act of rape itself and the way it is dealt with after the event were part and parcel of inter-clan relations: in prosecuting rapists clan authorities are inclined to seek the best outcome for the clan rather than for women. Fowzia's chapter notes that rape in 'normal times' and rape in warfare are defined differently by Somali society. She comments on the need for assistance to raped women to be adapted to the social and cultural environment.

NOTES

1. Mark Bradbury (1993) *The Somali Conflict: Prospects for Peace*, Oxfam Research Paper No.9 (Oxford: Oxfam).
2. C. Moser and F. Clark (eds) (2001) *Victims, Perpetrators or Actors? Gender, Armed Conflict and Political Violence* (London: Zed Books).
3. E. Rehn & E.J. Sirleaf (2002) *Women, War and Peace: The Independent Experts' Assessment on the Impact of Armed Conflict on Women and Women's role in Peace-building* (New York: UNIFEM).

1
Women's Role in the Pastoral Economy

Rhoda M. Ibrahim

After a journey so long
and tiring indeed,
Like a fully loaded camel,
tired as you are under the load,
You at last set a camp,
beside a hamlet with no blood ties to you,
Your livestock will need,
to be always kept in sight,
Your beast of burden will need
to be tied to their tethers.
The newly born baby sheep
have to be taken out to graze.
The house will always need
to be tidy and in shape.
Your children will always need
your comforting care and love.
Your husband will call for
your service in different ways.
And may at times scold you
for services poorly done.
And may at times beat you
for no apparent reason.
So stop whimpering
and perform as best you possibly can
The responsibilities and the duties
set out for you to do.[1]

Introduction

Women play a vital role in the Somali pastoral economy. On top of women's universal domestic tasks – child-care, food preparation and household chores – they also have important roles in animal husbandry, the mainstay of the national economy. They employ considerable technical skill and knowledge in the construction and maintenance of the nomadic home (*aqal* – which they unpack and repack each time the family moves on), as well as in crafting utensils and containers and in administering natural medicines to livestock. Recurrent drought has obliged both women and men to adapt their economic roles. The conflict which has affected Somali society since 1988 has broken up families and required many women to take sole responsibility for their families.

This paper sets out to record the typical roles and lifestyles of girls and women in the pre-war pastoral economy of north western Somalia (now Somaliland), as I experienced it during prolonged visits to relatives. This personal experience is supplemented by research I carried out in 1992 and by more than 18 years' experience as a development worker in rural Somalia and Somaliland. I also refer to research carried out since the war by Vetaid and the Pastoral and Environmental Network for the Horn of Africa (PENHA).

My ethnographic description of the nomadic pastoral family shows how the family's division of labour, herd management, mobility, marriage patterns and lifestyle adaptability are all essential factors for everyday survival in an extremely difficult environment. I describe a girl's *rite de passage* into womanhood and her preparation for marriage. I describe some of the coping mechanisms pastoral families may resort to in times of severe drought, including the long-term or even permanent separation of the male head of the family from his wife or wives and children. I then try to trace some of the known impacts of the war and collapse of state structures on the pastoral way of life and on pastoral women in particular. These include loss of adult males through combat and migration to urban centres and the resulting changes in gender relations at the level of household decision-making and livelihood as well as household mobility. Among the questions my paper asks are, are these changes in gender relations going to be long-term and are they actually empowering for women? And what does the widespread male urban migration mean for the marital prospects of pastoral girls and the future of Somalia's nomadic pastoral economy?

What I describe here is representative of the pastoral way of life throughout Somalia although there will be some regional variations.

The pastoral economy

Pastoralism, the movement of households following seasonal grazing patterns, has been practised among Somalis for centuries. The movements of pastoralists and their livestock are directed by the seasons and by the availability of grass and water. In Somalia there are two rainy seasons (*gu'* and *dayr*) and two dry seasons (*haggaa* and *jilaal*). Pastoralists move between rainy season grassland with seasonal water supplies, and permanent water sources which they concentrate around during the dry season.

The main diet of the pastoralists depends heavily on animal products and is composed principally of milk from all livestock, and ghee and meat. Cereals are bought with cash from the sale of livestock. Since the commercialisation of livestock in the 1970s and 1980s pastoral communities have shifted towards urban-style food and clothes.

The pastoral economy depends on families herding a variety of species for production and for sale. Sheep and goats are herded as domestic stock, while camels are the family's main asset, valued both for their resistance to drought, for their market and social value, and for their varied uses in transport and as food. Camels represent the most important gifts – such as the bridewealth (*yarad*) given by a prospective husband's family to the family of his wife-to-be. The *yarad* will consist of one male and several more valuable female camels and sometimes a gun and a horse.

If a murder or wounding occurs, of all the livestock the perpetrator's family can give to the victim's family in compensation the camel will be the most important. The exact number of camels and livestock to be handed over will be carefully calculated to match the 'value' of the dead or wounded person and the impact of the damage caused. Livestock are the pastoralists' currency and the camel is the highest denomination. Up to 100 camels could be given (or their equivalent in sheep and goats) in the most serious cases of male homicide.

Female animals usually constitute the majority of a productive herd, while male herds are used for commercial purposes, being exchanged for town commodities such as grain, sugar, clothes and shoes. They are also kept for slaughtering for feasts, funerals and other social events. A family needs both male and female camels but will keep more females than males. The female camel is the most valued as an exchange asset and because it is the source of milk.

Male camels are important as stud and burden-bearing animals. Only male camels are used for transportation. Specially selected before they reach seven years old, the males chosen for transport camels (*gaadiid*) will be first castrated. Camels are extremely strong and to castrate one needs several strong men. Once castrated they will be broken in by the 'camel boys' (teenagers who may be sons or cousins of the family) and then trained by the men. Camels are not docile animals by nature; training takes up to a year. The camel is trained to sit for a long period whilst its back is loaded, to walk with a load for a long period of time, to wear a saddle and halter, to be led and to stand still, to obey commands. Somali pastoralists do not use camels as riding animals: only the very young, very old or sick are carried on the camel's back. It is to carry the family's house and household equipment that the camel is trained.

Once trained each transport camel can carry one house (*aqal*). Until they are sufficiently experienced the newly trained transport camels (*qaalin* or *gaadiid*) will be entrusted with carrying unbreakables only. An obedient and reliable transport camel is a highly valued asset. The older, most experienced transport camels, *hayin*, will be trusted to carry children and young livestock on the long journeys to find a new place to settle. *Hayin* are patient and obedient; the less experienced *qaalin* will be tied to and led along by the *hayin* to prevent them running away and destroying their burdens.

While female and castrated male camels spend much time in distant grazing areas with the camel-boys, transport camels will always be kept near to the household, and are thus available when needed by women to bring water from a distant water source, or to transport milk to be exchanged in town. When the time comes for the whole household to move on, the women work out how everything will be transported, which camels will carry what and how many camels will be needed. A family will only have a certain number of transport camels of their own (relating to the number of *aqals* in the household), but families will lend each other their transport camels if necessary, known as *gaadiid qaad*.

In very difficult times the household may be forced to sell some of its camels or may lose them through sickness or prolonged drought. But a family would never sell its transport camels while it still had options available. Without its transport camels the pastoral family is unable to survive; such a family is in a state of complete poverty.

The uncastrated male camels (*baarqab*), which are not selected for breeding or training as transport animals will be sold or slaughtered for meat. A household with 100 head of camels will keep just one or two stud camels for breeding. Although they graze with the herd for the rest of the year, during the breeding season stud camels are kept close to the family home, needing strong and experienced men to look after them. Breeding is carefully planned; to avoid interbreeding within the herd stud camels may be temporarily exchanged between families. There are stories of stud camels being given herbal medicines with aphrodisiac properties to improve their performance, or sometimes to calm them down.

Women's role in the pastoral economy

Somali society is a strongly patriarchal one. Sets of families (*qoys*), each with a male head, and usually related through the male line, settle and move together, forming a *reer*. Women continue to be members of their *reer* even after they have married and moved away to live with their husband's family, and this provides women with a measure of protection against mistreatment by her husband's relatives and clan family. A group of several *qoys* who settle in a common grazing area during a given season forms a *beel*.

The division of labour in the Somali pastoral family is clearly defined. Women view their role chiefly in relation to child-bearing, child-rearing and household tasks. Women are also the key contributors to the family economy through their production of livestock by-products such as ghee and milk. As mothers, they bear Somali culture, and foster among their children the distinctive role-playing which determines future male and female patterns of behaviour.

Women are an important part of the labour force, and polygamy is common as a means of providing additional hands and an additional source of income. Typically, each wife and her children form a separate unit, each with her own hut (*aqal*) and the animals that she is allotted for her own use over which she has primary rights of ownership. In addition to productive animals, her livestock will include one or two male camels for transport as well as newly-calved female camels for milking.

The working day for nomadic women starts before sunrise, soon after dawn prayers, and finishes after the sun sets and the last prayer has been made. Women's main role in animal husbandry concerns milking and the management of small stock. Women are responsible for deciding what proportion of milk should be used for family consumption, feeding of young animals, sale as fresh milk, or processing. In herd management, women are responsible for selecting animals for sale, slaughter, and breeding, and for arranging these activities accordingly.

Pastoral women divide the grazing work between their children according to their age and ability. Children under seven are responsible for young livestock grazing around the house, while those between the ages of seven and ten are sent out to look after the adult livestock grazing further afield. Women count the number of livestock leaving in the morning and coming home in the evening. Older daughters are responsible for fetching water, and for cleaning the fence once every three days to protect livestock from ticks, pests and diseases.

Pastoral women are also responsible for selling surplus products such as *harar* (mats), excess milk, processed meat and wild fruits, exchanging these for commodities needed for household consumption.

Women cook food for the family, collect firewood, and do the washing. Elderly women are responsible for entertaining children, often by telling folk stories. Women also treat and feed sick animals, using medicinal skills and knowledge about local herbs.

As people move from one place to another in search of better grazing and water, women are responsible for arranging the transport, and for dismantling the *aqal* to load on to camels. When they reach their destination women again erect the *aqal*, check the animals and feed the family. It is women's responsibility to weave the mats of the *aqal*, shape the frames, and undertake all the crafts required for its construction, from its coverings to the smallest pin.

The *aqal* is a round hut made from grass and trees. Pastoral women make everything needed for it and the household items inside using raw materials from the surrounding environment. The frame of the *aqal* differs according to different localities but has common features and is usually made from roots of the *galool* tree (a type of acacia with very long horizontal roots), and consists of eight to 12 strong, crescent-shaped supports called *dhigo*, as the foundation. A further 15 to 25 *lool* (shaped the same but longer and softer) are spread over the frame and tied down to strengthen it. If the *aqal* is big then a large supporting pole, known as *udub dhexaad*, is placed in the middle of the house. The women then cover the frame with *harar*. There are about 15 types of covers made from grass and sisal. The size of each mat and the time taken to make it varies according to the size of the *aqal*. The longest type of mat (*dhudhun*) is about 9.5 metres in length and 4 metres wide and takes an average of 10 days to finish. The shortest, 7 metres long and 3 metres wide, takes seven days to complete.

The *aqal* frame can be the hardest component to find and prepare as the materials need to be of the right length and strength, and cut from the tree when still green. Men may help with cutting the *galool* roots but it is the elderly women of the household who prepare and bend them. Bending takes several days: the cut root is fixed into the ground at one end, arched over until it is in the desired shape and then fixed into the ground at the other end. Left arched and fixed for several days the green wood gradually dries out and a permanently arched and strong frame should result. Once a suitable site has been found, erecting the *aqal* takes half a day.

Pastoral women produce household containers for milk and water, and other food utensils from leather, palm leaves and sisal. Examples include *qarbed* and *sibraar*, both made from the hides of goats or sheep to transport water and milk. The milk containers *dhiil, haan, doobi*, are made by weaving and sewing palm leaves and are used to store milk from a few hours to days or sometimes weeks. Fresh milk, soured, sheep's, goats' and camels' milk will all be kept in different containers. Sheep and goats' milk, used for ghee production, stays fresh for only a short while. Camels' milk lasts much longer; it may be fermented, soured and even dried.

Women have always managed the milk trade. They send their containers of milk to a middlewoman in the town. Her container will have her 'mark' on it, the same as branded on her family camels. Tied onto the side of the container is a string of knots, the number and size indicating to the middlewoman what goods she wants in exchange for her milk.

Women make protective padding for transporting animals from by-products of *aqal* manufacture (old clothes, used leather, sacks, and so on). Women also produce items for cleaning out livestock quarters, like *digo xaadh* and *dhiriq*. The first is a flat piece of wood to clean out the animal den, while the second consists of branches tied together with small sisal ropes to collect and remove manure.

Yeesha are hide-ropes used by nomadic women to tie the frame of the *aqal* to the camel when they need to transport it. *Mareeg* are light tethering ropes made by women to keep small goats and sheep from running away and to protect their mothers from suckling before milking time. Women plait all these ropes from sisal and bark fibre (*xig iyo maydhax*) and sometimes travel long distances in their search for raw materials. In the days when there were still many wild animals, they faced danger of being attacked.

In summary, women's role in livestock production and in maintaining the household (both the human beings in it and the fabric of the dwellings) has always been crucial to the survival of the pastoral system. It includes important contributions to animal production and to the technical aspects of nomadic movement, as well as food production and domestic responsibilities. Decision-making beyond the level of the nuclear family is regarded as the domain of men, all of whom over the age of 16 are eligible to participate. The kinds of decisions that need to be addressed at this level include: dealing with newcomers coming to share resources with the host clan associated with the territory; resolving conflicts and settling disputes; payment of *diya* blood money; when and if to go to war. Recent research by the Somaliland Women's Research and Action Group (SOWRAG) concludes that 'there are indications that women were consulted privately on the matters under discussion. But in order not to undermine men's decision-making powers, women's "invisible" role ...was never publicly acknowledged.' (Amina Warsame 2001)

Rites of passage and the *aqal*

The transformation of a girl from childhood, adolescence to adulthood is mirrored and signified by changes made to her hairstyle; her age and status can be determined by her hairstyle and the different names given to different styles. As an infant and until she reaches the age of circumcision at six or seven years her head is almost completely shaved, leaving only a little topknot, *dhoor*, the common name by which such girls are known. After circumcision and until puberty all of her head is shaved except for the front where the hair is left to grow; this is called *food*. At the time of her first period the *food* is shaved off and she begins to grow her full head of hair and will braid it. At this stage she is known as a *gashaanti*. Her head will remain uncovered until she marries, when she covers her hair with a *gambo*, a black head-scarf.

From three years old girls are given responsibilities within the household. Along with boys of the same age their first task is to look after sheep and goats which are kept to browse near the family *aqal*. The older girls and women will be nearby for much of the day, sitting under a tree weaving and constructing materials for the aqal.

From about six years old, the boys will join their cousins and brothers to look after camels in the distant grazing areas. From the same age until puberty the girls will take responsibility for sheep which graze some distance from the family *aqal*. They will also help older sisters collect the grass needed for the preparation of their wedding *aqal*. At this age girls start to learn basic sewing and plaiting, preparing the sisal threads for the *aws* (woven walls of the *aqal*), called *dhumbal* in central regions.

Once she reaches puberty and wears her hair as a *gashaanti*, her family stop her looking after the sheep and goats so that she has time to prepare her own *aqal* and learn the skills that she will need when she becomes a wife and is in charge of the household's sheep and goats. These skills include counting the animals, learning about animal health and illness, and cooking. Although it may be many years before she does marry, her time will be taken up accumulating and preparing the materials for the *aqal* which she will not construct or live in until her marriage.

For a woman the importance of creating a fine *aqal* cannot be overestimated. Her future marriage could be affected and her value as a good wife may be measured by how well she has woven her *harar*, the coverings for the *aqal*. Proverbs and poems exploit and reinforce the use of the *harar* as a metaphor for a woman's worth. The greatest compliment is to describe a woman's *aws* as *aws hariir*, which is a silken cover.

Much of her time will be spent finding the correct grasses and fibres for her weaving and then practising transforming dried grass and sisal into the weather-proof, strong and decoratively pleasing woven walls needed for her marriage home. Weaving a fine *aws* is an art that takes years of practice. Test pieces made by *gashaanti* will not be thrown away but will be used as padding for the transport camels' backs. A woman will continue to practise her skills until she has perfected them and can produce an *aws* that will keep the rain, dust and wind out, withstand transportation and provide a pleasing pattern to look at inside the *aqal*. A well-made *aws* can last many years if kept in good condition.

To progress her transformation into adulthood and marriage, when a girl becomes a *gashaanti* she is given a *buul aws*, a small *aqal*, of her own to live in. Situated within the family compound for protection, the *buul aws* is intended to give her enough privacy to meet a prospective husband. She is given responsibility for deciding who she will and will not associate with and it is usually her choice which one of her suitors she marries, although this varies in different parts of Somalia. The trust placed in her by her family is expressed in the saying, *kun way la hadashaa kowna way ka guursataa*, meaning 'A woman – maybe a thousand men will talk to her but she finally chooses just one.'

Grazing land is always common and therefore shared by different clans. As the household moves each season they will have new neighbours from different clans. In this way there is usually a range of eligible men (*heerin*) for the *gashaanti* to meet. When this is not the case several women may go together to another settlement area to find out about *heerin*. As a girl cannot become a *gashaanti* with her own *buul aws* until her elder sister is married, there is some pressure within the family for suitable partners to be found.

Since all the men are away with the herds throughout the dry seasons, young men and women get to know each other during the rainy season when the households and herds are closer together. At these times there will be all-night dancing, *iyargud*.[2] The dancing provides opportunities to exchange words through songs and so develop relationships. Marriages only take place during the rainy season.

The clan system traditionally provides protection against rape; if a woman is raped it is an insult to her clan because it shows that they could not protect her. Under normal circumstances any man who violates a woman invokes the revenge of her sub-clan against not only himself but also his own sub-clan. Thus he not only risks his own life but that of his family and wider network of paternal relatives; and indeed he risks disaster for both clans as they would have to go to war. The only way such a disaster can be averted is for the rapist to take the woman he has raped to be his wife. In some circumstances a couple who wish to marry but fear strong opposition may resort to staging a rape in order for the marriage to be condoned. (See also Chapter 3.)

The effects of drought and other hardships

Somali pastoralists use risk-averting strategies to survive and measures to predict and adjust to ecological dynamics. Multi-species herding in different ecological zones, and splitting the herds into different grazing areas, are the most common strategies. They maximise their herd size and keep high proportions of female animals for rapid recovery from lean times. They have also developed water systems such as reservoirs lined with cement, concrete and stones (*berked*) in addition to more traditional forms of water catchment including earthwork dams, in order to prolong the availability of grazing and ground water. Pastoralists try to match suitable livestock numbers and types with the quantity of water in the *berked*, aware of the need to conserve shared resources.

Water is such a precious commodity for the pastoral household that its use is severely restricted. Women will use transport camels to collect one week's to 10 days' supply of water from the nearest source (which could be half a day's walk away or more) and take it to the household. One 60-litre or two 30-litre containers of water will last the family a week. Water is used only for cooking, drinking, toilet ablutions and ritual cleaning after sexual intercourse. The family wash themselves only during the twice-yearly rains; if clothes are washed it will be because the household is camped near to the water source. Little water is actually drunk, as milk is preferred and usually plentiful. Teeth are kept clean and strong with a stick brush without the use of water.

Pastoralists have their own system of signals to warn of impending drought. Information networks enable families to find out where the best rains have fallen and whether a long dry season is coming. Groups of clans have their own signal, or code, known as *baaq*, which members use to recognise one another during times of conflict, or to bring people together during household and herd movements when individuals can be far apart driving stock through hostile terrain.

Women and men prepare in different ways to cope with disaster. Women's role is to make food ready to store against drought. The first thing they do is to identify the animals strong enough to resist the drought and sell some of the weak ones, using the cash to buy food for the dry season. They also slaughter some animals and preserve the meat for the dry season either by smoking or by drying it in the sun and then frying it.

Early in the dry season women also dry milk from both camels and goats. Camel milk is fermented until the curd precipitates and the whey separates; it is then filtered through cloth and dried until it becomes like powered milk, to which water can later be added.

At this time men go off to look for better grazing and water. They also go to the towns to buy grain. Sheep and goats are readily marketed during the early stage of a drought. The price of goods from town increases while livestock prices sink.

Elders of each grazing area meet at this stage to exchange information and decide what to do next. Families split their stock into three: lactating sheep and goats go with the children, and lactating mothers and pregnant women are moved to nearby villages for closer access to water; the rest of the family and sheep and goats remain in the bush; and unmarried men and young boys move camels far away from the families.[3]

Livestock numbers and management vary according to topography, from the Haud, the Ogo plateau, the Gollis mountain range to the coastal area. A family in the east may commonly have as many as 1,000 sheep and goats which they keep for meat not milk, as well as camels, which would sustain all the family's needs; towards the Haud in the west, the wealthiest family might have no more than 300 sheep and goats which they would milk, and would probably be engaged in some livestock trading or mixed farming.

Likewise, in times of stress there are variations in coping mechanisms, but a common practice would be to keep lactating animals with lactating human mothers and small children so as to maximise the children's chances of survival. It is not unheard of for camel herds to be driven as far as Eritrea and even further southwards into Uganda in order to find grazing during severe drought.

Deaths of animals occur, and sometimes deaths of people. For pastoralists the loss of transport camels is a crisis for they simply do not have the means to continue moving to better grazing areas. Families have few alternatives at this stage but to abandon the *aqal* and other possessions and trek to the nearest village or water point with their animals.

New situations often demand lifestyle changes. Destitute pastoral families (who have previously lost their livestock) will often try to return to the pastoral way of life if they can, rather than stay in towns and become dependent on others. But to return to a pastoral way of life the family needs the means to re-stock and to obtain at least one transport camel.

When conditions are bad, the male head of the family will look for employment or other means of providing a living. In times of severe crisis, like the drought of 1974, if he is unable to get a job he might abandon his family. His original decision to go to town to search for work will have been a joint one, made with his wife. But if he fails to find work the decision to leave his family will be made by him alone. He will base his decision on the knowledge that he can no longer contribute to his family's needs and it is shameful for him to be around them at such a difficult time unless he can be useful. From this perspective, by leaving his family he is relieving them of having to provide for him. Many of the Somali men who migrated to ports such as Cardiff, Liverpool and Aden came to be seamen through such circumstances. During the drought of the 1970s pastoralists went to the Gulf countries as labourers; in the 1980s drought many from the north west joined the Somali National Movement (SNM).

A woman whose husband has left in this way would remain with her children overseen by his family's household, and wait for his return, never remarrying unless news comes that he has died. With this news she is allowed to remarry and most commonly will wed one of his brothers, whose responsibility it is to take care of her. If her husband returns after many years (couples have been known to be apart for 15 years or more) and his wife is past child-bearing, he is likely to take another wife. Women in urban settlements on the other hand will tend to seek divorce and remarriage if difficult circumstances mean their husband has abandoned them and he has not been in contact with them for more than three months.[4]

The impact of the war on the pastoral economy

More research is needed to assess the relative impact of the war on pastoral, settled agricultural and urban communities. What is already apparent from research conducted among the pastoral communities of Somaliland is that the pastoral economy has survived the war, probably better than the agricultural and urban economies, but with some major constraints and changes. These can be best understood from a gendered perspective.

Most of the fighting parties relied on pastoralists for personnel, equipment, logistical support and food. The war also restricted the movement of pastoralists, causing excessive grazing and the spread of livestock diseases. During the civil war young men left their pastoral responsibilities to join the opposition movements. Unknown numbers died in the war, others survived, kept their weapons and joined armed gangs or bandits (*dey-dey*).[5] In Somaliland many were subsequently demobilised and transformed into the new army and police forces. Others remain unemployed war veterans for whom, as a result of *qaad* addiction (see opposite and below), the town remains more attractive than the harsh life of a pastoralist.

Thus the years of the civil war have left women, the elderly and very young to the traditionally male tasks of camel castration, herding, milking, camel training and scouting for new grazing. Without the men, less movement of the herd will be possible and so the mobility of the household is restricted. There is evidence[6] of a post-war shift from a nomadic way of life to a more sedentary one and that this is having a dramatic impact on the environment. For example, impoverished pastoral families who have lost their animals are increasingly fencing off land and turning to agriculture, which is creating new restrictions on remaining herd movements as well as potential for conflict. Once fencing of land for planting becomes established for some families, it is only a matter of time before others follow suit in order to protect their staple food supplies.

Traditionally the father in the pastoral family is constantly on the move for the benefit of the family and clan – travelling to town to sell stock and buy dry supplies, scouting out better grazing areas, checking up on the herd, gathering information on which clans are moving where, participating in clan and sub-clan meetings. Nowadays men are always seen in villages or towns and it is not for the benefit of the family. One reason they are in towns is that during the civil war urban relatives with whom the pastoralists came into contact introduced *qaad* chewing to clan meetings. Many men have now become *qaad* addicts and need access to towns and villages where daily fresh supplies are sold. *Qaad* chewing is both time- and money-consuming and is a new and destructive phenomenon in the pastoral economy.

Qaad chewing

Qaad is the name of a plant (*catha edulis*) cultivated in parts of Ethiopia, Kenya and Yemen in particular. When chewed the leaves produce a mildly stimulating sensation and result in a loss of appetite. *Qaad* was banned for a while under Siad Barre. Chewed mainly by men, but also increasingly by women, it is now an important component of men's social gatherings. It is sold in the markets mainly by women traders who buy from male (and some female) importers (see Chapter 5).

Nowadays *qaad* chewing is widespread throughout Somalia and among male refugee populations, including those in the western diaspora. In most of Somalia the climate is not suitable for growing *qaad*, so the vast quantities required to satisfy the daily demand are imported from Kenya and Ethiopia. It is estimated that annual imports from Kenya alone in 1996 were worth US$3.1 million. *Qaad* chewing is a colossal drain on household and national resources. It is often blamed for increased family social and economic breakdown since the war.

The extensive migration of men to towns in search of employment, prolonged political instability, war and drought have combined to force changes on the traditional position of women in pastoral society. Many women have become heads of their households and manage their families with the help of their children. Women are taking on non-traditional economic tasks; for example, many nomadic women have become livestock traders, some travelling deep into the Ogaden in Ethiopia to buy livestock to trade in Hargeisa in Somaliland. Nowadays men and women sell their livestock side by side in the market place. Women can even be seen touching the hands of men in the course of dealing and bargaining. This was totally unheard of in the past. (Amina Warsame 2001)

Participatory research by Vetaid in 1997[7] notes with some surprise that men are aware of this change and instrumental in transferring to women almost all of the decision-making powers relating to livestock production that had traditionally resided with men. Similarly, women reported that men are willingly relinquishing control over the family's income and interfering little with the family income as long as they contribute little to its production. The report did note that men continue to be the decision-makers on the major external issues that may also affect the family. The researchers comment that 'Whatever such changes may show, it is how much the average family income exceeds expenditure which will actually determine whether men have just handed over trouble to women or voluntarily empowered them.'

As well as in trade, changes will be seen in the management of camel herds, the pastoralist's main asset. Camel boys may still be available to do the early breaking of camels, but other tasks such as training transport camels, castration, breeding and milking are likely now to be left to women. Shortage of labour in pastoral areas has led to an increase in labour-hiring, especially of children from poor families to look after livestock. For this, families are repaid in kind, which may enable them to re-stock. For settled pastoralists, animals such as chickens, cows and donkeys, are now being kept that are more in keeping with a settled lifestyle.

According to the Vetaid research (Vetaid 1997), when women were asked to prioritise their problems they placed shelter next to water, although shelter was a problem rarely mentioned by men. As noted earlier, women are traditionally responsible for the construction of the *aqal,* and traditionally a woman is partly judged by the quality of her house. Being displaced or returned refugees who have lost their *aqal* in the conflict and who have had difficulty in making a new one, women who have grown up with traditional concepts and values will not be satisfied with living in makeshift shelters. But it is not difficult to imagine that with the loss of the majority of adult and adolescent male household members, women have no time for making and repairing the traditional house and utensils. Almost every *aqal* visible from the roadside now has a covering of the blue plastic sheeting provided by UNHCR to refugees, and empty milk cans replace the handmade woven milk containers. Where the arched *lool* supports of the *aqal* frame have been lost or impossible to obtain without extra help, or required too much time and effort to prepare, women have constructed their *aqals* in more of a 'wigwam' design, *bebe*, from straight pieces of wood gathered locally.

One impact of the war on the pastoral way of life has been the high number of *gashaanti* girls and women unable to find men to marry and who are likely to become *guun*, that is unmarried women over 40 years old. In fact, the war seems to have had a profound impact on the traditional pastoral way of marriage. Vetaid's research confirmed that one impact of conflict-related factors such as destitution and the loss of male labour to manage the herd is a trend away from the traditional pastoral system of marriages between distant clans (exogamy) towards the intermarriage of closely related families (endogamy). (See Chapter 2) Anecdotal evidence suggests this shift towards marrying within one's clan is also widespread among the settled urban population. Reasons given are that all male relatives and offspring of the marriage will be of the same clan and should therefore never find themselves opposing one another in a clan war.

Impact of the collapse of the state structures[8]

Pastoral communities have suffered badly since 1998 when import bans were imposed on livestock from the Horn of Africa by Saudi Arabia, the largest importer of Somali livestock (usually sheep and goats). The bans were imposed to prevent the spread of Rift Valley Fever, which was identified in southern Somali livestock in 1997–98. The war led to the collapse of regional veterinary certification mechanisms. As a result Somali exporters are unable to provide acceptable proof regarding the health of their livestock and therefore the ban is still in place. The economic impact of the ban has been tremendous both for the national economy, which depends on the livestock trade for the major part of its revenue, and within pastoral communities.

Other problems have been exacerbated by the collapse of government structures. These include the impact of recurrent drought, environmental degradation because of unregulated enclosure of grazing areas and the privatisation of land; lack of management of gullies and water run-off created by the road system; and the exodus of the young pastoralist population. Compared with urban communities, the pastoral community is marginalised from whatever development or rehabilitation progress has taken place in the past five years; most of the young pastoral population feel left out as they lag behind in social service delivery, lack of infrastructure and other economic prospects. All these issues reduce livestock productivity and mean that the family income is not good enough to provide a strong future for the pastoral family.

Conclusions

Studies of the pre-war pastoral economy and way of life have tended to be from a male perspective. The result has been that the role of pastoral women has not been extensively recognised. Some research is now under way[9] to understand the impact of the war on pastoralism, and includes gender-sensitive approaches. What is clear is that profound changes to men's and women's roles and responsibilities have taken place and may have equally profound impacts on the environment, natural resource management and social and political organisation in the future.

In Somaliland PENHA's research and advocacy have resulted in more attention being given to the pastoralists' problems as government institutions and national and international agencies look for ways to improve life for the pastoral communities. Range rehabilitation, proper policies and schemes to tackle environmental and social issues are being channelled towards them. In PENHA's assessment the situation is improving and many pastoralists are for the first time feeling served and resourced. In terms of the inclusion of women in these changes, PENHA notes that

> while in general, consultative meetings and conferences are made on understanding the situation of the pastoral community, women are not much included because of lack of time from their side and cultural and religious stereotypes and barriers that hinder women to attend such meetings. There is a trend of empowering pastoral

communities by creating pastoral associations and every attempt is so far made to include women in such associations. It will require a huge effort and time to bring pastoral women into the forefront of development.[10]

TESTIMONY 1: HABIBA OSMAN

Editors' note

More immediately obvious than the impact of the war on pastoral families is its effect on Somalia's agro-pastoral communities, the Rahanweyne of the south. The Rahanweyne inhabit Somalia's most fertile region, the area that lies between the Shabelle river in the north and the Juba river in the south. The great majority combine transhumant, or regular seasonal, livestock herding with sedentary cultivation of rain-fed sorghum, maize and legumes. Having resisted, but failed to curtail, Italian colonial domination and expropriation of their fertile riverine lands, the Rahanweyne people continued to suffer political and economic marginalisation at the hands of the post-independence governments, from 1960 onwards.

This first-hand account, by Habiba Osman, a midwife from an agro-pastoral family, begins in the months preceding the outbreak of war in the south, when armed conflict was developing between major clans of the Darod family, the Ogaden and Marehan. Under Siad Barre's rule members of the Marehan (his own clan group) accumulated the greatest power and wealth. The Ogadenis were also a favoured group, given prominence in the army and key military posts; but Barre's rapprochement with the Ethiopian regime in 1988[11] and the growing power of the Marehan within the military eroded Ogadeni support for the regime. In April 1989 Barre sacked his (Ogadeni) defence minister, sparking a mutiny among Ogadeni soldiers and leading to the formation of the Somali Patriotic Movement (SPM). For most of the war against Siad Barre the SPM constituted a southern front, destabilising the regions south of the capital. (Bradbury 1997)

Habiba describes how government soldiers terrorised civilians, including herself, in her home town, Baidoa, the commercial centre for the Rahanweyne people. These events were a foretaste of the violence that was to come to the largely unarmed Rahanweyne people.

For following the collapse of Siad Barre's regime in January 1991 his forces withdrew to their strongholds in the southern inter-riverine regions, including Bay and Bakool (see map). Well-armed and vengeful, they pursued a scorched-earth policy against the politically marginalised and less well-armed agro-pastoral communities, systematically destroying the infrastructural and resource basis of the country's economic wealth as they went. By the end of the year the Rahanweyne agro-pastoralists had become trapped in what became known as the 'triangle of death', the area between Mogadishu, Baidoa and Kismayo; surrounded by the three competing forces of Siad Barre, General Aideed and Mohamed Hersi 'Morgan' (Siad Barre's son-in-law). Each force rampaged through the agro-pastoral lands and settlements in waves of looting, rape and violence.

By the time Siad Barre's forces had been driven from the country in mid-1992, the region was in the grip of a man-made famine in which an estimated 500,000 people died. Throughout 1992 Aideed's forces prevented relief food shipments from reaching Baidoa and other parts of southern Somalia. Baidoa became known as the 'city of the walking dead'. In September 1992, 5,979 people were recorded to have died – nearly 200 a day. As Habiba records, some of her own close family members were among those who perished from malnutrition and famine-related disease. Taking her small daughter, Habiba fled the famine and war, travelling more than 1,500 km by road to the northern port of Bossaso. There she found a boat that could take them to Yemen where they live today.

Habiba's story

In 1989 I was working for the Ministry of Health on a World Health Organisation (WHO) project in Baidoa, Bay Region. I had been offered a post with another health organisation, AMREF, and I was called to Mogadishu to sign a contract. I had two dependants, my daughter aged one and the seven-year-old daughter of my younger brother, whom I had looked after since infancy. I sent a message to my mother requesting her to come and care for them in my absence, and I hurriedly prepared to depart for Mogadishu. It was Friday afternoon (18 July). As I was about to leave, the officer-in-charge of Baidoa security, whose wife was in her last hours of labour came to see me asking if I could help. I realised that I wasn't going to make it to Mogadishu that day. After the baby was delivered I returned home. It was nearly 10pm.

At midnight a group of thieves, heavily armed with an AKA machine gun with two loaded ammunition cases, broke into my house. One held his gun less than an inch from the side of my head. The others looted our home, taking gold, money, clothes, food, utensils and the health supplies that I used for my work. Imagine, six men loading all my belongings onto their truck for at least an hour while another held a gun to my head.

As they were leaving one of them said that if I made a sound during the next 30 minutes he would come back. He said he knew that we didn't have anybody to protect us.[12] He told me not to shout or tell anybody that the perpetrators of this crime were actually soldiers, not ordinary thieves. As soon as they left I tried to get the numberplate details of their vehicle but could not as it was dark outside. Early in the morning I went to the police station to report the incident. To my astonishment the police told me that they couldn't do anything for me. I went back to my looted home.

From then on thieves came every other night in Baidoa, looting the homes of civilians. Two nights after my home had been looted the health school compound was looted. I decided to leave Baidoa and on returning to the house I packed what was left of my belongings and told my mother that we were to leave. That day we left Baidoa for a small village near Burhabo [between Baidoa and Burhakaba] where our own family was settled. I then went on to Mogadishu and resigned from my job with the Ministry of Health and signed my contract with AMREF who posted me to work in Luuq, Gedo Region (see map).

During the period of my work in Luuq the peace was deteriorating day by day. Most of the inhabitants of Luuq had left with the exception of some of Siad Barre's troops. Even refugees[13] in the nearby refugee camp had evacuated and disappeared. While I was in Luuq I heard that nine trucks coming from Mogadishu, owned by Marehans and containing vast loads of money and ammunition, had been seized by a group of Ogadeni people about 9 km out of Luuq. Some of the trucks' passengers walked by foot into Luuq and told of these events. Some of the people commandeered vehicles in order to reach the robbed group of Marehans. The vehicle I used for my work was among those taken for the rescue. At I am someone knocked at my door saying that there were injured people at the hospital. I went to the hospital and found 10 injured people; many more had died. The victims were the rescue party. One of the vehicles following the thieves was blown up by a landmine that they (the thieves) had planted.

Days later we were attacked by a group of heavily armed men who took the office car. A few days later they broke into a neighbour's house; the husband was absent and the wife had given birth six days before. As she lay on the bed with her new-born baby they raped her.

I was extremely frightened and the director decided to evacuate women to Mogadishu, leaving men behind for the time being.

I had been in Mogadishu for a week or so when there was an announcement that all foreigners should leave the country [this was advice from the UN Development Programme office responsible for coordinating international development assistance in Somalia]. AMREF's foreign nationals left and I was delegated to take over the office responsibilities. Insecurity was worsening daily. We received a telegram telling us to go to Nairobi in order to attend a seminar. I am not sure whether the real objective of this seminar was to evacuate us from Somalia or not (a few international organisations did try to help Somali colleagues find ways out of the country during this period). I travelled to Baidoa in order to say goodbye to my mother and children. It was 30 December 1990.

While returning on the bus from Baidoa to Mogadishu I learned that war had broken out in Mogadishu between the opposition militia and Siad Barre's soldiers and that heavy artillery shelling was taking place. We were advised by a passing bus from Mogadishu to stay where we were. The driver of our bus asked the passengers to get off. One of the passengers threatened the driver with a pistol, demanding that he continue to Mogadishu. Shaking with fear, the driver drove to a distance of 7 km outside Mogadishu and again requested that the passengers get off the bus. But all of the passengers refused. Finally everyone got off the bus at the bus station about 4 km outside of Mogadishu. I lived on Avizione Road and I heard that there was heavy shelling going on in this area. Out of fear I decided to go to my brother's house in Madina (a district of Mogadishu), where I learnt that our property had been looted for the second time.

My younger brother at this time was living in Xamar Jadiid [another district of Mogadishu]. Over the phone he told us artillery bullets [shells] had missed them by inches, that they were down to their last bag of pasta and that food supplies were scarce as all shops were closed. My elder sister, who was staying with us in Madina, suggested we join our brother and his children in Xamar Jadiid saying that 'we should die with him and his children in the same place'. So the next day, 13 January, at 6am we left my brother's house. On the way we passed 12 dead bodies in military uniform, and a further four dead civilians. They were being carried on mats by a group of women.

As we walked gunfire was all around us. I was hit in my shoulder by a bullet that took with it a part of my clavicle bone. I saw a small chip of bone fly in front of my eyes and I fell to my knees. I asked my sister to knock on doors to find water. At the fourth door a kind old lady gave us water. Blood was flowing from my body. I did my best to apply pressure to stop the bleeding. Eventually we reached my brother and his children. During the night we could barely sleep for fright and in the morning we all headed back towards Madina. I found the journey back difficult – I would take 20 steps and then had to sit for 10 minutes. The next day we decided to leave for Afgoi (a small town 30 km inland from Mogadishu).

On the way from Mogadishu to Afgoi I could not believe the number of people walking on the road. One could see infants on their mothers' backs, children, and older people being transported in wheelbarrows. The events that we encountered on our way to Afgoi were really very frightening. We saw a lady in her late 30s giving birth in the road. She was crying and nobody was paying any attention. Even though I was injured I tried to help her deliver the child. Further along the road we passed a boy who was dying. I felt extremely miserable. We arrived in Afgoi at sunset. Our group consisted of my elder sister with her two sons, my elder brother with his three children, his mother-in-law, his sister-in-law, three children and the son and daughter of my eldest brother. We stayed in Afgoi until Siad Barre had been overthrown in Mogadishu [26 January 1991].

The consequences of the war for Baidoa

Whilst I find it painful to recount the effect of the war in Baidoa I nevertheless feel it necessary to inform others, who were not there, of what happened. While Siad Barre was fighting in Mogadishu [in January 1991] Baidoa had been overrun by the so-called Somali Patriotic Movement (SPM – an Ogaden based political and military movement). On their arrival in Baidoa from Ethiopia nothing had happened for the first three or four days. In fact Baidoa people gave the SPM group a warm reception as they believed these people would fight Siad's forces in Mogadishu. And they did seize all the military munitions of the 60th Division of Siad Barre in Baidoa and proceeded towards Mogadishu. On their way to Mogadishu in Afgoi town the SPM forces were halted by USC [United Somali Congress – the Hawiye-based military force led by General Aideed] forces and retreated towards Baidoa. After a couple of weeks war broke out in Baidoa between the SPM and the civilians of Baidoa region. The well-equipped SPM were driven out of Baidoa by the civilians whose only weapons were bows and arrows.

Just after this Siad Barre mobilised his forces from Kismayo and Baidoa was overrun again. What resulted was the worst genocide, plundering and looting that has happened in Somalia. Women, infants, children and elderly people were killed and raped. Underground food stores along with camels, cattle, sheep and goats were taken. The whole population of Baidoa tried to flee for Mogadishu while the nomads of Bay Region split into factions in the countryside.

The revenging [sic] forces of Siad Barre reached the town of Dafed near Afgoi [heading for Mogadishu]. The USC forces prepared an attack that drove them back to Bur-dhuube, Bay Region. While USC forces were driving back Siad's army both groups plundered whatever property they came across. All this misfortune happened to the innocent population of Bay Region. Serious drought struck the region and as a consequence of war and famine almost half the population in this region died.

The impact of the war on my family

The perpetual war in and around Baidoa and Bay Region touched our family [the Haji Osmans] and many others. The consequences were very saddening. We have lost lives including children and parents. We have lost possessions, assets, our homes and finally each other as our family [members] have joined the dispossessed and have fled to other foreign countries: Yemen, Ethiopia, Canada, and some still remain in Somalia.

The worst disasters happened soon after the war had begun in Mogadishu. We had fled back to Baidoa and, as Siad Barre attacked Bay Region, we moved to a little village called Mood Moode and from there to Mogadishu again. It was during this part of the war that we lost my father, two children and a sister and a small girl of my sister. We had left behind in our home in Baidoa our father and with him our oldest brother and a sister. Our father was over 80 and had refused to go with us so two of the family stayed with him.

Like a line of tied camels made up of 23 persons, we were making our way through the thorny bushes of the thick forests to reach Mood Moode when the revenging forces of Siad Barre reached Bay Region and wreaked havoc on my family and others.

My father suffered from high blood pressure. By the time we reached Mogadishu we heard that he was seriously sick. He sent a message saying that his medicine had run out and that he needed more. I managed to find somebody going to our father's area who would take medicine for him. Three days before the man reached him my father died. May Allah bless him. I believe everyone will die on his/her day, but his death left us with great grief and came about because of my family's forced separation brought about by Siad Barre's revenging forces in Baidoa. It was an act of the divine might of God the merciful, may he bless those as we grieve their absence from this world. God may give them the water of Fardusa Paradise. I will express here how much we miss those members of our family and how they died.

My brother, who was married and with four children, had a good herd of camels but they were all stolen from him when Siad Barre's forces attacked Baidoa. While the militia were driving his camels away he pleaded with them to leave him one or two of the female milking camels in order to give milk to his children, but they shouted at him and then they shot him dead. God bless him! He left behind him four children and their mother. Those plunderers took all our camels.

My older sister who was married and had two daughters really died because of malnutrition. May God bless her also. Another brother of mine had died because of chronic dysentery including vomiting and swellings. He left behind him a small daughter and his wife. Another brother's daughter died from measles. She couldn't be vaccinated because of the war. That little child would have survived if it had not been for the war.

Mogadishu

After being a few weeks in Mogadishu the war broke out between the Hawiye factions, the Abgal and the Habr Gedir.[14] Fighting continued for at least seven months. Because of the heavy artillery bombardment and shelling, every day we believed that if we didn't die today then surely we would die tomorrow. One of the worst days was when a lorry full of people and cargo stopped near our house while we were having dinner. We were five people sharing a dish. My mother, brother, my little daughter, the daughter of my sister and me all having dinner under a tree. Suddenly bullets, flinging dust and stones, fell on our rations. In spite of my mother shouting at me to stay in and not to open the door, I opened the gate and caught sight of two dead bodies at the side of the road. I looked ahead and took a few steps then saw two more corpses. The lorry, full of people trying to leave Mogadishu, had been on its way to Kismayo when it was attacked.[15] The following day we moved out of our house. One terrible night our neighbour was robbed and looted, the daughters were raped and their gold was taken with some cash sent to them by relatives in Italy, along with everything of value in their house.

Another horrifying event: in a house very close to ours there resided an old man with his elderly wife. [One day] the house was attacked and the old man was shot while he was praying to Allah; and the elderly woman was threatened with death. Jewellery, gold and all valuable possessions were stolen.

After these terrible incidents my mother suggested that I and my little daughter leave Mogadishu. My mother decided to join a brother of mine who was a cattle herder in Qoryoley [a town about 100 km south of Mogadishu]. That day I decided to leave Somalia for Yemen. I would travel north to Bossaso port and take a boat from there.

From Somalia to Yemen

With my daughter I left Mogadishu and went to Afgoi where we stayed for five days. Two things in Afgoi astonished me. The first was the high density of the population in this little town, and the second was the infestation of mosquitoes – because of which my daughter fell sick with malaria. On the sixth day we left by bus. The bus had no seats apart from the driver's so everybody had to sit on the floor. The fare was unusually high: each passenger had to pay 1.5 million Somali shillings. We set off towards Baidoa along the tarmac road until we reached Dafed town and continued [on unpaved tracks] towards Bulo Berti. We arrived there after a terrible journey because the roads were very rough [the bus had taken a cross-country route to avoid roadblocks on the tarmac road].

We felt a little happier when we discovered that we were back on the main road. By the time we had arrived at Bulo Berti [about 150 km from Beletweyne] I had very little to my name. What made my financial situation worse was an old woman with a number of children in her charge who had no money at all. Whenever I ate some food with my little daughter I had to give the woman and her children something.

By the time we arrived safely in Beletweyne we had hardly any money left. We managed to go on to Balanbale town. There it was common for the inhabitants to ask new arrivals which clan they belonged to. If you did not declare which you belonged to nobody in Balanbale would sell you anything. For the whole day we were there we ate nothing, but we drank water.

Eventually we started north, towards Abudwaak, and arrived there safely. My daughter and I, along with the old woman and her accompanying children, stayed there for three days. The bus driver had kindly helped to arrange for us to travel to Bossaso [more than 1,000 km further north] on a Fiat Model N3 trailer. Because we had no male companion to secure a suitable position at the front part of the trailer we were forced to travel at the back, with all the indescribable dust. The truck was an old one and it took almost three days to reach Bossaso, where we stayed for five nights. On the sixth day my daughter and I began our journey by boat across the Red Sea to Aden in Yemen. The US$50 boat fare for my daughter and I was paid for by a former colleague of mine. In the good old days we had worked together. He helped us a lot and we owe him many thanks and regards.

The boat sailed from Bossaso but lost its way. Without knowing which direction we were sailing we stayed awake for three nights. By the mercy of Allah on the fourth night we arrived in the Port of Aden in the Republic of Yemen. It was the first day of Eid Al Fitr, 4 April 1992.

As soon as our feet touched dry land we prayed to our great God. Although most of the other passengers were quietly dismayed, my little daughter and I felt quite happy. Luckily we were taken to the refugee camp and spent two days there. I cannot express in words the poor health condition of the inhabitants of this camp. Sanitary standards were also poor. Most of the children were really sick. On the third day my little daughter caught bad flu so I immediately decided to leave the camp to find better conditions. I eventually found my brother in the northern town of Sada, where I was later able to find work in the hospital.

After leaving Mogadishu I had fallen fell sick many times. I was extremely homesick and worried for my family back in Somalia. Many key members of my family have been lost or are now unable to find an income. With my salary I look after myself, my daughter and many relatives of my extended family, both in Somalia and in the diaspora.

Although I am now in the relative safety of Yemen, members of my family remain in Somalia and continue to suffer from the ongoing war. In May 1995 I was able to meet my mother during the holy pilgrimage (*Hag*) to Mecca in Saudi Arabia. She told me what had happened since I had fled Somalia. One remarkable thing my mother told me was that, although our house had been burned down three times, our wooden wok (*kurbun*) had survived. We had used this wok for storing coffee seeds before they were ground and brewed. I remember seeing that wok around our home since my childhood.

NOTES

1. Composed by a Somali woman whose name is not recorded, the poem above, the Somali recording of which has been lost in the destruction of Mogadishu, is the voice of a pastoral woman as she prepares her daughter for the hardships of life ahead as a wife and mother. (Hassan *et al* 1995)
2. Known as *dhaanto* in other parts of Somalia.
3. In order to leave what scarce resources there are to women and children.
4. According to Islam, a woman is entitled to divorce her husband if he has left her without support and contact for more than 90 days.
5. Known as *mooryaan* in Mogadishu and *jiriir* in Puntland.
6. Communication with Pastoral and Environmental Network for the Horn of Africa (PENHA).
7. Vetaid (1997) *Pastoralism and Sedentarisation in Waqoyi Galbeed Region, Somaliland,* A report for Oxfam (Edinburgh: Vetaid).
8. PENHA established a research and advocacy programme in Somaliland in the late 1990s; we are grateful to PENHA for providing the information included here about the impact of the livestock export ban and other challenges facing pastoralists.
9. For example, the PENHA has a research and policy advocacy programme examining the current situation facing pastoralists in Somaliland/north west Somalia. Also involved and playing a key role in gendered research is the Somaliland Women's Research and Action Group (SOWRAG).
10. Personal communication with PENHA.
11. Rapprochement with Ethiopia triggered dissent because, since the colonial division of Somali territories, the lands of the Ogadeni people have been within Ethiopia's borders. It was to reunite them with the rest of Somalia that Siad Barre launched war on Ethiopia in the Ogaden Region in 1977.

12. Habiba's husband was out of the country at this time, and did not return.
13. These were refugees from the Ogaden region of Ethiopia who entered Somalia after the 1977 Ogaden War.
14. Once Siad Barre had been deposed the loose coalition of forces that had defeated him collapsed and Somalia disintegrated into factional fighting. In Mogadishu the main fighting was between the Abgal forces of Ali Mahdi, and the Habr Gedir forces of Aideed, both sub-clans of the Hawiye.
15. Such violent attacks on people fleeing the war were common and usually combined looting and killing. Halimo Elmi's account later in this book describes some of the hazards for those caught up in roadblocks and attacks.

2
Traditions of Marriage and the Household

Sadia Musse Ahmed

Editors' note

> 'After that day I decided to rely only on myself, and not any man ... the civil war taught me that a woman *can* live on her own.'

This Somali woman was reflecting on the day during the war when she learned that her husband had decided to divorce her, leaving her and her year-old daughter to fend for themselves.

Marriage is encouraged and expected in Islam and in Somali tradition; and a man is expected to protect and provide for the family just as a woman is expected to bear and nurture children. But marriage has significance beyond the nuclear family. It is an institution vital to the maintenance of the social, economic and political organisation that underpins a nomadic pastoral society. It has developed, and is maintained through, strongly defined rules and customs.

This chapter[1] describes marriage in Somali society and women's position in the household and clan. It examines the ways a marriage may come about, including socially sanctioned elopement and as a way of sealing a peace agreement between warring clan groups. The chapter is intended to provide an overview of the 'traditional' system of marriage and kinship. For this reason it uses the present tense to describe these 'traditional' patterns, even though they are not all still current.

The chapter focuses particularly on clan-exogamous cross-cousin marriage. This provides an insight into the experiences that a number of women in this book describe, and why and how women can act as peace envoys between warring clan parties. Anecdotal evidence of changes in women's attitudes suggests women are increasingly preferring their daughters to marry within their own clan. This is a direct result of the family break-up and conflicts of loyalty women have experienced in the civil war that stemmed from exogamous marriages.

Under normal circumstances an exogamous marriage can be a woman's best protection from spouse-related domestic violence. Future research will be needed to assess whether or not the trend away from exogamous marriage is permanent and whether or not it is accompanied by increased domestic violence; such a trend would seem to be developing within some of the diaspora communities but whether or not this is linked to the absence of protection from male blood-relatives and extended family remains a matter for conjecture.

The full impact of life in the diaspora on the institution and practices of marriage in Somali society, particularly as experienced by second-generation Somali girls and boys brought up outside Somalia and their extended family, is another area awaiting research.

Forms and stages of marriage

Marriage in Somali society is a contract between families or lineages (groups of families linked through male ancestors). There is a preference for this bond to be between groups not already related by clan lineage, or not closely related or living in the same area. In other words, young people are encouraged to marry into a group where new relations can be established. This is known as exogamous marriage.

The type of marriage most encouraged is that between cousins who are the children of a brother and a sister (*ilma abti*). Since such cousins are likely to be from different lineages (the sister's child being a member of the lineage of his or her father, not the mother), marriage between them establishes relations between the lineages, or strengthens such relations if they already exist. A person grows up envisaging their father's sister, or their mother's brother, as a potential mother- or father-in-law, since their children will be from a different lineage; and these kinsfolk will command particular respect.

Marriage between the offspring of two brothers or two sisters is discouraged, rare, and believed to be not blessed. Marriage between cousins whose fathers are brothers (*ilma adeer*) would be marriage within the same lineage, and is discouraged. Same-lineage marriage is discouraged because if the girl needs help and support, or protection from abuse by her husband, her father's brother's son would normally be the one to take revenge for her or take responsibility for her welfare. If he marries her, then that obligation will disappear and the girl will have lost her only defender.

Men value their relations with other men highly, be it in-laws or otherwise. This is illustrated by the saying: *Walaasha iskuma hubtid eh seedigaa haysa seegin* ('You are not sure of your sister's position, so do not jeopardise your relations with your brother-in-law'). Men are fiercely protective of their relatives when the matter involves another clan but are more likely to safeguard the status quo than seek retribution when the insult or injury comes from within their own clan. For women this usually means an exogamous marriage affords greater protection from domestic violence than does an endogamous marriage. A proverb addressing a husband says: 'You only own her services but not her blood' – which means he is accountable to her family if harm is inflicted; but this proverb is hardly enforced in endogamous marriages.

Cousins whose mothers are sisters (*habra wadaag*, which means 'sharing mothers') are believed to be too closely related; marriage between them is taboo and almost considered incest.

Commonly, marriages are arranged by elder kinsmen of the spouses. There are two types of arranged marriage. In most cases the pair has a long secret courtship in the course of which the girl asks the man to approach her family for consent. The man then tells his father or his closest relative of his intention to marry, and the latter arranges to approach the girl's family to seek consent. If her family refuses, the girl may influence the situation by making clear to her kinsmen her desire to marry the man. The family might decide that it is wise to accept the match. If there is a problem that could justify her family's decision to stand firm against the marriage, she will have a choice to make between her family and the man. By siding with the man, she risks making herself an outcast from her family, which could have drastic consequences for her if the marriage fails.

The second type of marriages are those arranged without the consent of one or both of the couple. The girl is selected mainly for admirable characteristics possessed by her family, such as their wealth, her mother's diligence, and the girl's rating among her peers. Girls wishing to resist such a match stand a better chance if they win their mothers over to their side. However, the father or other male relative is likely to try to limit this option by formalising the marriage before announcing his intention to the family. This practice was abolished by the Family Law of 1975[2] by which a father could not formalise his daughter's marriage without her consent in the presence of the officiant. Even though the Family Law has ceased officially to apply since the demise of the Siad Barre government, women in urban areas who know about it still use it as a basis for their cases.

But the effects of war and the collapse of the judiciary have undermined its effectiveness.

Elopement is a third possibility and a common way of avoiding arranged marriages. If a girl realises a marriage is being arranged for her while she is being courted by another, she might elope with the one she wants, risking her family's wrath. If a man cannot afford the marriage payments required for a successful match, his only option is to elope with the girl. Elopement is the most detested marriage arrangement among Somali nomads, yet it is the most effective way to avoid an unwanted marriage or payment of an expensive bride wealth. It is also the most dangerous form of marriage as it could cause a feud between families. It could be disastrous for the girl if the relationship goes wrong before she makes peace with her family. It brings no prestige for either spouse and is frowned on by society.

There are two other types of marriage. In the first, a woman or a group of women, is given in marriage as a peace offering to seal the resolution of a conflict between two groups. The receiving group is expected to select virile men with the highest integrity to be the girls' husbands, to assure the sending group that their offering has been received with respect. In this type of marriage, neither spouse has any say at all. In the unusual event of a boy or girl refusing, then the next one in the family will take his or her place. Most girls promised in such a marriage are very young and find it hard to refuse unless they elope or unless there is some resistance to the marriage within the family. Sometimes after a conflict both groups exchange women, underscoring their mutual commitment to honour the decisions of the peace negotiations. In this type of marriage women are treated with utmost respect: any wrongdoing by the husbands or in-laws is seen as harmful to the peace.

If a woman found herself single at an age where she might be seen as a spinster – which could be as young as 20 – she would feel forced to take drastic action. Such women could in the past initiate marriage by selecting a husband and going to his house, a practice known as *u gelid*. The man selected would have to marry the girl or face a compensation demand and the wrath of the community. This type of marriage still apparently occurs in Djibouti but no longer exists among ethnic Somalis in Somalia; it died out when spinsterhood lost its taboos. There was no stigma attached to such a marriage but it was not admired as much as those that went through the normal channels.

Somali marriage is invested with a series of symbolic rituals followed from the time the bride's family is first approached until the wedding ceremony itself. There are five main stages.

First, the man's family announces their intention and makes an appointment for a formal meeting (*doonid*) in which, if the match is acceptable to them, they are received with respect by the girl's family.

Second, the groom's family makes a payment called *gabaati*, which is commonly distributed among the bride's kinsmen. This payment is not retrievable, nor is it counted as bride wealth; instead, it is considered as a token of respect to the girl's family and their kin. The girl is now officially considered as the groom's fiancee, but no sexual relationship is allowed until the wedding festival itself. Since most weddings take place in spring, when water and grass are abundant and people have fewer labour commitments, the gap between the two events could be up to a year.

Third, when the groom's family is ready for the wedding they bring to the bride's family the main payment (*yarad*) ranging from a few camels to 100 camels, a good horse and a gun, depending on the wealth of the groom's family and the position of the bride and her family within the community. The payment includes all the wedding expenses, with the exception of the bride's clothes called *marriin*, which are provided by the groom. These clothes must be varied and of high quality as they will be displayed in public by the girl's family.

Fourth, arrangements are made for the wedding celebration, which will probably be held near the bride's family. The latter provides the hut or *aqal*, most of which will have been woven by the bride herself. The mother and other relatives provide other items. A wedding *aqal*, including items specially selected for craftsmanship and quality, is built further from the bride's family dwelling as the couple's new home.

In a polygamous marriage the husband establishes a separate household for his new wife, set apart from that of his other wife or wives, and allocates livestock for her. This may be difficult for a husband who already has several households, or if he has grown-up sons who will themselves expect to marry from the same resources. Women detest polygamy and could sabotage the process. The first wife has a say in determining how much of the family stock can be allocated for a second marriage, and can hamper the husband's intention, especially if she has grown-up offspring. A woman may pre-empt her husband's remarriage by marrying off her sons, undermining his ability to pay a worthy bride price from the family stock. In second marriages, relatives' wealth contributions are limited; hence men have to rely on their own resources.

The fifth stage, the marriage celebration itself, starts with a religious leader tying the knot in front of two witnesses and formalising the marriage in the presence of the husband and the bride's representative. This is the formal religious ceremony. The husband promises money or livestock for the bride as a security bond (*meher*).

The festivities begin on the day the couple start living together as a family unit, and continue for three to seven days. The formal end of the celebrations comes with the opening of the *xeedho* – a container filled with meat, ghee and dates secured by string tied in a very complicated way. In this highly ritualised event, the groom's kin are challenged to unravel the string and open the *xeedho*, which symbolises the virgin bride. Sometimes they fail, and are obliged to cut the string and pay compensation to the mother of the bride. However, cutting the string is tantamount to abusing the bride, and is seen as being very offensive, creating problems between the two families. In modern marriages the mother helps the groom by pointing out where the end of the string is; in the past 30 years or so it has become a purely symbolic ritual in urban communities.

Eventually the new family unit prepares to leave the bride's family home and move to the groom's, unless the groom decides to live with his wife's family. Such a move usually happens within a year of the marriage. If his family do not have enough livestock then his kinsmen contribute. If the two families live far apart, planning is required to determine not only the timing of the move but also the means of escorting them. The husband goes back to his family to prepare his new wife's reception in his home. He and his kin receive the accompanying party, host them and treat them with respect.

If the *yarad* payment or bridewealth is large – for example, 50–100 camels, a gun and a horse – then at some future time the groom will expect to receive a share of the *dhibaad*, or gift given to the bride by her maiden family when she visits them after her marriage. The gift may include the *aqal*, preserved meat (*muqmad* – a highly prestigious dish[3]), some livestock and a transport camel. The groom's family now sets up his new herd.

Women can dissolve marriage by moving out and refusing to consider reconciliation. The man can deny her a divorce, but after a while even his relatives will urge him to let her go free. In such cases, some of the bride wealth might be returned if there are no children from the marriage because it was short-lived. The bride wealth will be returned in full if the marriage is not consummated. If the couple were married for a long time but with no children no bride wealth will be returned.

The importance of marriage in women's lives

Both men and women gain merit and respect through the achievement of their social tasks and responsibilities, which they learn from childhood. Women's work is seen as being crucial to society, and to some extent this is recognised in women's rights to inheritance and property. Nevertheless, for young people of both sexes, maturity and responsibility are mainly acquired through marrying, and through maintaining their own household. Young men become full members of society by gaining control of household resources such as herds and family labour. Women also develop their own areas of decision-making, principally by giving birth to, and bringing up, their children.

Women have opportunities to acquire economic resources independently. Sometimes young people accumulate wealth through inheritance, but this wealth will be managed by older relatives until the young marry. Livestock and other materials inherited by girls from fathers and other relatives are never taken over by the husband on marriage. Women also have the liberty of disposing of their wealth in whatever way they see fit.

Women's rights under customary law are limited; their main power-base is their family, relatives and her sub-clan who supposedly provide both resources and advice in troubled times. If a woman is ill-treated by her husband or in-laws, her family might intervene on her behalf, although this is not guaranteed. They can thus decide the fate of the marriage.

Cross-clan marriages create 'diplomatic' relations between groups, and are therefore treated with respect. The way men treat wives from a certain clan influences how other groups see them as potential partners. Hence if a man mistreats his wife other members of his group usually intervene, mediating between the couple with the help of her male kin.

The political functions of marriage

In northern Somalia the clan system involves relationships that Somali nomads utilise to create both war and peace. Marriage creates important ties between lineages. However, neighbourhood may be given greater importance than lineage. A Somali saying goes: *ood kaa dheeri kuma dhaxan tirto* ('a fence far away from you does not protect you from cold') meaning if a clan or family is far away, they cannot offer help in time of need.

Importance is also attached to relations with the mother's family (*reer abti*), and kinfolk, ie people who are not directly related to each other but are linked to each other via a third family (*xigto*), distant relatives (*qaraabo qansax*), and in-laws (*xidid*), all relationships created by marriage. For example, a mother's family regards their girl's offspring as very important, and treats them with the utmost respect. In-laws are usually valued highly, especially in cases where the husband treats his wife with respect and where there is harmony between them. In such cases the two families consider themselves to be especially close. These relations may prove more important than relations with other lineage members.

Somali pastoralists call on these ties in various circumstances. For example, when a trader is on long-distance journey through other clans' territories, relationships by marriage can provide safe passage. People traveling through territory belonging to another lineage will often select a highly respected name among the family whose territory they are crossing. Announcing the name of this protector easily deters any threat. Misdeeds encountered within the territory of that group will be avenged or redressed by the person whose name is quoted as protector. Travellers must have a strong claim on the person they trust with their safety (*magan-gelyo*), who will probably be a kinsman. For example, if a woman marries into another clan, her relatives can use her husband's name to travel through his family's area, or to seek assistance from members of her family in time of need. (See Amina Sayid and Halimo Elmi's testimonies, pages 59–66 and pages 127–37).

Family ties are also called on in other cases. For assistance when one is needy, for example when drought kills most of the family livestock, one can call on relatives for support and they are obliged to help. Kinsmen can be used as a 'bridge' in seeking the hand in marriage of women who otherwise would be unattainable. The assistance of relatives can be sought in redressing grievances committed in war, or in putting a stop to the looting of stock (when tribal cattle brands – *sumad* – are recognised by relatives). Another example of the importance of wider kinship links is that if a young man wanting to marry cannot acquire enough livestock by himself, he is given a long rope (*xadhig siin*) with which to collect livestock from kin. All his kin are expected to contribute.

These examples show that marriage often forms the sole basis for interaction between groups. The more marriages there are between two groups, the stronger the relationship between them. This enables land and other common resources to be shared between related groups. However, the existence of such relationships can become a constraint in times of shortages of resources such as water and pasture, and potentially create conflict between the groups concerned.

TESTIMONY 2: AMINA SAYID

Editors' note

As Sadia Musse Ahmed has highlighted, marriage ties across clan lineages have an important role in ensuring safe passage. During the civil war such family ties were a source of protection for many; they enabled family members to move through otherwise hostile territories equipped with a 'name' or contact relative who could act as their guide or protector (*magan-gelyo*). Many people were saved by relatives or friends temporarily 'adopting' them under their clan name.

Amina Sayid is a medical doctor from the coastal town of Brava, about 250 km south of Mogadishu. The Brava community, descended from Arab settlers, has a language of its own and is not part of the ethnic Somali clan system.[4] However, through her mother and her husband, Amina's extended family is linked with two of the Somali clan lineages. During the early part of the war these two clans (Hawiye and Darod) were at war, placing her husband and children in grave danger.

At the outbreak of war in Mogadishu many people fleeing the fighting sought refuge in Brava. The displaced included Bravanese themselves and Somalis from other parts of the country. Amina describes here how all who came to find safety were welcomed, whatever their clan. Among those displaced to Brava were large numbers of people from the Darod clan family, particularly the Marehan who had to flee Mogadishu because being closely associated with the injustices of Siad Barre's regime, they were a target for revenge attacks. As Amina records, whilst the Marehan were specifically victimised, anyone, particularly men, associated with the Darod clan family were vulnerable to attack.

Ironically, given the revenge-driven nature of much of the conflict in the early stages, and the deep shock of its people, it was the politically insignificant and unarmed Bravanese community that was decimated. Being outside the ethnic Somali clan system, the Bravanese community was an easy target for the rampaging militias of all sides who swept through the town in search of plunder and enemies during the first years of the war. The Bravanese were looted and even killed, with impunity.

Amina witnessed what happened in Brava in 1991; her testimony includes a first-hand record of the terror endured by her own family, neighbours and other residents of the coastal town, and those displaced from Mogadishu sheltering with them. Brava is on record as having suffered the worst violence of any community.[5] Affected by several waves of fighting in 1991 and 1992, Brava was terrorised and captured at different times by different clan-based militias. As a consequence of the looting, clan persecution and rape, those who could fled to the refugee camps of Kenya, (see Chapter 3) Yemen or in some cases Europe and America. A UN report notes that in August 1996 Brava 'looked deserted: there were very few young male adults walking in the streets'. (UNDOS 1997)

Amina's story

On 30 December 1990 civil war broke out in Mogadishu. I was attending a graduation ceremony at the Mogadishu Medical School when the first shelling started in the north east of the city. I had to rush, take a taxi and pick up my two daughters from school. On the road people were running to get public transport. At the school, parents, with fear in their faces, were asking each other what was happening. On the advice of the taxi driver, to reach our house we took a coastal road, which was safer, and we arrived home without difficulty. Fortunately we were living in the south western outskirts of Mogadishu, known as Kilometre 7, the opposite side to where the fighting was going on.

However, I was worried about my husband and my brother who were working in the city centre, and about my parents who lived in the inner city. It turned out that my husband and brother were safe and made it home by taking twisting and turning paths.

Meanwhile the fighting intensified and spread to the city centre. By sunset the fighting between Siad Barre's soldiers and the opposition militiamen [the USC] had stopped but the city was plunged into darkness, and people fell easy prey to looters and armed bandits.

At dawn the following day the fighting started again and the telephone lines were cut off. People began to flee the war zone. Waves of people were coming along the road near our home. This road, linking Mogadishu to Afgoi (a town 30 km inland), was one of the only ways to safety to the south. It was a parade of people in despair. Mostly they were on foot, carrying or dragging their belongings, with elderly people limping along.

Every means of transport was used. Wheelbarrows carrying elderly people and children, rented or private carts, old lorries, tractors and private cars. This terrible scene went on all day. As we were nearby, we took many people in, among them friends, relatives and acquaintances, who used our home as a stopping place.

The situation was worsening and everyone had guns in their hands. Looting was widespread, even in daytime. We decided as a family to escape to Brava, my home town 200 km south of Mogadishu. My husband drove us, our two daughters of seven and nine years old, up to Afgoi. We joined waves of people fleeing the fighting. Driving was not safe, as cars were highly sought-after by looters. So we had to drive very early in the morning. Afgoi had become a refuge for thousands of people. It was itself overcrowded and insecure.

Buses to Brava were not available and it took us four or five hours to find a place on a lorry – and then we had to pay four times the normal amount. My husband went back to Mogadishu to look after our house for a while.

Along the road to Brava exhausted people were travelling on foot for several days to reach places like Merca or Qoryoley, just 90–100 km from Mogadishu. Our journey took 14 hours instead of the usual six or seven. On our lorry I had no time to think as I was struggling to protect my daughters from being hurt, for we were packed in. The lorry driver took advantage of our desperate situation and crammed us into the back, creating tensions and disputes among the travellers. At stopping places those travelling in groups were luckier because they could send one or two of their group to get water and food supplies while the others kept their places on the lorry. These stops gave us an opportunity to exchange information. Many of the people on our lorry were missing members of their families, left behind in Mogadishu because they were out of the house when the danger forced the others to leave home. Some had witnessed killings caused by either shelling or opposition gunmen. It was very sad to know how these people [felt] to lose everything they cherished and be forced to flee without any plans for their future. They were all worried, hopeless and emotionally affected, probably with long-term consequences for their health caused by emotional stress.

Historically Brava is one of the most ancient coastal cities of Somalia. In 1991 its population was estimated to be 5,000–6,000 people. Thought to be originally Somali Arab settlers, the indigenous Barawans have their own language, Jimini, which is related to Swahili. Unlike most of the rest of Somalia's population, they do not use a clan system to identify themselves – during the war, for Barawans this characteristic could save you or be your death – and they traditionally practice cross-cousin marriage.[6] Culturally conservative, similar to other Arab cultures but different from the predominant Somali culture, most of Barawan society has typically not allowed girls access to further education. Women take the *hijab* head covering and after puberty girls are expected to stay in the home.

The town's traditional trade links with Mombasa and Zanzibar had stopped during the 21 years of the Dictator's [Siad Barre's] rule. The main livelihoods in the town were fishing, trade and small businesses and handicraft [Brava was famous for its leatherwork and cloth weaving traditionally done by men]. Brava is also well known for its peaceful tradition and strong religious values.

When we arrived in Brava our house was already full of relatives who had been displaced but I managed to get a room for myself and my children, and my husband who joined us after a week. The city was full of displaced people coming from Mogadishu. Community elders helped them to take shelter in public buildings; others were accommodated by friends and relatives, while many others made their own temporary shelters. The city was quiet and peaceful and the displaced had nothing to fear or protect themselves from. The only problem was the food shortage and inflation. Many displaced people were optimistic and believed that they could go back home once the fighting in Mogadishu was over. Displaced women became householders and started establishing small businesses in and around Brava. Some even risked going into the war zones to bring back goods to towns like Brava.

However, in January 1991 Barawans were unaware of the tragic events that were in store and were to haunt our memories forever.

At midday on 9 February 1991 when the market was full of people, suddenly, without any warning, the town was invaded by a huge number of heavily armed gunmen with 'technicals' [four-wheel-drive vehicles customised and mounted with heavy machine gun]. I realised that they were USC men[7] and that they were after male members of the Darod. They started shelling the town, killing several people and injuring many others. They were everywhere. I ran to the house. Seeing them coming down from the mountains behind Brava my youngest brother said: 'They are like birds coming down!' We closed our door so we could only hear the shelling. After a while when it stopped a little we opened the door to see gunmen coming and going everywhere [looking for Darod people]. We heard shouting and screaming from our neighbours. My mother, whose clan isn't from Brava though she was born in Brava, said we must do something; so she and I went outside and cried: 'Please leave us! These people are innocent.' But they said our neighbours were Marehan and why were we interfering? They said that if we did not go back inside they would shoot us. We went back into the house. Fortunately they didn't come to our house.

Throughout the night we heard the screams and crying of people. We were told by some of our neighbours that they were attacking the women. I couldn't eat for two days. I was so worried about my husband because he was Darod. My mother said we must leave by whatever means because someone might point out to the gunmen that my husband is from Darod. I learned that nine Darod were killed that first day. This was my worst two days ever. I couldn't believe what was happening.

After the shelling, the next step was indiscriminate looting, raping, torturing and destroying. Initially they looted cars and big things. We saw them take the earrings from an elderly woman neighbour.[8] We thought they were just after Darod but it was an excuse for the violence. We don't know why to this day. On that first night a lot of women were raped. In the morning there was a demonstration by men, taking the holy Koran and put it on their head saying: 'We are helpless. We are helpless. God help us!' Later on elders from Brava approached the warlords about what had been done to the people but the warlords just said: 'We can't help you. You should have been armed. You should arm yourselves and defend yourselves.'

We don't know how many women were raped but we know it was a large number and it included the Darod women who were displaced in Brava. The raped women were desperate because we don't rape in our culture. Brawani women were very conservative and this was the end of the world for them. They were shocked and traumatised. Some denied what had happened to them. You would hear about a mother and a daughter who had been raped. Brothers and husbands were desperate but couldn't do anything to help them though they tried to protect them. Maybe in one or two cases raped women were divorced by their husbands but mostly the husbands stayed and tried to help them.

The town was living in a nightmare. In all its history nothing like this had ever happened before. What was most shocking for the people of Brava was the humiliation and the violations. We were not armed. We Brawanis keeping saying: 'Why? We're not involved in politics, we're not involved in anything. Why did these things happen to us? We are defenceless.' Brawanis had never expected the war to affect them.

After that first night people started to leave by whatever means, many trying to get to Mombasa on small fishing boats. There were few boats available so they were overcrowded. People had been robbed so they had little to take with them. There was no time for preparation or planning, unlike in Mogadishu. Some people I met later told me they had drunk sea water. Some left elderly family members behind to save their girls from being raped.

Fortunately, after three or four days we found a family friend's bus. He came to Brava to transport people and so for my husband's safety we went back to Mogadishu [so that he could escape further north; Mogadishu itself was now a dangerous place for Darod]. We couldn't go to Kismayo because that was also full of armed people. The bus was very overcrowded. So many wanted to leave Brava that only the strongest managed to get on. The fare was 50,000 Somali shillings [compared to 6,000 before the war]. Many people couldn't pay so they started walking along the coast. On the road there were many checkpoints looking for men mainly from Darod. At one checkpoint a young member of an armed gang (*mooryaan*) came on to the bus pointing out some of the men ordering them to get off in order to check their clan. So it is lucky for those [like my family] who have someone to protect them, and it was an advantage to have been born into a different clan [from the group being targeted as this enabled us to help people get through unharmed]. I was frozen. Terrified. We were lucky to have my uncle with us. Along the road we had seen a lot of men's bodies lying dead. Killed just because of their clan. Thinking about the people who were helpless and didn't have any other clans to protect them is awful.

I left Brava a town eviscerated by human predators and abandoned to its hopeless fate as a city conquered by cruel enemies. Mogadishu was itself in a state of total anarchy. Everyone was armed, regardless of age, and clashes between armed bandits for control of a given area were frequent. We moved back to the same area as before. Our house was OK; it had been looked after by some neighbours. But everything was difficult, finding food especially, because we were living far from the market and the way was dangerous. A big group of women would go to the market together and a man would go with us and bring us back.

Even then we believed that everything would soon be sorted out and the war would end. All this time our daughters were terrified. They studied our faces and felt our fear. They couldn't go to school because it wasn't running so they stayed at home, although when they could they went to Koranic school in the mornings. I worked as a volunteer in the Banadir Mother and Child Hospital for a while but my main objective was to find a way of escaping the war. The hospital had been looted. Although many people were still using it, there were no drugs, surgical equipment, materials. I came back to work at the hospital because it was better than sitting at home. We had lost our jobs, we had no salary. The Red Cross supplied weekly food rations at the hospital, which helped. It wasn't safe to work there. From my house at Kilometre 7 to reach the hospital 2 km away was very dangerous. The way had become an empty road with big, looted buildings along the way with gunmen patrolling. Some mornings I found other people going to town whom I could walk with; if I couldn't find others to go with I stayed at home.

When Darod tried to recapture Mogadishu I witnessed in Wardhigley [a district of Mogadishu] many Hawiye women running along the road carrying cutlery and kitchen utensils and shouting to the opposition fighters [USC]: 'Give *us* the guns! Take these [the cutlery]! You, go home and do the cooking! You are the women, *we're* the men!' They went to every military checkpoint and threw their knives and forks and spoons at the men. [The women's actions were to humiliate and goad the now tired militia into fighting against the returning forces of Siad Barre, which threatened to overrun the city.]

In another period of heavy inter-clan fighting I saw many women running in the street wearing *weer* [white headbands to signify mourning]. I stopped one and asked her what was going on. She said the women from both sides of the fighting had gone wherever the fighting men were to be found and had called on them to get out from their holes: 'Stop fighting or we will go naked [uncover our heads]!'[9] They went to men on both sides of the conflict. The men were ashamed and stopped fighting.[10]

While we still had some money I needed to find a way out for myself and my daughters. [It had been too dangerous for Amina's husband to stay with them in Mogadishu so he had left some months before to make his way north.] There was no security for us in Mogadishu. On 15 May 1991 I managed to get tickets for a boat going directly to Mombasa, Kenya. It was quite a small fishing vessel. There were 90 passengers on board, mainly women and children. It took a week to reach Kismayo where we stopped for two days to pick up other people. We all slept in the open. My daughters and I were very sick.

There was a woman giving birth on board the boat and I had to assist her. The crew let us use a cabin. It was her first baby and she was circumcised. I couldn't suture her without a kit but I stopped her bleeding and when we reached Kismayo I went to the hospital and found an old colleague who gave me some antibiotics for her. Fortunately, both she and the 'boat baby' that came to join our desperate community survived.

Two days out from Kismayo our boat [ran out of fuel]. We were stuck in Kenyan territorial waters, miles from land. An old seaman on board suggested we should put a sail up. Finally we reached a place where we could see land. We stayed in this place for nine days because the Kenyan authorities refused to give us any assistance and ordered our boat to go back to Somalia, which was impossible without fuel. We waved for help from passing fishing boats but no help came. Everything ran out. We were starving. We cooked together once a day. Those who got on at Kismayo shared their rations with us and some people managed to catch some fish which we cooked by burning bits of the boat but by the last three or four days there was no food. Water was OK because the boat had a filtration system so we could make fresh water. This saved us. It was terrible: the children begging for food, the elderly fainting from hunger.

The boat had a radio. One day on the BBC Somali Service we heard a Somali journalist for the BBC based in Kenya [reporting] that our boat had been transporting arms and there had been an accident at sea and all passengers were dead except two. This was a cruel lie and a terrible thing to hear. We could only imagine the pain and distress it caused our loved ones. It was not until the next day that we could send a radio message to Mogadishu informing our relatives that the announcement had been a lie and we were all OK.[11]

Our plight continued until the boat owner, from his Kenyan residence, finally persuaded the Kenyan authorities to allow him to take supplies to the boat. We received food and fuel and had to make our way back to Somalia. Our boat dropped anchor in Kismayo and from there I went back by bus with my children to Mogadishu via Brava. I had no choice. Mogadishu was the only place where I could find a way to safety.

However, the situation in Mogadishu was worsening further and the relatively free movement of people that had been possible during some hours in the mornings now became very dangerous due to new hostilities between sub-clans. Things were really bad.

I remained stuck in Mogadishu for a further six months. We came together with my elder brother's family to share things, which helped us get by. I did not lose hope. I never stopped trying to find out about escape routes either within or outside Somalia. Some who organised these escape routes made their fortunes, even though often they used inadequate and unsafe transport.

I heard from colleagues at Banadir Hospital that there would be some flights leaving from Mogadishu to Garowe [in the north east]. My friend and I went to the airport to see if I could manage to pay. At the airport we found a young boy of 18 or 20 who was a mediator [between the plane's owner and passengers]. We asked him if he could sort out seats. He agreed for US$200 per seat. He said he didn't know for sure which day the plane would take off so I was to bring my children every day to the airport and to be ready.

It was 21 November 1991, almost a year since the war had started, when my two daughters and I left Mogadishu on this small aircraft which landed two hours later in Garowe, in the Nugal region of north eastern Somalia. Although I didn't know anyone I recognised someone, who helped us to find a hotel, and from there we travelled to Bossaso to join my husband. Eventually, from Bossaso, along with many other displaced people from the southern region we crossed by boat to the refugee camp in Yemen, in search of the chance of education for our daughters now that all the schools were closed or destroyed in Somalia. Having first sought survival, we now sought life.

NOTES

1. The information in this chapter comes partly from Sadia Musse Ahmed's own experience and partly from research she conducted in the early 1980s on women's issues in the Somali Academy of Sciences and Arts in Mogadishu. Some is borrowed from her MSc thesis, submitted to London University in 1994. (See references)
2. The government of Siad Barre implemented reforms in the Islamic family laws to promote equality between men and women.
3. Lean meat cut into small pieces and deep-fried with oil or ghee and herbs, then cooled with purified ghee. This meat could be kept for a long time.
4. See Mohamed M. Kassim, 'Aspects of the Benadir Cultural History: The Case of the Bravan Ulama', in Ali Jimale Ahmed (ed.) (1995) *The Invention of Somalia* (Trenton NJ: Red Sea Press).
5. UNDOS (1997), *Studies on Governance 1, Lower Shabelle Region* (Nairobi: UNDOS).
6. Parallel cousin marriage.
7. The United Somali Congress (USC) was headed by General Mohamed Farah Aideed, leader of the Hawiye clan-based military force. The USC led the attack on Mogadishu to overthrow Siad Barre. USC forces targeted members of the Darod clan group, which had carried most power and wealth under Siad Barre. The coastal towns of Merca, Brava and Kismayo and the inland towns of Baidoa and Bardera suffered waves of invasions by inter-clan fighters.
8. In 1992 an aid agency noted that in some badly looted communities such as Brava women were found inside their homes on the verge of starvation, unable to go in search of food or help because all their clothes had been stolen.
9. The threat to remove their headscarves is traditionally used by women to break up fighting between men. In an Islamic culture, for a woman to uncover her hair in front of a man who is not her husband, let alone a group of such men, is considered shameful.
10. This and the account of women goading men to fight illustrates that women were not neutral or passive in the war but could act either as

promoters of war or peace, depending on their interpretation of the situation.

11. Allegedly the boat owner was from a Darod clan and the journalist from the Hawiye, the opposing sides at this point in the conflict. It is assumed that by issuing what he presumably knew to be a false report the journalist was inflicting pain on those he regarded as his enemy.

3
War Crimes Against Women and Girls

Fowzia Musse

Editors' note

The wars in Bosnia and Rwanda drew the world's attention to the use of rape and sexual violence in war. But systematic rape during wartime is nothing new. From the ancient Romans to the Vietnam war, sexual violation of women and girls has been a means to conquer the enemy.[1] What is new in the case of Bosnia and Rwanda is that the United Nations Security Council established an international war crimes tribunal and included rape as one of the crimes against humanity that the tribunals are empowered to prosecute.[2] On 23 February 2001 three Bosnian Serbs were given jail sentences of up to 28 years for the rape of Muslim women – a watershed for women around the world.[3]

Journalists' exposure of what was happening to Bosnian women, combined with detailed reports by human rights organisations and others,[4] ensured that the rape of thousands of women and girls in the Bosnia and Rwanda wars was acknowledged and will, in part at least, be addressed.

In contrast, the world is ignorant of the wartime rape of thousands of Somali women and girls between 1991 and 1994,[5] which a decade later was still going on in some parts of the country. Atrocities carried out by individuals and militia groups against women and girls in Somalia between 1991 and 1992 were unprecedented in Somali history. Traditionally, in Somali pastoral society feuding and conflict were bounded by codes and social conventions.[6] Along with the elderly and the sick, women and children were immune from attack. That is not to say that women were never targeted but if they were harmed there were rules about retribution and compensation. In the inter-clan warfare from 1991 onwards these traditional laws have played little part, and women as well as children and other non-fighters were attacked by warring factions with impunity.

Among the worst of the atrocities were the 'rape camps', particularly in Mogadishu in the early 1990s. Militiamen abducted many women, imprisoning them in villas where they were subjected to repeated rape and other forms of sexual abuse.[7] Although all women and girls were vulnerable, rapists tended to target female members of opposing factions, or those with weak clan affiliations and therefore little clan protection. The most violated women were those from minority groups, and especially the coastal populations of Mogadishu, Merca, Brava and Kismayo. (See Amina Sayid's testimony, Chapter 2) These groups were generally unarmed and offered little retaliation since they were not part of the clan lineage system.

Many of these women and their families were among the thousands of Somalis who fled the country between 1991 and 1993, some by boat for Yemen and Kenya, and some overland to the Kenyan border. Women and children made up about 80 per cent of the estimated 300,000 who had sought refuge in Kenya by October 1993. They had fled to Kenya to escape the Somali civil war but, as Fowzia Musse describes in this chapter, many found themselves facing sexual violence. In the words of one refugee quoted in *The Nightmare Continues* (African Rights, September 1993) 'We ran away from the lion, but we have only found a hyena.'

By the end of 1993 reports from the UNHCR[8] and international human rights organisations[9] were documenting the shocking scale of sexual violence occurring inside Kenya's refugee camps. Fowzia Musse was the Somali social researcher recruited by the UNHCR in early 1993 to investigate rape and other forms of sexual violence inside the camps and to recommend ways to respond. In this chapter Fowzia presents information from her work with refugee rape survivors. She summarises the main findings of her investigation for the UNHCR, which she describes as 'the tip of the iceberg', and examines concepts of sexual assault in Somali society and how society traditionally deals with rape. She describes how women who had been raped responded, what preventive measures they and other women tried, and the UNHCR's interventions which she was instrumental in establishing and coordinating as Project Coordinator of the Women Victims of Violence project from 1993 to 1995. Reflecting on how best to assist refugee survivors of sexual assaults as well as to prevent further attacks, Fowzia presents the thinking behind the UNHCR's response, part of which focused on helping women reconstruct their social and economic networks and status in society.

War crimes against women and girls

The scale of sexual violence against women refugees

The exact number of Somali women who were raped in Kenya's North Eastern Province following their arrival as refugees is not known because until the UNHCR intervention in 1993, women had no incentive to come forward and report what had happened to them. They were also fearful of reprisals by their attackers and reluctant to speak about their ordeal. Based on reported cases, the total number of women raped in the camps is likely to have been in the high hundreds or even thousands.

From February to August 1993 I interviewed and documented reports from 192 survivors of rape or attempted rape in the Kenyan refugee camps. Just over 100 incidents had occurred after the refugees had crossed into Kenya, while 85 had occurred in Somali territory. The age-span of the victims was from four years old to 56. In August 1993 alone 42 additional cases of rape were reported. All of these occurred in the camps in the North Eastern Province, in the Dadaab area. The majority of attacks in Kenya were attributed to armed Somali-speaking bandits or *shifta,*[10] who would have included both Somali nationals and Kenyan Somalis. Seven attacks were said to have been committed by members of the Kenyan security forces. Most women attacked by security force personnel refused to report the crime to the authorities for fear of reprisals.

Women say their attackers were usually people they knew,[11] that they were well armed, and that they attacked in groups. Some women were forced to submit when militiamen threatened to destroy their homes with their children locked inside. Some were raped inside their own homes in front of their husbands who were forced to watch at gunpoint. Many victims were raped in front of their children and relatives. Sixteen rape survivors whose cases were documented by the UNHCR reported that they had been raped over the body of their dead husband, child, sibling or other relative.

Almost all the attacks were carried out by more than one attacker. Sometimes as many as ten men took part in a gang rape. They would be armed with rifles, grenades, daggers, bayonets, clubs and walking sticks. Some used flashlights when attacking at night to blind their victims. They used physical force against their victims, including hitting with rifle butts on the upper body and the legs; unrelenting fist blows to the head; striking the woman violently when she was lying on the ground; using razor blades, daggers or bayonets to remove the 'external virginity' or infibulation of women and girls who had never had sexual relations, often inflicting severe injuries. (See below – 'Female genital mutilation')

Women known to have money were tortured to reveal the whereabouts of their assets, their attackers typically cutting parts of their bodies with daggers or bayonets. Some women reported being blindfolded with their hands tied before they were raped. Some were held to the ground by several assailants if they tried to resist. Some attackers even sat on the woman's head while others raped her.

Female genital mutilation (FGM)[12]

For Somali women, the physical injuries caused by being raped are compounded by the almost ubiquitous practice of female genital mutilation (FGM – also known as female circumcision, or *gudniin* in Somalia).

Different forms of FGM are practised in many parts of Africa, and it is also common in the southern part of the Arabian peninsula, along the Persian Gulf, in the Middle East among some populations in Indonesia and Malaysia. Mistakenly thought of as a Muslim custom, FGM predates Islam and is found in Christian, Animist and Muslim societies. Among such societies a girl will be considered unclean, improper or unmarriageable if she does not undergo this operation as part of her rites of passage.

Somali women subjected to genital mutilation in their childhood have generally undergone the most severe form of FGM, infibulation, known in Somalia as *qodob*. This involves the removal of the clitoris and the labia minora and parts of the labia majora. The remaining surfaces are then stitched or fastened together. Only a small opening, sometimes the size of a match-stick, remains for the flow of urine and menstrual blood.

One of the reasons given to justify infibulation is that it is believed it will stop girls from being raped or sexually active.[13]

Any form of sexual intercourse for women who have undergone this operation is painful or impossible unless infibulation is reversed. Typically this is done on marriage and consists of making a short incision to separate the fused tissues.

Some refugee women and girls who had never had sexual relations before recounted how their attackers removed their 'external virginity' using razor blades, daggers or bayonets.

Some women were attacked in the daytime while in the bush collecting firewood. Most were attacked at night in their tents and either raped inside or taken to the bush. When assailants came in groups they tended to attack several women in the neighbourhood. Sometimes they rounded up victims in one compound, took them to the bush, and raped them collectively. Gang rape seems to have been a feature of most attacks. Only a few survivors reported being raped by one assailant while the majority described between two and ten. Many women reported being raped on more than one occasion.[14]

Nearly half of the refugee women who reported being raped during 1993 had previously been raped in Somalia, the majority in Kismayo town. This previous experience had driven them to become refugees in the first place.

According to the victims, most of the attacks in the camps were clan related. Since most of the refugees came from southern Somalia the clan and sub-clan tensions in Somalia were transferred to the camps.[15] Many women said that the rapists would ask their clan affiliation or demand to know the location of the dwellings of a particular clan.[16] The attackers would then target the women of that group. Women who were from the same clan as their attackers were often spared from being raped and were only robbed.

The majority of rapes also involved looting and robbery, even of the victims' refugee food ration cards and kitchen utensils. Intimidation and extortion influenced the incidence of rape and sexual violence: a number of women who ran successful trading businesses in the camps became targets if they did not pay protection money. Women were targeted who had some form of income, usually from petty trading within the camp such as selling meat or firewood, or from working for a relief agency in the camp.

Many women, especially those from the Harti sub-clan of the Darod, became exposed to sexual violence when their husbands, brothers, fathers and male relatives left the camps to return to Kismayo town. Some of these men left to take part in the fighting in southern Somalia. However, many left because their lives were at risk in the camps owing to clan tensions – for example between the Harti, Ogadeni, Marehan and Hawiye. As men are seen as the progenitors of clans, their death jeopardises the propagation of the clans. In the eyes of many women, it was preferable for them to be without the protection of their male kin than to risk the life of the clan.

Testimonies

1. Maryam, a 38-year-old woman of the Marehan clan, arrived at Ifo camp in north eastern Kenya around July 1992. A month later she was sleeping at the hut of a friend when they were attacked by nine unknown assailants. In Maryam's words:

> They came around 9pm. We were in the house sleeping. They came into the house with guns and knives and told us to give them our money. We didn't know them. They were wearing black jackets, trousers and hats. We were so scared, we gave them everything. Then they began to beat me. They beat me for hours and then six men raped me. After the rape I was in so much pain I could not walk. The doctor had to come to the hut to see me. (Interview, Marafa camp, Kenya, 23 July 1993)

2. Asalim, a 20-year-old Ogadeni, had been recently married and was expecting her first child. In March 1993 she and her husband were asleep at night when two unknown men entered their house. She described them as being dressed in olive-coloured jackets and trousers and both carrying guns. They threatened Asalim and her husband and stole the few belongings in the hut. Asalim explains:

> They took me to the bush outside the camp. I was so scared that no sound was coming from my mouth. They asked me what clan I was and then told me to remove my clothes. Both men raped me – each twice. (Interview, Dagahaley camp, Kenya, 26 July 1993)

As a result of the rape Asalim suffered a miscarriage.

3. Hibaq, a 40-year-old woman, was raped by three unknown assailants in the middle of the night at Liboi camp in March 1993. She was sleeping in her hut with her three children aged 21, ten, and eight years old.

> I live in a compound with my husband and his second wife, and I was woken up by a torch shining in my face. I asked who it was and they told me to shut up. There were three men dressed in black with white

> scarves around their heads. One of them had a gun. They dragged me out of the house and then searched the house for money. They couldn't find any so they dragged me back inside and began beating me. I started crying and screaming: 'God is great, God is great and my God is watching you.' They said: 'Fuck your God.' They slapped me on my ears and even now I can't hear in one ear. No one came to help me. They were too scared. Then all three raped me in my own house while my children were there. One of them held a gun at my throat while the other raped me and then they changed places. For one hour they raped me and then they went to another house. (Interview, Liboi camp, Kenya, 19 July 1993)

When Hibaq's husband discovered she had been raped, he kicked her out of the compound where the family was living and took her belongings, including her food ration card. After an intervention by the UNHCR and the committee of elders in the camp, her ration card was returned and she was allowed access to her children but her husband refused to have anything more to do with her.

4. Bishaw came to Ifo camp with her five children in April 1992 after walking miles from Kismayo, Somalia.

> In July 1992 nine *shiftas* with guns came into my house at night. They were wearing black trousers, black jackets and hats pulled low. I did not know them. They all had guns and big boots like soldiers. They pulled my arms behind my back and tied my hands. They told me not to scream and pushed knives into my upper arms and head, They kicked me with their boots. They told me to give them all the money I had. I traded at the market during the day and they must have followed me to know where I stay. After they tied and cut me I gave them the money which I had buried in a safe place. Then three of the men caught me and dragged me into my home and raped me. One man raped me while another held a gun at my head and told me he would kill me if I made a noise. My daughter of 10 years woke up and cried and they beat her on the head with guns. Up to today she has [mental] problems [and chronic ear infections]. I tried to shout but the *shiftas* shot in the air and so people ran away.

Terrified by the attack, Bishaw and her family moved to another location in the hope that the attack would be the last. Bishaw, however, was targeted a second time by *shiftas* in August 1992.

They came back again in the middle of the night. This time with more men – so many men I couldn't count. Four of them came into the house while the others guarded outside. My friend was sleeping in the house as well as two of my children. Both of us had been raped before. This time they did not beat me. They came into the tent and told us to give them all our money from the market. I think they knew me from the market. We gave them the money. After that two of the men raped me, and the other two raped my friend. Then we heard a shout outside and they all ran away.

The third time I was raped was in March 1993. It was just as I was eating the dawn breakfast in Ramadan. I saw about 40 men with guns. Six of them came into the hut and took my money. I didn't know any of them. They were not wearing uniform. Thankfully they didn't beat or hurt me – but two of the men raped me.

Bishaw reported each of the rapes and robbery to the police at Ifo. After taking a statement, the police took no further action. (Interview, Marafa camp, Kenya, 23 July 1993)

Source: Africa Watch Women's Rights Project, *Seeking Refuge, Finding Terror – The Widespread Rape of Somali Women Refugees in North Eastern Kenya*, 4 October 1993, Vol.5, No.13, pp 9–18. Names of the women were changed by Africa Watch to protect their identity.

Traditional responses to rape

Within traditional Somali society it is the duty of a woman's family to protect her honour and status. In cases of sexual assault or abuse her family or clansmen are charged with seeking redress. The social ramifications of the assault, and thus the type and amount of compensation sought, vary according to the woman's marital status.

Assaulting an unmarried virgin has the greatest ramifications. Such assaults are believed to destroy the sexual purity of the victim. As a result she is regarded as socially dead. Due to the gravity of this offence the compensation demanded is correspondingly high. The relatives of the girl or woman generally demand not only payment for the offence but also the *diya*, or blood payment, given to the relatives of a murder victim. In addition, the relatives demand that the assailant, or a member of his clan, marry the victim.

Concepts of sexual assault in Somali society

Somali society has two distinct terms for acts of sexual aggression: *kufsi* which is most closely analogous to the western term 'rape'; and *faro-*

xumeyn which may be translated as 'sexual assault'. These terms are often interchangeable. Traditionally, Somalis define *kufsi* as penetrative sexual intercourse with a woman by an assailant using force, against her will. The term *kufsi* comes from the word *kuf*, literally 'to fall down', implying both the use of force to make one fall down and a drop in value of the honour and prestige of those who are forced to fall.

Faro-xumeyn, literally 'bad-fingered', consists of any malicious actions intended to produce physical or psychological harm to women, from the more 'socially accepted' acts such as inappropriate physical contact, to wife-beating and rape. *Faro-xumeyn* is often used euphemistically to connote rape.

Rape as a consequence of war, however, is only one form of sexual assault Somali women face. Other situations involving sexual abuse, recognised and defined within Somali culture, are:

Rape to force a marriage occurs primarily within nomadic society. In Somali pastoral society women are valued for the bride-wealth they will bring to their father's house. However, in their quest for financial security fathers often demand amounts of bride wealth which are beyond the means of eligible suitors. So groups of eligible suitors will sometimes conspire to have one of their number rape a local girl whose bride wealth is considered too high. The suitor is then able to negotiate with the victim's family to obtain a reduction in the payment, since they will be anxious to arrange a speedy marriage. Often the victim is an unwilling participant in these marriage arrangements but is forced to take part by her family in order to uphold their honour. Many such marriages soon end in divorce or separation. Such a marriage can in the long term lead to trauma for the victim.

Dhabar-garaac, meaning forced marriage, occurs in nomadic society when a girl is abducted by raiders and then forced to marry one of her captors. This practice is extremely coercive, with the girl being beaten, starved and otherwise physically and psychologically abused until she agrees to marry. The abducted women are allowed to return home or contact their families only after they have become pregnant (when the marriage arrangement can no longer be annulled). This practice had begun to disappear but underwent a resurgence with the outbreak of civil war, when there was an increase in the numbers of women without traditional networks of protection. There were a number of reported incidents of *dhabar-garaac* within the refugee camps in Kenya.

Laheyste-galmo means literally 'sexual hostage' and most people say that it was unheard of before the war. Some, however, say that it did occur in the past, mostly during times of inter-clan warfare. Such instances occur when armed men raid the settlement of an opposing clan and either kidnap women and young girls, or occupy the settlement making the women hostages in their own homes. While in captivity the women are forced to cook, clean and watch the herds of their kidnappers as well as provide them with sexual services. Marriage almost never results from this kind of sexual abuse and any children born belong to the mother. Captivity may last for months. Many girls and women suffering from the effects of rape in the Somali refugee camps had suffered such attacks. Some of these had happened within Somalia, others in camps in Kenya, probably the work of bandits preying on women gathering firewood.

In the case of assault on a married woman, the perpetrator or his clan is forced to pay the equivalent of the woman's bride price (*meher*) to her family. This is intended to create the legal fiction that the victim was married to her assailant at the time of the attack. The fictitious marriage is considered valid only for the period of the attack, not thereafter. Its purpose is to preserve the woman's social reproductive capacity – that is prevent her from being ostracised. If the woman becomes pregnant the child belongs to the real husband, although he will often seek a divorce. Compensation is given to the woman's relatives and not to her husband.

In the case of assaults against divorced or widowed women the compensation demanded is the same as that for an unmarried woman except that her relatives do not demand the *diya* payment.

In all of the above, terms of compensation are 'ideal' types implemented when the assailant is not related to the victim by blood or clan. In cases where the woman is related to her attacker, or if he is of the same clan, compensation is generally less and sometimes dispensed with entirely. Even in cases where compensation is given, almost all of it is kept by the elders of the clan or the male members of the woman's family, leaving little of it for the woman herself.

In the case of rape during war it is the responsibility of the clan to avenge the attack, and in such cases compensation is not generally sought. In these instances the clan has a responsibility to look after the interests of the victims. For example, if she is single they must find a suitor to 'clean the shame', or if she is married the elders will encourage the husband not to divorce her even if a child results from the rape. These are traditional interventions by the elders resorted to in times of intermittent clan-based warfare, when cases of rape are relatively rare. In a protracted war such as during the past decade, when rape is common and at the same time fewer marriageable men are available, clan elders tend to forsake this duty.

In the case of raped women in the refugee camps in Kenya, elders were eager to seek the highest compensation possible for rapes committed against their clanswomen. Many victims complained that the reason for their zeal was primarily a desire for material gain when resources were scarce, rather than a concern for the honour of the victim or the clan. The UNHCR research in 1993 found that many elders at that time were reluctant to report attacks to camp authorities partly because they stood to gain more if they pursued the case through traditional means. It was reported to the UNHCR that local Kenyan police often preferred to allow clan elders to handle the case in exchange for a portion of the compensation payment. This situation did change as a result of the UNHCR's awareness-raising work with elders and the Kenyan police.

Some women who preferred to settle their cases through negotiation and compensation agreed by the clan elders noted that the compensation was derisory. Each of the elders who negotiates on the woman's behalf, as well as her close male relations, is entitled to a share of the compensation. Moreover, the assailants generally go unpunished. Even the clan elders became frustrated at seeing the same men committing the crime repeatedly, so that eventually it was they who were encouraging the women to go through the legal system. On the other hand, when cases went to court, assailants' families strongly resist the accusation, because of the violence and physical brutality in Kenyan jails. Another factor which encouraged women to seek settlement through the courts was the fact that rape is a felony against the State of Kenya; thus women come to court as witnesses in a criminal investigation, as well as being victims seeking to redress a wrong.

The social consequences of rape in the refugee camps

A strong cultural stigma is attached to rape in Somalia, as elsewhere. Women who have been raped face not only physical and psychological trauma but also the likelihood of rejection by their families. Although, in general, the social consequences of rape include rejection by husband, family and community, the outcome varies according to marital status as well as the social and cultural backgrounds of the victims. For an unmarried woman or girl who loses her virginity through rape her goal of finding a husband disintegrates.

One 16 year-old Somali girl who was raped stated: 'Now I am treated like a prostitute. The only thing I want is to be buried alive and disappear from this world.'[17] Similarly, older women who have developed their status and influence over the years find both shattered in the eyes of the community when they are dishonoured by rape. For married women the jeopardy lies in mixing her children from her husband with an unwanted child born as the result of rape. Although husbands are culturally bound to provide moral and financial support for the child, they often divorce their wife rather than live with the 'shame'. If he remains with his wife, a man's own social status suffers as the husband of a defiled woman. Daughters of marriageable age may also suffer as suitors may not wish to marry into a family with a mother-in-law who has been defiled by rape. Meintjes *et al* put it thus: 'Rapists strip women not only of their economic assets (food, clothing, jewellery, money and household furnishings) ... but also of their political assets, which are their virtue and their reputation.'[18]

It is not surprising, therefore, that deep fear of being stigmatised prevented many women refugees who have been raped from coming forward to seek medical help or report their ordeal to police, or participate in the UNHCR mission to research and respond to rape in the camps. 'To admit to being raped is an admission of guilt in Somali society', according to one female lawyer assisting the UNHCR project.[19] This is one reason why the exact numbers of rape incidents that occurred as a result of the war will probably never be known.

Within the camps, women who have survived rape attacks generally withdrew from the social and economic activities of the community. They refrained from collecting food, firewood or water. Many petty traders allowed their businesses to collapse. Women reported that their main reason for withdrawing from such activities was the ostracism they faced in public places. The children of these women also faced similar discrimination and harassment as a result of their mothers' misfortune. Many children were left severely traumatised by witnessing their mother's rape and refrained from regular social interaction with other children.

After being raped many women felt unable to conduct their household chores such as cooking food, and this caused their own and their children's nutritional status to deteriorate. Women who gave birth as a result of being raped suffered severe trauma during the post-natal period causing nutritional problems for both mother and infant.

1 Somali women refugees in Kenya, where more than 500,000 people fled, use traditional techniques to build a shelter for them and their children. Women like these sought safety in the refugee camps of northern Kenya, but they found only more insecurity and terror as sexual violence and rape were prevalent there during the early 1990s. Between 1991 and 1993, the war created more than 1.5 million refugees. (Betty Press/Panos Pictures)

Women's own responses

Because of the lack of trees inside the camp firewood collection had to take place outside the relative safety of the camp boundaries. Many daytime attacks on women took place as they were collecting wood. To reduce the risk of rape and attack women in the refugee camps organised themselves into groups, some members armed with machetes (*pangas*) for firewood collection, rather than go alone or in twos and threes. This strategy could succeed when the women encountered small groups of unarmed men but it did not deter attackers who carried guns. Women interviewed said that they chose not to allow male relations to accompany them during the dangerous task of collecting wood because they knew that attackers would kill any man they encountered from a warring clan whereas they would 'only' rape a woman.

Some women tried to thwart attackers by changing where they stayed at night. Women had noticed that bandits often attacked tent compounds that had cooking areas attached because it was obvious that women lived there. Most single men living in the camps do not cook and so do not build cooking areas. So women moved out of their compounds at night to sleep in tents for single men. At first women reported that many of them had escaped attacks. Unfortunately, as the bandits got the news of what they were doing they began searching the tents of single men.

In 1993, prior to the UNHCR interventions, as the incidence of rape attacks worsened women in different camps decided to take action to prevent their virgin teenage and young daughters being raped. They began sending their daughters to sleep at night at places they identified to be safe havens. These included the mosques and hospitals inside the camps which are near to the police stations and are heavily fenced and guarded. As the number of minors and teenagers sleeping in these areas increased, the authorities intervened and stopped them. In the case of one hospital, the reason given for ejecting the girls from the hospital grounds was that their being there could draw bandits and an attack that might injure hospital in-patients. The only alternative solution the Dagahaley camp authorities could find was for the girls to be allowed to sleep inside the police compound. However, the mothers and older women refused to accept this, expressing their fear of their daughters being attacked by the police themselves.

The UNHCR's response

As a Somali woman it was clear to me that the recovery of women who had survived rape attacks depended on the reconstruction of their social and economic networks, that is, reconnecting them to their social environment and rebuilding their status in society. I believed that anything which the UNHCR could deliver to improve their material status would also help to ameliorate their psychological trauma.

I also believed it essential to introduce more systematic and lasting measures to prevent further attacks, to provide long-term assistance to those who fall victims of such violence, and to strengthen the skills and capacity of the police force to deal with rape cases.

Accordingly, the UNHCR set up a multi-faceted project initially called Women Victims of Violence, which encompassed a variety of activities and interventions. Perhaps the most important was the counselling programme. 'Counselling' is perhaps an inaccurate word to describe the process set up to assist rape survivors in the camps, since it may suggest a particular style of support derived from western psychiatry. 'Guidance' may be more appropriate, since the service aimed to make the survivors aware of the assistance they were entitled to in the camps. The counsellors were Somali social workers, counselling was done in the presence of family members, and the survivors were encouraged to use traditional healing systems such as the recitation of specific Koranic verses over their bodies, and rituals such as spirit possession (*zar*).

An aim of these sessions was to create space for the women to begin to talk about their experience. Contrary to western perceptions about Muslim societies' reluctance to discuss sexual matters, Somali women have shown themselves extremely anxious to talk about their ordeals. These sessions were generally the most emotional and traumatic for the women, especially for the Barawe and Bajuni women from Hatimy and Jomvu camps (originally from coastal towns of southern Somalia such as Brava and Kismayo, and from islands off Kismayo) who had traditionally led a secluded life and who had never before had a public voice. Counselling often provided women with an opportunity to express their feelings and expectations for the first time, in a society which often prefers to suppress their tragedy, blaming the victim for her calamity rather than helping her cope with it.

Replacing clothing was an important psychological support as many women who had been raped, too poor to obtain new clothes, were forced to continue wearing the same clothes in which they had been raped. For most this was a source of severe psychological trauma, the clothes serving as a constant reminder of their ordeal. Some reported that, even after washing their clothes repeatedly, they could still smell the body odour and semen of their attackers. Similarly, others stated that by not being able to change their clothes, they were in a perpetual state of ritual impurity and thus unable to perform religious duties such as their daily prayers.

The UNHCR sought to help empower women by encouraging them to report cases of sexual assault to the UNHCR, and thence to the Kenyan police. Such encouragement, combined, in many cases, with legal action by the Federation of Women Lawyers (FIDA), did much to help women give voice to their predicament and give them hope that something can be done to alleviate their plight. The project also attempted to improve women's economic conditions by providing them with skills and opportunities to undertake income-generating activities such as handicraft production. Engagement in such activities contributes to the mental rehabilitation of rape survivors as well as increasing their economic welfare. Over time this became a major component of the project.

The UNHCR provided practical support to raped women in the form of referral to medical practitioners. Most women interviewed still bore the scars of knife or bullet wounds. Ongoing medical problems included miscarriages among women raped while pregnant; haemorrhaging; inability to control urination; mutilation of the female genitalia; venereal diseases; and insomnia. Where appropriate, women were transferred to another camp, or to another section within the same camp, where they felt more secure or had relatives. The project provided essential items such as blankets, clothes, kitchen utensils, tents and jerry cans for water, to replace those lost during the incidents.

The project also introduced a number of preventive and awareness-raising measures including improving camp security, strengthening the capacity of the Kenyan police in terms of equipment and specialist staff (including female case workers), human rights training for staff of agencies and for police working in the camps, and a training manual on refugee rights for the Kenyan authorities.

The UNHCR's interventions had some problems, among them the title 'Women Victims of Violence', which further stigmatised women victims and deterred some from coming forward for assistance. But an immediate consequence of the project's activities was a dramatic reduction in the number of rape incidents, dropping from an average of 26 cases each month during the first three months of the project (October–December 1993) to nine per month in the following seven months.

The project also played a crucial role in raising the general level of awareness about sexual assault within the refugee camp system in Kenya, not only within the camps but also on a wider scale among members of both national and international communities. The project was able to communicate the existing crisis within the camps to non-governmental and governmental agencies, journalists, and international human rights organisations, consistently highlighting the continuing security problems surrounding the camps – to which women living in them were particularly vulnerable.

Many rape survivors were helped to cope with rape. They were able to receive counselling as well as material and medical assistance. Channels were established whereby they could report incidents to the proper authorities, which helped them to realise for the first time that they could do something about their situation. It provided many with the opportunity and the means to bring their plight to the attention of the wider world by allowing them to speak unhindered to journalists and human rights activists.

Refugee elders were encouraged to become aware of the problem of rape in the camps and to manifest their concern over it. In the beginning, refugee elders showed little concern about the sexual violence taking place in the camps but over time this attitude changed and they became an important component in the prevention and treatment of rape in the camps. Among the roles elders played were mobilising refugees to plant live fencing around the camp and supporting violated women to report their experiences to the police or the UNHCR, and advise them on how to preserve evidence that could support their claims of rape.

TESTIMONY 3: A GROUP VIEW

The experience of women during the liberation struggle in north west Somalia, 1980–88[20]

Editors' note

Somalia came to the world's attention in 1991 when the Siad Barre regime collapsed with the outbreak of war in Mogadishu but what is often overlooked is that civil war had been going on in Somalia since the end of the Ogaden War with Ethiopia in 1978. The brutality of the post-1990 conflict, and the use of sexual violence, had precedents in the government's war against its own people: first in Muduug Region, Somalia's central rangelands, in response to the formation of the Majeerteen-based Somali Salvation Democratic Front (SSDF); and then in the north west of the country following the foundation of the mainly Isaq-supported Somali National Movement (SNM) in 1980. Both the SSDF and the SNM launched their armed struggles from bases in Ethiopia with the support of the regime of Mengistu Haile-Mariam. The SSDF insurgency collapsed in 1986 when a rapprochement between Somalia and Ethiopia led to the arrest of its leader.

The SNM claimed to be a pan-Somalia movement; its aim was the overthrow of the Siad Barre government. From the late 1970s onwards Siad Barre's regime increasingly discriminated against the Isaq population of north west Somalia (the area now known as Somaliland). There was unequal political representation, there were unfair economic practices and development resources were unevenly distributed. The population of the region faced growing hostility from Ogaden refugee paramilitary groups, which had been set up and armed by the Barre government. Draconian emergency legislation gave extraordinary powers to the military and police. As this group testimony describes, these powers were used to repress the Isaq population. Between 1982 and 1991 the forces responsible for the nation's security carried out mass arrests, detentions without trial, extortion, extra-judicial executions, rape, looting and torture of innocent citizens.

> The military became established as the political elite in the north west, sustaining their position and privileges through violence. Their interests … were not solely political. Corruption was rife. After 1982, military transfers to the north west were much sought after as an opportunity to make money.[21]

The women speaking in this testimony say that arbitrary arrests and torture were a common means of extracting money. People who were unable to buy their release were commonly killed or died of ill-treatment. In reference to the trade in human lives, Hargeisa police station was nicknamed the *saylada dadka*, 'the meat market'.

Men were the primary target of arrest, detentions and killings. Many were snatched away never to be seen or heard of again. One man who lived in Hargeisa at the time, and whom the regime imprisoned, said that Siad Barre saw men in general, particularly Isaq, as 'enemies of the revolution'.[22]

As a consequence of the regime's policies towards the north west, public services barely functioned and corruption was rife. Freedom of movement was restricted in 1986 as vehicle owners were forced to get written permission to travel between towns, and livestock and other property was taxed and confiscated. The rural population was subjected to the same scorched-earth policy of asset stripping, killings, destruction of water reservoirs, burning of farms and planting of landmines that had been used against the Majeerteen in Muduug Region in 1979–81 when thousands of civilians had been killed. Isaqs faced discrimination in employment and access to services. For the many innocent people targeted there was no possibility of legal help or protection. The government was at war with its own people.

The women whose collective testimony is recorded here are Amina Yusuf, Shukri Hariir Ismail, Zamzam Abdi and the late Noreen Michael Mariano. All lived in Hargeisa during the government repression and counter-insurgency in the north west, and after the war took on important roles in the community working to rebuild society and a secure peace. Interviewed in Hargeisa in 1999 they recall life in the city under the military regime of Siad Barre, the impact of the civil war on men and women, and the roles women played in trying to counter the repression.

The group's story

Between 1981 and 1988 many men and boys in north west Somalia left their families and homes to join the opposition or to live in the Gulf countries. Those who stayed behind were constantly under threat of arrest by Siad Barre's forces on suspicion of being SNM supporters, so over time more and more men chose to leave. The situation was worst in Hargeisa and Gebiley because that's where the SNM drew its strongest support. It was bad in Woqooyi Galbeed, Burao, Sheikh and Berbera, but less bad in Erigavo.

After the SNM was formed it became unsafe for any Isaq man to stay in Hargeisa or other towns. Women had to shoulder many responsibilities on top of their normal tasks because so many men had either taken up arms to fight, had been put in prison, or had fled.

As well as caring for children and older people during the conflict years, women provided vital support to the fighters in the villages and rural areas held by the SNM. Women also served as intelligence gatherers, messengers, and fundraisers for the SNM. Others joined as nurses and paramedics while a small number fought alongside the male fighters.

We tolerated all kinds of degradation under the military and their civilian supporters. There were different ranks and types of people involved in the repression: the 'victory pioneers of the October Revolution', known as the *guulwade*, who were community vigilantes involved in surveillance; the security forces of the Central Intelligence Department and the National Security Service; the military police (*hangesh*), the military intelligence (*dabar jabin*), known as the 'backbreakers', and the *koofiyed cas* or Red Berets who were the Presidential Guard made up of men exclusively from Siad Barre's own sub-clan.

Starting in 1981 or 1982 there was a curfew. It was common for it to be enforced from 2 o'clock in the afternoon until 7 o'clock the next morning. You were not allowed to break it even if you were in labour or a person was sick and needed to go to the hospital.

You never knew what would happen to you or whom you could trust. The military would come to the houses, forcing down doors, taking people away, taking money and looking for our gold.[23] People would be imprisoned for no reason and then the family would have to pay for their release. Sometimes fathers were taken from their homes and killed. Then the next day the elders and mothers were taken to see the bodies of their loved ones – to humiliate us. You couldn't mourn – they would be staring into your eyes to see if you were crying. Women and girls were raped in front of their families. For many of us our worst fear was that we might be raped in front of our fathers.

Orientation Centres were originally used as centres for socialist propaganda teaching. This was where you had to go to get married (usually with a group of other couples). They were a symbol of the regime's control over our lives.[24] In the 1980s you had to go the Orientation Centre to report any new person who came into town, even if they were only coming for two or three days; they would be allowed to stay for a certain period and if they overstayed you would be taken to prison. They wanted to control everyone's whereabouts and movements. One of the jokes at the time was that a man reported his new-born baby to the orientation centre as a newcomer to his house.

The government imprisoned the rich merchants and traders so that they could not support the SNM. If they weren't imprisoned then they were forced to report to an Orientation Centre every morning to prove that they were still in town, and to degrade them. No matter how much wealth an Isaq had they were not allowed to drive new cars or Land Cruisers. At the port imported goods would be seized if they belonged to an Isaq. To get them back would involve paying out large sums of money, usually, but not always, to one of Siad Barre's clansmen. These people were eager to be posted to Somaliland (north west Somalia) because they could get rich there.

No form of community organising was permitted. Any social action was seen as a threat and was heavily repressed. In 1980 a group of young professionals who had raised funds and mobilised the community to improve conditions in Hargeisa Hospital were all arrested and given long prison sentences in solitary confinement. Three were even sentenced to death for treason (the sentences were not carried out). When students demonstrated outside the courtroom against their arrest, the *dabar jabin* fired on them killing some of them, and arrested some 200.

There was enormous suppression and control of information. It was forbidden to talk about the war or what was really going on. It wasn't easy to get information in or out. To find out what was happening and what might come next or what we needed to do, we needed to be good intelligence gatherers but very careful of giving away our interests and being caught. Women were important in this role as we were less of a target than the men were. We would meet informally every morning and pass on details of what we knew about the latest arrests or disappearances and so on. Every morning we would gather information from our sources and from each other, and pass on what we'd learnt to the next person.

As the SNM grew stronger the government punished the civilians more. When the SNM killed one person, the military would kill scores in retaliation. In 1984 the government murdered 40 Isaq men (and women) in a reprisal for the SNM having killed the leader of the force charged with targeting the Isaq. In the same year 45 men were taken and killed in the centre of Burao for 'helping the SNM'.

Some women took their children and went to live in Mogadishu or Ethiopia but the majority of people stayed until forced to flee in 1988. Few ordinary people in the south had any idea what was going on in the north west. The regime was expert at controlling information, repressing reports, preventing journalists from visiting. Even after thousands of us had fled to Mogadishu in 1988 we feared to talk about what had happened to us and it was difficult to get people to believe us. Nobody wanted to believe it. Those that were able to left the country completely. You couldn't feel safe knowing that your own government wanted to exterminate you.

TESTIMONY 4: SHUKRI HARIIR

Editors' note

In May 1988 the SNM attacked and briefly captured Burao and Hargeisa, the two main towns in the north west. Siad Barre's response was genocidal: days of aerial and ground bombardment of both towns by the Somali Armed Forces, backed up by South African mercenary pilots; the round-up and summary execution of hundreds of civilians; the complete destruction of the towns' infrastructure; and the displacement of hundreds of thousands of people.

By the time the bombardment had ended the city of Hargeisa was in ruins and thousands were dead. Unknown numbers of people had been massacred and buried in mass graves;[25] more than half a million people had fled south and to the border. Anti-personnel mines were planted in streets, houses and livestock thoroughfares to kill, maim and deter return. Some 50,000 civilians were estimated to have been killed between May 1988 and March 1989. Such was the government's suppression of information and the lack of media interest that this war was barely reported in the international press. (Amnesty International & CIIR/ICD 1999)

Shukri Hariir, a broadcaster for national radio, was the mother of six young children and at the time heavily pregnant. She lived through the bombardment. Through the detail of how she and her family made their escape we learn something of the dilemma that faced parents of young children as they tried to flee the city on foot, loaded with their infants, in darkness and under constant fear of detection and death.

Shukri's story

On the morning of 27 May 1988, as newsreader for Radio Hargeisa, I reported that the Somali National Movement (SNM) had invaded and captured Burao the previous night. Having made this announcement I immediately excused myself from the Service and went downtown to my mother's small food store to collect bags of food, charcoal and store water in case of war. We had reported that the SNM were on their way to capture Hargeisa and would come soon.

On the night of Tuesday 31 May 1988 we were woken by the thunder-like explosions of war. The sky was red with shell and rocket fire. We were not used to the incessant sounds of heavy artillery and rockets. A 'Stalin Organ' or 'PM' gun and a tank situated close by filled us with fear and restlessness and as a result my husband, myself and my six children lay awake until morning.

In the morning non-uniformed forces in more than 40 armed vehicles entered Hargeisa from the west. They were led by Jeeps equipped with heavy anti-tank guns. This procession passed by our house, which was located on the main Hargeisa–Gebiley road. We realised they were SNM forces and wondered if they had captured the *faqash* [derogatory slang for the forces of the government] in one day. An hour later we found that our area was in the hands of the government army. At 8am we went here and there trying to get information and talking to neighbours who belonged to Barre's tribe. But our neighbours would not greet us and looked on us with hostile eyes. Two passed by near us: one was a *ma'alin*, or teacher, at a Koranic school located near to our house, the other was a National Security Service office watchman. Both were armed with AK-45 rifles. Partly because of their old age and partly because I imagined that *sheikhs* and elderly men would not be moved so quickly to engage in war, I did not expect these people to take up arms. From the way they were holding the rifles it was apparent that this was the first time they had ever taken up such a weapon. When we asked about the situation, they answered with angry expressions on their faces.

'Are you not aware of what your kinsmen have done? Then what are you expecting?' My husband responded: 'Things will be as God wishes.' Three more armed men appeared leading an unfortunate woman, she was blindfolded and her neck was tied with a rope on which they were pulling, as though she was a camel. Her clothes were torn and bloodied. The poor woman looked as if she was shaking with pain. Although we knew one of the three men pulling her along we did not talk to them. One of the men glanced at us saying: 'The most dangerous spy is caught!' They reached a point about 100 metres away from us when an exchange of fire nearby could be heard. They suddenly threw the woman down on the ground and shot her dead.

Bodies were scattered here and there, not all of them government supporters. We saw the bodies of nine dead government supporters and two SNM. We saw through the window women who had just learnt about the death of some relatives; [they were] stabbing three dead bodies with knives. We were afraid that these women would rush and kill us. Luckily, at this point this idea had not entered their heads.

On the night of Wednesday 1 June we stayed in our house discussing our way out of the situation. We felt the SNM had captured the northern part of Hargeisa and that the east–west would be the front line. We were convinced that we could not cross the front line, which was north of us. We decided to go to my mother's house in southern Hargeisa. We believed the people from my husband's family were cut off from us by the front line. I was six months' pregnant. The oldest of my six children was a boy of six years, the youngest were my twin boys aged one. Two of my children could undertake a long march but it would prove difficult for the others so we needed people to help us carry the children.

On the Wednesday morning we saw one of our neighbours, a government supporter called Ahmed, leading three tanks to us. While they were passing the house he told them something about us. The tank directed its barrel towards us. Instinctively we rushed the children into the dining room on the other side of the house. We were just in time – the tank devastated two bedrooms and the sitting room with six heavy shots. Miraculously we were not harmed, although we were very frightened. They clearly thought that we were dead. After a few minutes they were distracted by heavy firing nearby, and the tank moved on.

We immediately set off to a neighbouring Isaq family. We were explaining to our neighbour what had happened when armed men knocked at the door. When the door was opened the men asked: 'Who is the man who fired at us?' They were told that nobody had fired anything. But they ordered all of us out of the house while firing into the house to terrify us. Seven of the armed men looted everything useful from the house, including the curtains. Both of our households decided to escape while we were still alive. We left all we had except for SSh20,000 [equivalent to US$50] which the looters had failed to find. We walked 3 km to reach my mother and displaced sister with her five children in the southern part of the city.

We felt some relief in the morning because the war was not so near, although government troops were moving on the roads near us. But in the evening we moved to another house to get away from the government's artillery bombardment of all the houses and the resulting exchange of fire. We relocated to a house situated in the southern tip of Hargeisa.

Everybody was thinking about how to escape. All were convinced that anyone staying behind would be killed by the defeated troops of Siad Barre or by civilians whose relatives had been killed by SNM troops. On the fourth day of the war I met the unfortunate Asha Yusuf who told me the menfolk in her group, including her husband, had been slaughtered and that even the babes in arms had been checked to determine their sex; and four baby boys including her only son had been slaughtered. As she was recounting this story tears were streaming from her eyes. I cried too, as did the others who were with us.

Kadra Ali, a girl who was with us told us that she had witnessed something similar. She had been hiding in thick shrubs when around 50–60 people were shot dead while trying to escape – two babies were left crying over their mothers' dead bodies. Kadra could not tell us whether the babies had been eaten by animals or whether they had been taken by people. She said these troops remained there until dark dividing the looted wealth among themselves and checking the pockets of dead bodies for money.

I couldn't get anyone to help me carry my children and without help we couldn't make it. The families who had strong members had a better chance of escaping.

On the tenth day of the war we decided to make our fourth escape attempt, determined to join the settlements of the displaced populations located in the north of Hargeisa. When we were almost halfway across, somewhere near the eastern side of Hargeisa, troops intercepted us and ordered us to sit down in a line. They watched us closely as if they had caught the highest commanders of the SNM. We were sure they would kill us all. After we had been sitting there for an hour and a half, a door of a house nearby opened. I looked at the person who had stepped outside and recognised him as a colonel called Hassan Wiif who was known to my husband. I called to him to help us and release us. We did not expect a positive response because of our experience during the past days. But the man did order our release. Despite the reports of his troops which identified us as SNM, the colonel ordered the release of all the people. Luckily for us this man did not have the poor tribal mentality that so many others had sunk to the level of.

Those people who were not carrying small children continued their attempt to escape. But we could do nothing but return to the house we had set out from that morning.

Day by day people were beginning to adapt to the awful situation. In the early days of the war large groups would try to escape after sunset – the only time of day when it was possible to move unnoticed. At other times you could be easily seen by the government troops, who would ambush people en route. On the day we decided to try to escape we got together with many families and planned to begin after midnight. It was six weeks after the war had started. At 1 o'clock in the morning we started out. We were not less than 300 people. A man who knew more about the route we would escape by was assigned to guide us. We walked in single file without making the least noise. Although heavily pregnant I carried my year-old twin boys, my mother carried the next youngest. Some people were reluctant to escape in a group with young children for fear that the children would cry out and alert attackers. All the way I prayed that my children would be able to keep silent. They did, and I wondered if the smallest ones had been 'trained' by such awful experiences that they had been through.

After four hours walking south west the guide told us that we had passed through the hostile area. We were so relieved and pleased. After another hour of walking we reached Gerebis, a village 30 km south west of Hargeisa. We rested for a few days and then continued our journey, still on foot, to the refugee camp in Harshin and later to Harta Sheikh in Ethiopia.

NOTES

1. For more on the historical incidence of rape in wartime, and for a feminist analysis of rape, see Tamara L. Tompkins (1995) 'Prosecuting Rape as a War Crime: Speaking the Unspeakable' in *Notre Dame Law Review*, Vol.70, p 4.
2. On 27 June 1996 the UN International Criminal Tribunal in The Hague made an historic decision by announcing the indictment of eight Bosnian Serb men in connection with rapes of Muslim women during the Bosnian war. Spokesperson for the court, Christian Chartier, said: 'This is a landmark indictment because it focuses exclusively on sexual assaults ... it is of major legal significance because it clearly illustrates the court's strategy to focus on gender-related crimes and give them their proper place in the prosecution of war crimes.' In previous post-war courts evidence of rape was heard, but it was treated as a secondary offence. (Reported in Coalition Against Trafficking in Women (1997) *Coalition Report* Vol.4, No.1) The court cases ended on 23 February 2001 when three of the men indicted for rape were given jail sentences of up to 28 years.
3. Tompkins 1995, p 850.
4. For example, African Rights (April 1995) 'Rwanda: Death, Despair and Defiance', Human Rights Watch, *War Crimes in Bosnia Hercegovina* (New York: Human Rights Watch).
5. Reports of systematic rape and sexual violence in the Kenyan refugee camps were published by African Rights in September 1993 and Africa Watch in October 1993, but little is documented about the widescale use of rape as a weapon of war in southern Somalia following the overthrow of Siad Barre.
6. Called *biri-ma-geydo* (spared from the spear) these unwritten codes or rules of war are like a Somali version of the Geneva Conventions; they are not enforceable but dependent on reciprocal obligations defined in unwritten customary law. From Mark Bradbury (1998) 'Rights, Responsibilities and the Somali Conflict' in *Human Rights in Somaliland: Awareness and Action* (London: Amnesty International & CIIR/ICD).
7. Fowzia Musse, *Women Victims of Violence*, report for UNHCR, Nairobi 1993, cited in Mohamed S. Hamdi, 'The Somali Refugee Women's Experience in Kenyan Refugee Camps and their Plight in Canada', in Hussein M. Adam & Richard Ford (1997) *Mending Rips in the Sky. Options for Somali Communities in the 21st Century* (Trenton NJ: Red Sea Press).
8. For example, Fowzia Musse (1993) *Women Victims of Violence. Report on Refugee Camps in Kenya*, prepared for UNHCR Nairobi.
9. See for example, African Rights (September 1993) *The Nightmare Continues. Abuses Against Somali Refugees in Kenya*; Africa Watch Women's Rights Project (October 1993) *Seeking Refuge, Finding Terror. The Widespread Rape of Somali Women Refugees in North Eastern Kenya*.

10. Kenya's North Eastern Province is sparsely populated by nomadic pastoral groups, mostly ethnic Somalis. Government policy towards ethnic Somalis keeps them isolated and politically marginalised. The nomads have increasingly resorted to cattle rustling, banditry and poaching and are described as *shiftas*, meaning bandit, in Kiswahili. See Africa Watch 1993.
11. Similarly in the case of many Bosnian women, the rapists were men they knew, sometimes well as in the case of teachers and neighbours, see Tompkins *ibid.* For others, although they may not have known their attackers individually they nevertheless could recognise the factions with which they were affiliated.
12. Drawing on Raqiya Haji Dualeh Abdalla (1982) *Sisters in Affliction. Circumcision and Infibulation of Women in Africa* (London: Zed Press).
13. Hamdi S. Mohamed (1997) 'The Somali Refugee Women's Experience in Kenyan Refugee Camps and their Plight in Canada', in H.M. Adam & R. Ford (eds) *Mending Rips in the Sky: Options for Somali Communities in the 21st Century* (Trenton NJ: Red Sea Press).
14. Of the 107 women who reported being raped in 1993, 16 were raped on two different occasions and three on three different occasions. (Musse 1993)
15. There was evidence in 1993 that rape attacks inside Liboy refugee camp on the Kenyan border were linked to events happening in Somalia. For example, at a time when General Mohamed Said Hersi Morgan's forces were fighting the Ogadeni in Somalia, the rape of Ogadeni women in Liboy camp increased.
16. Of 192 interviewed in 1993, 137 were Darod, 24 Hawiye; and 87 were from Mogadishu or Kismayo.
17. 'Sexually Assaulted Refugee Women', UNHCR *Information Bulletin*, October 1993, cited in Hamdi S. Mohamed 1997.
18. S. Meintjes, A. Pillay & M. Turshen (eds) (2001) *The Aftermath – Women in Post-Conflict Transformation* (London: Zed Books).
19. Cited in Marie Wandera (1995) 'The Unheeded Cry. Refugees and Sexual Violence: A Gender Analysis of Sexual Violence and Somali Women Refugees in Kenya' (unpublished dissertation for the University of East Anglia).
20. For more details of this period see Africa Watch (1990) *A Government at War With its Own People. Somalia, Testimonies About the Killings and the Conflict in the North* (New York, Washington, London: Africa Watch Committee).
21. CIIR/ICD & Amnesty International (1997) *Human Rights in Somaliland: Awareness and Action* (London: CIIR).
22. Personal communication, Dr Adan Y. Abokor.
23. Somali women, in common with many women across Africa and the Middle East, typically try to 'bank' any capital wealth they may have in the form of items of gold jewellery.
24. Dr Adan Y. Abokor writes: 'The Orientation Centre was a place established in every section of the city for surveillance and security. It was mainly for brainwashing. The people who worked there were mainly the "pioneers of revolution" (*guulwade*), mostly from the minority groups

who because of the discrimination they suffered had a grudge against the oppressing majority. Women were called out from their houses to listen to lectures and sometimes to take part in dancing and singing revolutionary songs. The Orientation Centre created conflict among wives and husbands by asking the women to report if their husband stopped them from coming to the Centre; such disputes usually ended with the husband behind bars. Women also were encouraged by the Centre to ask for a divorce from the district court, which happened quite often. It was another way of humiliating and frustrating men.

25. The Independent Committee for the Investigation of War Crimes was established in Hargeisa in 1997, after heavy rains exposed a mass grave containing some 200 bodies of prisoners executed by Somali government forces in May 1988. Many more mass graves have since been uncovered and the Committee's work to research and document war crimes of the Siad Barre regime continues.

Part 2

Women's Responses to the War

Section 1
Changing Roles and Responsibilities in the Family

Introduction by Judith Gardner

In Hargeisa in 1992 three elders were talking. One was well dressed and prosperous and other two – one of whom was ill – were quite poor. The sick elder said: 'Can anyone change my sons into one girl?' When asked why he wanted this he replied: 'Because the well-dressed elder has two daughters, one takes care of his clothes and the other his food. I on the other hand have four sons – and look at me!'

This story was recounted by a Somali woman at a CIIR workshop in 1997 juxtaposed with the Somali proverb 'One boy is equal to four girls'. She told it to explain how, in her experience, one positive impact of the war has been that women and girls are valued more highly than they were in the past. Research in the north in 2000/01 by the Somaliland Women's Research and Action Group (SOWRAG) supports this view. SOWRAG's research concluded, however, that this change of attitude is linked to the increased economic importance of women since the war rather than a fundamental change in attitudes. The research notes that 'most Somali men and women still think women are naturally inferior to men'. (Amina Warsame 2001)

In 'Changing roles and responsibilities in the family', three Somali women explore the impact of the war on family life, how women's responsibilities and position within the family have changed, and some of the consequences of these changes. Three different contexts are described: life for women refugees in the Canadian diaspora; urban women traders in the north of Somalia; and the personal experience of an educated, urban professional woman displaced by the war to a remote rural area in a part of Somalia she had never visited before.

The war's impact on family livelihood systems

Chapter 1 of this book highlighted the important economic role that rural and poor women in Somalia have always played in the family.

Because of the impact of the war on the family and household nowadays almost every family – urban and rural, educated and uneducated – depends on the economic productivity of women to a far greater extent than before. And whereas in the past it was shameful for a man to be financially dependent on a woman, in many households, including within the diaspora, women are now the main breadwinners.[1] A major factor promoting this change is the war's effect on the male population and by extension, the typical livelihood /economic system of the extended family. This is explained below, drawing on the editor's interviews with women and men in Somalia and the diaspora.

Historically in Somalia pastoral families have tried to deploy their 'human resources', male and female, strategically in order to spread economic risk and increase opportunities. For example, it would not have been surprising to find that an extended family includes: a son who lives as a nomadic herder in the rural area taking care of the extended family livestock; a daughter who is also a pastoralist, living with her husband in the rural area; another son at university in the capital training to be an engineer; a son working in a Gulf country who sends back money regularly to his relatives in Somalia; a daughter who trained as a teacher and is married to an army lieutenant; another son who runs a business in town using his brother's foreign currency to buy imported goods; an unmarried daughter who is a bank clerk; and a grandson studying computer science in the US. Within this web of livelihoods income or resources in-kind are transferred or negotiated between family members so as to support and maintain the whole.

What the war has done to many extended families is to separate menfolk from the rest of the family, sometimes permanently. Taking the above example of what an extended pastoral family's network might have included before the war, and based on real life scenarios, it is possible to imagine that the impact of the war on this *hypothetical* extended family might be as follows:

The son who is a nomadic herder left the rural area to take up arms. After demobilisation he settled in a town where he could more easily satisfy the *qaad* addiction he developed as a combatant; he depends on irregular income from the sale of ghee and milk passed to him by his wife and other relatives who maintain the remaining livestock.

The daughter who was a nomadic herder has lost her husband who fled to a neighbouring country to escape being killed and has not returned; whether he is dead or not, he no longer contributes to the welfare of the herd or the family. Many of the herd have been looted or died from disease; caring for the sheep and goats that are left, the daughter and her own children have settled on land near a town where she sells livestock products. Any income is shared with her parents.

The son at university left his studies when Mogadishu went to war; he joined a militia group for a while then escaped to Kenya where he spends all his time searching for a way to get to the West to continue his studies. He rarely finds work that he is willing to do, and when he does he spends any earnings on *qaad*. He depends on support from his mother's relatives, also refugees in Kenya, for his day-to-day needs.

Still in the Gulf, the migrant son is now the only son providing income to the family; he remits dollars to his older sister, the former teacher, who is now internally displaced and trying to set up a shop with another displaced woman. She is separated from her army husband who fled to Kenya. He is not working but hopes to become involved in any new government in the south. Their two sons are also in Kenya living with one of his sisters, a refugee, who depends on remittances sent to her from another sister who lives in Canada.

The son who was a businessman died early in the war. His oldest son was also killed. His wife and the younger children finally reached a refugee camp in Kenya and now live in a slum area of Nairobi with her brother's family.

The unmarried daughter who was a bank clerk is now living as a refugee in Yemen. Her family sent her with two of her nieces early in the war to prevent them being raped. She works illegally as a cleaner and remits money to her sister and mother when she can.

The grandson in the US had to give up his studies when his father died and his funding stopped. He no longer has a valid visa to remain and exists in a state of permanent insecurity surviving on what illegal work he can find and occasional support from an aunt who is also in the US and works in the travel industry.

These hypothetical but realistic examples show how, within the extended family, economic relationships have been transformed by the war whereby women now tend to be the key providers and men, if they are present, the dependants. A woman interviewed in the southern district of Kurtanwarey, in 2001, explained:

2 Members of an internally-displaced women's cooperative near Bardera collect wood to sell. One consequence of the war and the collapse of the state was the increased economic burden carried by women from all sectors of society, many of whom became their families' main provider. (Betty Press/Panos Pictures)

> Earlier, it was men who used to be breadwinners for the family and on whom the family depended. Now men have lost this role. At times, men just stroll around and come back with nothing while the children are crying. Previously women didn't know business. Some went to collect grass for cows. Today, work has shifted from men to women – be it business or collection of grass, it's only women who do it.[2]

For the majority of women their economic activities are at survival level, barely earning them enough to feed the family one meal a day. A woman interviewed by ACORD in 2001 as part of the same research project, describes her circumstances which are typical of many other women in this region:

> For ten years now I [have been] struggling to bring up my children alone. We have no information regarding their father. We have lost hope of finding him. We have taken him to be dead ... I work for my children. There are many children's diseases: two of them have already died. The remaining two – I cultivate a *jibaal* [a hectare of land] for them. I leave the house in the morning and return at 5pm. Whatever I get, I pass the market and buy them food. That is how I give them food at night and in the morning I leave them. I have [endured] misery and sufferings in the struggle to bring up my children. My children have suffered and I have also suffered. From when my husband went missing I have laboured for my children. Nobody assists me in their upbringing. (ACORD 2001: 17)

Although some women own their own small-scale businesses such as restaurants and cloth shops they are relatively few. Some women in urban areas organise themselves into traditional savings and credit groups, known in the south as *shollongo (hakbad* in the north), in order to raise funds for their small businesses. Opportunities to earn income are more limited for rural women in the northern pastoral regions but nevertheless they are getting involved in economic activities traditionally associated with men, such as livestock trading. (Amina Warsame 2001)

Changes in gender relations within the family

Women's increased economic role in the family implies a change in gender relations at household level. With the family no longer economically supported by a man, and often without a productive man in the household, many women have become the household head responsible for decision-making. ACORD's research found that 'male interviewees say that they have accepted their wives as head of households and obey them, minimising family friction at this time of crisis'. (ACORD 2001: 28) One man said: 'Now we obey our women. Women sell tomatoes, maize etc, the men are supported by their wives. They are taking us through this difficult time.' (ACORD 2001: 27)

But whether or not this change is 'merely circumstantial survival mechanisms which have few implications for the future' (ACORD 2001: 43) or a precursor to transformation of the position of women in Somali society remains to be seen. For now, how the change in gender relations at family level is 'experienced' by women depends on many variables, not least their clan, economic class, whether they are urban or rural based and what kind of breadwinners they are: widows, abandoned women with children, women with a male partner who provides them emotional if not economic support, women with or without a support network of relations close by. Our research for this book indicates that becoming the breadwinner and experiencing increased economic power and decision-making at household level is more likely to be an empowering experience for urban-based, educated women who are emotionally supported by their male partner or have a close network of support from relatives than it is for uneducated women without a male partner or close support network – whether rural or urban.

Widows, and women separated from their husbands and left behind with their children, have experienced great emotional suffering as a result. 'Probably the most painful impact of the conflict to many interviewees is disintegration of the household.' (ACORD 2001) Thus it should not be assumed that because it brings a change in power relations at the family level the majority of women prefer to be the sole breadwinner or to live without a male companion. In insecure and alien environments such as refugee camps, or where the threat of a resurgence of armed conflict prevails, a woman without adult male relatives or an adult male companion of the appropriate clan family is likely to feel the absence of male 'protection' keenly. Not surprisingly, under such circumstances seeking to build a relationship, short-term or otherwise, with a suitably armed, connected or otherwise qualified male companion or marriage partner is one survival strategy that some women and girls adopt. In rural families on the death of a husband it is customary, if there are young children, for the widow to become the responsibility – and sometimes the wife – of her husband's brother or close kin. But since the war and the departure of so many men this traditional practice no longer functions. A widowed woman's chances of remarrying to find male companionship and support are remote. Women separated from or abandoned by their husbands are allowed under *shari'a* to seek divorce. For many women this is a shameful prospect and they remain faithful to their absent husbands who may have fled to a neighbouring country and since remarried. (ACORD 2001)

Where men are present, many are unemployed and find their job prospects shattered. Men who were previously urban-based and employed in the formal or public sector, appear to have found it hardest to adapt to a situation where the kind of jobs they used to hold or aspire to are no longer available. Many men in the south of Somalia have been displaced from irrigated farmlands, as their livestock has been looted and their livelihoods and capital lost. Also it is difficult for people formerly employed in the public sector to take up a new economic activity such as farming because they generally do not own land. Insecurity, intimidation and extortion still prevail in the south to a far greater extent than elsewhere, factors that severely affect the ability of some men to engage in productive activities such as irrigated farming and livestock herding. Where they have no choice men, and women, work as casual labourers for those who have displaced them from their farms, receiving such a pittance that 'if you work the whole day whatever you earn cannot buy you anything'. (ACORD 2002)

Unlike many men, women, who have also been hit by the lack of formal or public employment, have been less selective about how to earn an income, and have been willing to take on the most menial tasks and activities in order to bring the family food and basic necessities. A man interviewed by ACORD explained:

> I cannot work and I cannot assume her household roles either. I cannot sell maize [in the market] or roast bread. Can I sell tomatoes? Can I do these jobs? That is the problem. My wife told me instead of our children perishing with hunger, I will work, you stay at home. That is how we are. (*Ibid*)

More research is needed to understand why 'while a woman will not hesitate to trade in all kinds of items without fearing loss of pride, a man will be hesitant to engage in all economic activities he sees as "degrading" and "unmanly"'. (Amina Warsame 2001)

A Somali woman in the European diaspora talks about why women have fared better as refugees:

> By the time they arrive here in Europe, the men will have lost their dignity and all the privileges attached to being males. They are no longer the kings of the household. Here they find themselves in a nuclear couple, with the woman their equal. Since neither men nor women are likely to be given a job commensurate with their status, you find both doing the same kind of low job. Women are more used to that, probably because they used to do it at home! It has brought about the absurd situation in which women are the breadwinners and men the dependants. And then the men refuse to help at home.[3]

ACORD's report has more sympathy for the men's case:

> When they lost access to their farms and livestock the affected men were unable to meet expectations of providing for their families, thereby losing their sense of worth as men. It is part of the strategy of war, whereby one patriarchy attacks the worth of the other. (ACORD 2001: 30)

Whilst some men are taking on household duties such as cooking and looking after the children, by and large domestic responsibilities are still seen as women's work. Where there is access to schooling, the true cost of the change in gender relations at family level is paid for by daughters, for whom the chance of even attaining primary level education, already low before the war, significantly diminishes when their mother is the breadwinner and needs their assistance in the home.

NOTES

1. In a 1993 survey Save the Children found 38 per cent of women in the six major towns in Somaliland were de facto household heads.
2. Ibrahim Nur (2001) 'Somalia Case Study', *Gender Sensitive Programme Design and Planning in Conflict-Affected Situations* (London: ACORD, unpublished).
3. Nurrudin Farah (2000) *Yesterday, Tomorrow – Voices from the Somali Diaspora*, (London: Cassell) p 157.

4
Domestic Conflict in the Diaspora – Somali Women Asylum Seekers and Refugees in Canada

Ladan Affi

Traditionally Canada has welcomed immigrants and refugees from around the world, particularly those of European heritage. Although the percentage of immigrants to Canada has remained relatively steady since the Second World War, their cultural backgrounds have not. Figures published by Statistics Canada reveal that the ethnic diversity of new Canadians has increased dramatically during the past decade.

Further, within the past few decades the composition of immigrants has changed dramatically, from approximately 80 per cent from countries with European heritage to almost three-quarters from Asia, Africa, Latin America, and the Caribbean. Almost half of Canadian immigration now comes from Asia. Between 1971 and 1986 the number of Canadians who had been born in Africa, Asia, and Latin America grew by 340 per cent. Over the past two decades there has been an increase of immigrants and refugee claimants from African countries such as Somalia, Ethiopia, Eritrea and the Sudan. Within a five-year period (1988–93), the Somali population in Ontario increased by 613 per cent with 70,000 Somalis living in Canada, 13,000 of whom live in Ottawa.

This chapter presents an overview of the situation faced by many Somali women, particularly married women and single mothers, adapting to life as an asylum-seeking refugee in Canada having fled southern Somalia in the early 1990s. It also describes ways Somali women have sought to overcome their adversities as well as helping other refugee groups through joint advocacy initiatives. It is based on first-hand experience as a refugee woman and a voluntary worker with the Somali refugee community in Canada.[1]

The chapter begins by examining the first challenge of arriving as an asylum seeker – the immigration process. It highlights how women and girls who are rape survivors face a difficult choice in deciding whether or not to reveal their experience in order to claim asylum status under Canada's progressive, gender-sensitive legal frameworks. It then explores the challenges facing mothers, particularly single mothers, and the family's dependency on women to be the wage-earners and sources of remittance payments to relatives 'back home' as well as the means of sponsoring other family members, including their children, to join them – the motivating factor for many women who endure the low-status, low-income jobs shunned by most men.

Tracing some of the consequences for women of this increased economic role and responsibility, the chapter looks at the trend of domestic violence and high divorce rate within the Somali community in Canada. A link is made between marital breakdown and the loss of the extended family, which, in Somalia would normally intervene to help resolve serious or violent marital disputes. The issue of conflict between mothers and children brought up in and 'at home' in the diaspora is also touched on. Finally the chapter describes ways in which women and other members of the Somali community have developed self-help advice and advocacy initiatives.

Somalis in Canada

Somalis first entered Canada in 1988 after the destruction of north western Somalia, and in larger numbers in 1991 after the outbreak of civil war in the southern part of the country. The majority of refugees originally arrived in the United States and, after long and harsh cross-examinations, received refugee status in Canada.

The growing Somali community is considered to be one of the most disadvantaged among the visible and ethnic minorities. The majority have had to cope not only with living in an alien culture without the traditional support system of the extended family, but also with not being able to speak either of the two official languages, English or French.

Somalis experience a high rate of unemployment and, in general, struggle to survive. Settling as claimants (asylum seekers), Somalis were ineligible for many government programmes available to newcomers. For example, landed immigrants (those granted refugee status as well as other, non-refugee immigrants) receive effective government programmes established to assist them in integrating into Canada such as language classes and skill training. As such, many Somalis do not have access to such programmes until their claims are settled.

Women comprise about 60 per cent of the total adult Somali population and are arguably the most vulnerable sector of the community. It is estimated that the majority of Somali women in Canada are single mothers. Many have lost their husbands in the war, resulting in a great number of Somali families headed by single mothers. Single Somali women endure extreme obstacles in Canada including gender discrimination, language difficulties, and sole responsibility for child-rearing with a lack of any support system.

The immigration process

On their arrival in Canada women have to retain their own lawyer, attend numerous interviews with the authorities, write a coherent statement regarding why she should be considered a refugee and convince an immigration officer and the Immigration and Refugee Board of Canada that she has a legitimate claim. When making a refugee claim in Canada, the claimant has to remember exact dates and times of when events occurred. This is extremely difficult for Somalis who tend not to emphasise how far they travelled from one city to another, or the date of their departure. This often leads to their claim being rejected due to inconsistencies or for lack of facts.

Throughout this long process, the claimant lives with uncertainty and at the same time beginning the stressful process of appealing the negative decision. Women who have been raped or sexually assaulted are faced with yet a further barrier. Canada introduced, in March 1993, gender guidelines which are intended to take into account such factors as the abuses women refugee claimants suffer. Unfortunately, in Somali society the stigma of making a claim based on rape or sexual abuse is so great that Somali women are unlikely to mention the rape or assault in the context of their claim or hearing. Without this information, their claim may be rejected. Under such circumstances women are forced to reveal the violations or remain silent for fear of being ostracised or blamed in their community. (See Chapter 3)

Another obstacle claimants face was created by the new immigration law, Bill C-86, implemented in February 1993. This Bill requires that, even after being found to be genuine refugees by the Immigration and Refugee Board, claimants are still compelled to have documentation predating their entrance into Canada, in order to prove their identity. 'Our primary concern is not to enter a situation where we are landing people and we don't know who they are', says Jim May, Chief of Immigrant and Visitor Operations. This requirement directly affects more women than men because fewer women than men were in positions which gave them access to, or required, documents such as a driving licence, employer's contract, bank statements or passport. For women and men, documentation may have been lost when fleeing dangerous situations as a refugee. Refugees with their proper paperwork and documentation are rare. There is no system to apply for documentation proving their identity.

Some Somali women's claims are rejected on the grounds that they could live in safe areas, inhabited by their children's clan (i.e. the clan of their husband). Although the clan system is strong in Somalia, many clans are at war.

Refugee women also face sexism from Immigration and Refugee Board officers: one Somali woman was referred to by an Immigration officer as 'my dear lady' and 'little lady'. Such language is sexist and patronising. Some immigration officers refer to Somali women's dress styles, conforming to Islamic *shari'a*, as outdated and backward. Such attitudes may influence how a woman's claim is decided.

Economic responsibility for the family

Because many Somali women are the only adult in Canada from their extended family, there are certain responsibilities and expectations that they alone must fulfil, such as supporting family members back home by sending them money, and trying to sponsor other family members to come into Canada.

Single mothers feel the pressure more than two-parent families. Some women had to leave their spouse and children behind in Somalia. In many cases women fled Somalia with false passports and could only bring the number of children stated on these passports. The cost of bringing the children to Canada was also used as a factor to decide which children to bring. The decision about who would leave and who would stay is a difficult one since some mothers leave young children behind in the hope of sponsoring them once they themselves have become permanent residents. But this process takes, on average, over a year.

Sponsorship has been made more difficult under Canada's recently restricted immigration law, which only allows sponsorship of spouses and children under 19 years of age. Parents and grandparents, minor-age siblings, and adopted and orphaned children can be sponsored only if the sponsor is in work. Due to economic pressures and to be reunited with their children and other family members, women are thus forced to take any job they can get. These jobs are usually low-paid and result in having to accept two or three part-time positions in order to meet the minimum requirement for earned income set by immigration.

Immigrant women experience extreme difficulty finding decent employment at every level of the Canadian labour force, and Somali women tend to face the additional hardships of 'cultural and language barriers (Somali and Muslim) and discrimination (Black, female and Muslim)'. Somali women are highly visible in terms of dress and behaviour and this has major implications for both employment opportunities and access to services. The majority of Canadian employers ask for Canadian work experience and are not likely to acknowledge previous work and educational experience of refugees in their home countries. This forces most immigrant women into jobs well below their overall skills and almost always below their potential. Women also lack work experience as they might not have worked outside the home before.

Consequently the majority of Somali women are employed in some form of domestic work: there is minimum language requirement and such 'unskilled' jobs are available in greater numbers to women. Once in these menial jobs it is difficult to escape this employment ghetto.

Since the lack of English or French language skills is often not considered a problem with such low-paying jobs, the women do not have opportunities to improve their language skills at work. Women therefore remain ineligible for occupational training or upgrading. On the job these women have few opportunities to learn the official languages because their fellow workers and supervisors usually do not speak to them and the work is done in isolation. The long hours and exhausting nature of the work also make it extremely difficult for women to attend evening or weekend language classes. They are caught in a vicious cycle which makes them vulnerable to exploitation.

Families in conflict

Somali mothers, particularly single mothers, must cope daily with doing the household chores, disciplining and raising children and, as is the case for other women, they often they have to take low-paying unskilled jobs to help support family members, both in

Canada and in Somalia. Once they enter the system, however, they quickly learn that it was not designed for them.

There are several reasons why there are many single-mother heads of families. First, the Somalis who came as refugee claimants were predominantly women with many children and they chose to come to Canada because of its international image of helping and welcoming immigrants and refugees. For many, 'Canada is the first exposure to Western culture for the vast majority of Somali women'. Second, many families were forced to separate because of the war, leaving the woman to care for the children alone. And third, marital breakdown and divorce among Somali couples in Canada is high and results in many women caring for their children alone.

The conflicts that lead to marital breakdown arise mainly over the redefinition of traditional roles between men and women and the stress of trying to cope in a foreign country. For example, in Somalia men did not help their wives with household chores or childcare but there were many relatives helping out. In Canada however, this kind of support from relatives does not exist, yet women have to raise a family without the help of their husbands. At the same time men expect to be treated with respect and exert authority as heads of households as they once had in Somalia. These men are expecting to be obeyed without contributing very much to the well-being of the family.

Several other factors contribute to marital conflict, which sometimes becomes abusive. First, political conflicts in Somalia are often transferred to Canada. The effects are magnified, especially if the husband and wife are from different clans. This manifests itself in the form of who to send money to: should it be her clan or his? Her family or his? Or should they spend it on their own needs?

Second, a large percentage of Somali men are unemployed because of recession and lack of recognition from employers of previous work experience and education. Somali women, on the other hand, are willing to take dead-end, low-paying jobs in order to support their family in Canada and abroad. This creates a role reversal as women become financially independent of their husbands. As a result men feel alienated, useless, angry and frustrated, eventually taking out their frustrations on their wives and children. Many Somali women look to the police for protection.

The result is an extremely high rate of marital conflict and divorce. There is an increasing incidence of violence within Somali families where stress may be high and where abused family members do not know their rights or sources of help. In Somalia by contrast domestic conflicts that might lead to divorce are often solved by one's in-laws and extended family, thereby saving the marriage. (This is particularly the case in clan-exogamous marriages where there is more at stake than the relationship between two people.) In Canada social services and the police exist in place of the extended family but their intervention can unintentionally end up exacerbating a situation of domestic conflict. For example, one Somali woman who was angry with her husband called the police to teach him a lesson. Lacking knowledge of Canadian law she did not anticipate that the police would charge him, an outcome that made her situation far worse.

Because of the breakdown of the traditional support systems available in Somali, abusive relationships between parents and children, as well as among married couples, are increasing in the Somali community. Large numbers of children are growing up in Canada speaking either English or French and understanding how to use 'the system' to their benefit. In many cases they are abusing their mothers in the process. Somali refugee children in Canada tend to believe that they are deprived of the freedoms that Canadian children enjoy. This leads the children to threaten to call the police or the Children's Aid Society (CAS) and report abuse unless they get their way. Police and CAS intervention is the nightmare of most Somali single mothers in Canada, as many who have had contact with such agencies have had their children taken away from them.

Social marginalisation and racism

All of the above are only a fraction of the problems faced by Somali mothers. Housing has also been identified as a major issue. Families on welfare are asked to provide the name of a co-signer who has an income of Can$50,000 or over. This criteria cannot be met by many Somali single mothers and they have no option but to enter shelters in order to qualify for subsidised housing from the Ottawa-Carleton Regional Housing Authority. This, in turn, has led to an influx of Somalis into certain areas of the city.

Due to the increasing intolerance in Canada towards newcomers in general and towards the Somali community specifically, there has been an increase in conflict between Somalis and white Canadians who have stereotyped Somalis as abusing the social assistance system. Somalis are increasingly facing individual and systemic racism which has made their integration much more difficult. In many cases Somalis have been physically attacked and injured.

A poll in 1993 by *Maclean's,* a leading magazine in Canada, revealed an increasing intolerance toward newcomers and found that 34 per cent of those interviewed said immigrants should be encouraged to 'blend with larger society'. A poll by *Maclean's* in 1990 indicated that '40 per cent of the respondents ... said that new immigrants should be encouraged to maintain their distinct culture and ways'. These contradictory messages probably reflect a state of confusion over the meaning of multiculturalism to Canadians.

Recently the Somali community has faced increasing and systemic racism in the media, from government, and from the general public. Many Somalis have been charged with collecting multiple claims for welfare in order to send money to their warlords of choice. Even though these allegations have been shown to be false, the Somali community continues to face the repercussions of such false reporting.

Self-help initiatives within the Somali diaspora

Despite the difficulties described above, the Somali community in Ottawa-Carleton has organised to assist its members. Programmes have been implemented to make life easier for community members. Some community health centres such as the Carlington Community Health Centre and the Sandy Hill Community Health Centre have hired Somali workers to do outreach and counsel Somali single mothers and the Somali community. Carlington Community Health Centre has a Somali women's programme where the women get together, and decide on the topics to be discussed as well as who to invite as speakers. They have also attempted to recreate the support mechanism that they had in Somalia and have empowered themselves by finding out how the Canadian system works and how it can benefit them. Other governmental agencies, including the three levels of government as well as non-governmental organisations, have hired Somalis to render the services accessible and available.

Numerous heritage schools where the Somali language and culture is taught have emerged in the area. Women get together at weekends to teach each other skills and exchange ideas. Increasing numbers of Somali religious elders now do counselling in a way similar to that done in Somalia. During Ramadan, the holy month of fasting, Somali women organise locations to break the fast together and share prayers. During holidays such as Eid Al Fitr, women organise camps and picnics for the community.

Somali women have not only tried to improve life in Canada for themselves but have had a positive impact on other refugees and immigrants in Canada. In 1991 a group of Somali women in Toronto who were part of a support group being offered by the Canadian Centre for Victims of Torture, decided that they needed access to government housing which was not available to refugee claimants. The women did research, gathered support from other agencies and members of the provincial parliament, and then launched a lawsuit against the Housing Authority stating that they were being discriminated against. This has led to the law being changed to make all refugee claimants eligible for subsidised housing.

As the Somali community continues to face many problems in Canada, Somali women, as the majority of the Somali adult population, will continue to play a major role in solving them. Somalis have been victims of racism due to their vocal resistance to being discriminated against; and they have become scapegoats in the media, which makes them vulnerable to even worse racism and discrimination. Yet the Somali experience in places such as Ottawa has also played a significant role in policy changes that have benefited newcomers as a whole and which can be used as a model for organising Somali communities in other parts of Canada.

NOTE

1. A version of this chapter was presented at the Fifth International Congress of the Somali Studies International Association in 1993, and is published in Adam & Ford 1997.

5
Crisis or Opportunity? Somali Women Traders and the War

Amina Mohamoud Warsame

Somali women, both in rural and in urban settings, contribute substantially to their country's subsistence economy. During periodic droughts, famine and conflicts over resources Somali women take active responsibility for the survival of their families. When faced with economic crisis – whether at a personal level or at the wider societal level – women in towns take as central a role in saving themselves and their families from starvation as do their nomadic counterparts.

Trading is one of the strategies urban women resort to in order to combat such situations. Women's involvement in trade is not new. Their engagement in income-earning activities depends on, among other things, economic options, access to start-up cash, an alternative income provider in the family, an individual woman's desire to be economically independent, and the wider economic situation.

The long civil war has increased people's economic vulnerability. The almost total breakdown of the economy has put extra burdens on women to feed their families. Today more women than during any previous period in Somali history are turning to trade both in Somalia and outside the country.

In this chapter I present the changing role of Somali women in trade with special reference to women of Somaliland. The chapter is based mainly on material I collected during two field trips to Somaliland, in 1993 and 1994, for a research project on the impact of the civil war on pastoralists.[1] I first trace women's involvement in trade and then their struggle for economic survival amid the civil war and its aftermath.

I ask at which periods women's trading activities were strongest or weakest, and why. What pushes women into trade rather than other cash-earning activities? How does Somali society – specifically men – look on women's trading activities?

Because of Somali women's central role in their family's survival, and because of the collapse of the economy, an increasing number of women are forced to take to trade to make ends meet. However, many women do so for a more deeply felt need for some kind of economic autonomy vis-a-vis their husbands or other male relatives. For these women, their trading activities enhance their decision-making power in the family.

Much of the material in this chapter is taken from oral testimony in Somaliland and in Europe. For early historical periods, few written records giving information about women's involvement in trade are available at all.

Northern Somali women's role in trade (1860–1960)

Before colonisation by European powers trade in Somalia was limited to a few local commodities such as ghee, myrrh, ostrich feathers, livestock and gum arabic, and imported items such as rice, dates and clothes. Writing from the period makes no mention of women's involvement. However, oral sources suggest that some women, mostly elderly widows, accompanied caravans from the interior to the coastal towns to sell ghee, which was regarded as a 'women's domain'. With the money thus acquired they would buy dyed yarn – for making a carpet-like material (*caws*) used in building the nomadic hut – and sell it to other women.

As the economy became more commercially-oriented with the introduction of livestock trade by the British, many people began trading livestock to acquire basic commodities. This was initially in the hands of men. However, given women's important role in handling livestock products such as ghee, milk and meat, many took this opportunity to start trading in these items in the emerging towns. An observer in 1957 commented:

> Shops are concerned mainly with the sale of imported goods, while the open marketplace deals mainly with local produce and is dominated by women. Women bring in milk and ghee daily from the surrounding countryside and sell it in the market. They also sell woven bark containers, mats, rope and string, charcoal and grain, and some poultry and eggs, vegetables and fruit. (Lewis 1957)

Some rural as well as urban women were involved in trade. But they were limited to taking livestock and livestock products to the urban markets, selling them and using the money to buy basic supplies.

Elderly informants told how women, mostly elderly, started trading in sorghum. The sorghum trade increased during the Second World War, when Italy occupied Somaliland and the ports of Berbera and Zeila were closed. Many people were then forced to depend on grain from Ethiopia. Most sorghum traders were women, who took grain from Jigjiga in Ethiopia to sell in Somali towns. Known as *qumman* (a word connoting rich females) these were the first female traders to accumulate capital and become successful. According to an elderly man who when younger had worked for these women traders:

> The sorghum traders were tough women. Each one would hire a truck and two young men to load it. The truck would go straight to the farms, and after the woman had bought the sorghum, the other boy and I would put it in big bags. The women would then sew these and we would load them into the truck. We used to call these women 'mothers', because throughout the trip – which usually took four to six days – they fed us out of their own pockets. As soon as the truck reached town, we would unload it and receive our money. The traders had women agents in other places, whom they paid and who sold the sorghum on their behalf. (Author's research)

At about the same time other women went to Ethiopia to trade in goods such as ornaments, spices, household utensils and onions. These women were known as *qararaflay (*a word associating the women with the sound the items made upon loading) and were less successful than the sorghum traders. Unlike the sorghum traders, who were wholesalers, the *qararaflay* sold their goods in the market places.

Age, poverty and marital status were significant in determining which groups of women could normally engage in trade, or in any other sort of income-earning activity. There was a predominance of elderly women, poor women, widows and divorcees among the traders. It was thought to be shameful for young or married women to engage in trading, which requires sitting in public places or mingling with men.

With the establishment of towns and the gradual movement from the pastoral areas to these emerging administrative centres, many women took advantage of the increasing populations in the towns to diversify their trade. The kinds of things sold by women were mostly foodstuffs (traditionally considered a women's domain), including milk, thin flat pancakes (*laxoox)*, sheep and goat meat, deep-fried minced meat preserved in ghee (*muqmad*), fats collected from camel bone-marrow, household utensils and vegetables.

In the main, the types of trading done by women do not require a big initial investment, which could explain women's concentration in these petty activities.[2] Another reason could be the practice of buying commodities on credit through kinship networks. My study of market women in 1986 in Mogadishu showed both these factors to be significant in determining women's income-earning activities.

During the late colonial period the Yemeni port of Aden became an important trading centre, and some Somalis, among them women, migrated there. Most migrant Somali women did domestic work or were employed as incense cleaners. Some later used their earnings to trade between Aden and Somali towns. Other women living in the then British Somaliland would travel to Aden to trade. According to an ex-resident of Aden during the 1930s, they took gold and clothes from Aden and on their return home sold them to neighbours, or in the case of clothes, to retailers. From Somali towns they took ghee, dried minced meat and honey, to sell to the large Somali community in Aden.

The period following the Second World War saw progress and economic options for many men, and for a small number of women too. Soon after the British recaptured the country from Italy, in 1941, the authorities exempted people from taxes for six months, facilitating increased trade and diversifying the commodities brought into the country.[3] The post-war period was a significant era in northern Somali entrepreneurialism and in the build-up of economic resources.

Expanding trade opportunities (1960–88)

When the ex-Italian-administered Somalia (the southern region) and the ex-British Somaliland (the northern region) attained independence in 1960 and formed the Somali Republic, new economic opportunities became available because of environmental differences between the two regions. Farming was prevalent in the south since it had the only permanent water sources (the Juba and Shabelle rivers). Traders would take farm produce such as mangoes, bananas, sesame-oil, peas, grapefruit and water melons to the north. The building of a tarmac road connecting the two regions in 1973 facilitated this trade in perishables.

Although no studies were made of this internal trade, it is known that the majority of traders were women. They chartered trucks and, setting off from the north with the goods they planned to sell in the south, would buy fruit from farms in the south through middlemen. They then travelled back to Somaliland to sell the fruit there, or in some cases they would go further on to Djibouti. A former fruit trader I interviewed describes it thus:

> Most of the fruit traders worked in partnerships of two to three women. Because of the long route from the north to the south, women traders worked in shifts, i.e. one woman, usually with a young boy as a helper, would accompany the truck during each trip. A woman partner and I used to take fruit to Djibouti. We took mostly mangoes, grapefruit and watermelons. It took us five to six days from the farms to reach our destination. At one time the road from Jilib [a farming town in southern Somalia] was rough and when it rained the trucks stuck in the mud. The fruit would then go bad; it was a matter of luck. At other times our truckload would come in when there was a shortage of fruit and we would get a lot of profit. (Author's research)

Other commodities such as leather shoes were taken from the south to the north. Unlike the north, where only a few traditional shoemakers existed, catering mainly for the nomadic populations, in the south there were a number of small shoe industries. Moreover, some animal products such as ghee were much cheaper in the south. Like the fruit and shoe trades the ghee trade was mostly conducted by women. The traders would go deep into the villages, and through middlemen they would buy ghee which they then transported to the northern towns.

Because the seaport of Berbera in the north was close to the rich Arab states, many imported goods such as sugar and rice fetched higher prices in the south, especially during shortages. As one trader commented: 'As soon as we found out that a certain commodity was in shortage in one locality, we would seize the opportunity to take it from where it was plentiful to where it was in demand.'

Trade in *qaad* (*catha edulis*), whose leaves are chewed as a stimulant (see page 37), became an increasingly important trade item. Originally *qaad* was mostly chewed in northern Somalia. However, it spread to southern Somalia soon after unification, opening up new markets for *qaad* trading. Since the leaves are chewed fresh, the opening up of air services between the two regions further facilitated *qaad* trading. It was first taken by fast-moving Jeeps and Land-Rovers from Ethiopia where it is grown, to the northern towns. From there it was transported by plane to Mogadishu and surrounding towns.

At first it was mostly men who traded in *qaad*. But during the early 1980s, before *qaad* was banned, a significant number of women were trading both within the north and between the two regions. Traders would send *qaad* in small marked bags by aeroplane. The traders' agents would pick up the bags from Mogadishu airport and sell it.

Because of the increased dependence of both rural and urban populations on imported foodstuffs, some women took the opportunity to rent out storage space to wholesalers. In a famous Mogadishu market area known as Yobson, which was a trading transit and meeting place for people from the north, there were many of these rented buildings, known as *bakhaaro*, used for storing commodities. Many were owned by women, some of whom became wealthy and well known among northern entrepreneurs. There were similar storage buildings in the major northern towns.

With the growing number of Somali guest workers, especially northerners, in the Gulf oil-producing countries, trade flourished in the 1970s and early 1980s. It was facilitated by a semi-legal system of transferring foreign currency: a person working in Saudi Arabia or the Emirates would entrust money to a trader – usually a friend or close acquaintance from his or her own clan – to give to his relatives back home; the trader would use the money to purchase goods there; on arrival, and after selling the goods at a profit, the trader would give the original amount to the person or persons to whom it was destined. People working outside the country rarely used the banks to transfer money; instead, they used this system to send remittances. The relatives of the guest workers would get their money, and the traders would have access to hard currency with which they could buy commodities abroad.[4]

Many women used remittances sent by husbands or close relatives to start a trade. One such woman told me how she benefited from her trading activities:

> My husband migrated to Saudi Arabia in 1976, during the *dhabadheer* drought [one of the most disastrous droughts of the mid 1970s]. He got a job as an unskilled labourer in a construction company. He used to send me some money for our expenses every two months or so. Every time he sent me money, I would set

> aside some. When I saved a significant amount, I started to trade in women's clothes, perfumes and incense. My cousin was a trader who used to travel to Saudi Arabia and she helped to buy me what I needed from there. I would pay her for transporting the goods. In 1985 my husband was deported from Saudi Arabia as he didn't have the proper documents. By then I had a big clothes stall; we depended on the profits until we fled in 1988 after the war broke out. (Author's research)

During the post-independence period trading by women increased. Women maintained that they exploited opportunities to upgrade their position by gaining their own income. A survey carried out in 1987 among women in Bakaraha, one of the largest open markets in Mogadishu, substantiated women's yearning for economic independence. One said:

> When my husband divorced me I didn't have money because all the money he gave me was for our expenses. After the divorce I went to my brother and asked him for some capital to begin trading. Now, although I don't get much profit, I can feed myself without staying in another woman's *doc* [house]. I don't think I will ever again wait for a man's money.[5]

During the late 1970s and 1980s many women, either on their own initiative or through their relationship with the ruling elite, became wealthy by travelling to such countries as India, Pakistan and Italy and bringing back commodities such as medicines, clothes, and spaghetti. This trade was facilitated by the presence of Somali communities in these countries. Since most of these traders could not speak any language other than Somali they received assistance from the Somalis living there, who in return were given small payments for their assistance.

To illustrate the importance of Somali women's involvement in trade in one of these countries, India, on a visit to Bombay I was surprised to hear wholesalers in a shopping centre addressing me in Somali when they realised where I was from. These merchants, who were apparently familiar with Somali women traders, called out names of Somali cloth (*garbasaar* and *macawis*) as I passed. I learned from the merchants that they have Somali women clients who buy clothes from them; they thought I was a trader too.

Women's role in the economy during the war

Even before the outbreak of war in 1988 the economy was severely depressed and it was impossible for ordinary people to survive on one source of income. The value of wages halved in real terms between 1970 and 1978, and a high proportion of trained and experienced personnel sought employment in richer countries. These hard economic times caused more women than ever to take up diverse trading activities.

When war broke out in 1988 between the northern opposition Somali National Movement (SNM) and the troops of the central government headed by Siad Barre, the latter used air raids and artillery bombardment to flush out the opposition, which had captured two main towns. As a result, the majority of the population in the bombed cities, as well as a large rural population, fled to neighbouring Ethiopia where several refugee camps were set up.

As the people recovered from the initial shock of the disaster, women in the camps were the first to start trading with whatever money they had fled with. Some traded some of their rations to get hold of capital. Others sold their gold in Ethiopia (if they were lucky enough to escape with it) and used the money to start trading. In this way, refugee families were able to supplement their food rations with other necessities.

Soon the refugee camps became trade and exchange centres. Goods from as far as the then capital in the south would be brought to the camps and further forwarded to surrounding Ethiopian and Somali towns. Grain would be bought from families in the camps and traded for pastoral products in the countryside. In the same way, goods would be taken to the soldiers and their families and anyone remaining in the deserted northern towns.

The majority of the traders were women because it was safer for women to cross enemy lines. (Africa Watch 1990) Making use of their dual identity (their clan of birth and that of their husband and children – see Chapter 7) women traders travelled far and wide to bring commodities from every corner of the country for sale.

Apart from their dual clan identity, Somali women also exploited another clan-related factor enabling them to cross enemy lines, namely that revenge killings only apply to men, since according to Somali perception no woman is worthy to be killed in revenge for the killing of a male clan member. It must be mentioned however, that trading across enemy lines was not always risk-free. As Africa Watch for example has reported, many rapes were committed by government soldiers during this period. (*Ibid*)

In addition to their involvement in trading activities during the war years, women served other important functions too. Women traders would also take remittances or other material assistance from the Gulf States and from families living in the capital, and pass them on to the senders' relatives in camps or nomadic areas. In this way these women served as mobile banks.

This was especially the case during the first years of the civil war when many families from the north joined their relatives in Mogadishu (the population of which doubled) while others fled to the countryside or refugee camps in Ethiopia. Until the war spread to the south, financial assistance from abroad was sent to and from these family members through women traders. The women traders made use of the cash sent through them. As it was less safe for them to carry cash long distances through the territories of different clans, they used it to purchase goods, repaying the beneficiaries from the sale.

During the war remittances from abroad – i.e. from the Arab states, Europe and North America (where a large number of Somalis fled to) – were a significant way for many traders. Some got income from relatives living in neighbouring Ethiopia or Djibouti, while others could get their commodities on credit, which is an important way of making profit without having cash.

Making ends meet in the post-civil war period in Somaliland

With the defeat of the regime in January 1991 the war between the SNM and the government came to an end. Voluntary repatriation from the camps followed after the declaration of independence by the ex-northern regions of Somalia. For several months ex-refugees returned to ruined towns and villages with no infrastructure, no social services and collapsed government institutions. Several conflicts erupted that added to the already precarious situation. The post-civil war period was characterised by renewed displacement of people, political tensions, clashes between the armed clan militias and rivalry within different factions over power and limited resources. The situation was further aggravated by the proliferation of weapons, which facilitated banditry and insecurity. Faced with total destruction and a collapsed economy the newly declared but unrecognised state of Somaliland had little prospect of viability. Formal unemployment was total and most people had lost everything in the war. Moreover, *qaad* chewing, involving many hours of idle sitting, spread among the male population. Not for the first time, the burden of coping with the new situation fell on women.

Today Somali women are involved in an important economic activity in increasing numbers, greater than at any other period in history. In the markets of the partially reconstructed towns as well as in rural areas, one can clearly see more women than men. Women have assumed a key role in travelling around the country to trade in vital commodities – cereals, vegetables, fruit, milk, *qaad* and meat as well as a variety of imported goods. They are active not only in important service and trading activities within Somaliland, but also in trade with countries such as Ethiopia, Djibouti, Saudi Arabia and the Arab Emirates.

A survey conducted by Save the Children in 1991 described women's role in the wheat trade in this way:

> The wheat grain is very largely imported from Harta Sheikh, just across the border in Ethiopia and the location of the largest refugee camp. The grain is collected by traders at the market there or directly from the refugee camp on the Dula'd plain outside the town. The traders operate on various scales. Many are women who hire space on trucks, and can be seen arriving at Hargeisa on top of their cargo of some 10 to 20 bags for each woman.

In another survey by Save the Children in 1993, covering all the major towns of Somaliland, the most common source of family income was found to be market activities, of which 56.8 per cent was conducted by women.[6] A more recent UNICEF survey, carried out in 1996, found the proportion of female-headed households to be very high, up to 40 per cent in some areas, and the proportion of households where mothers were the major income providers was also high at 30 per cent.[7]

Most recently, women have also ventured into trade in areas thought of as male domains. A case in point is the increasing involvement of women in the *qaad* and livestock retail trades. For although some women took part in the former it was predominantly a male area. Today, an increasing number of women are involved in the *qaad* trade and, like men, are making an income by selling it (though not to the same extent as before the war), despite the alleged harm to society of *qaad* chewing. Women are also increasingly getting involved in the livestock trade, although on a much more limited scale than the *qaad* trade which needs little capital to get started.

Society's view of women's income-earning activities outside the home

Society in general, and men in particular, have in the past had a negative attitude towards women owning property, even an *aqal* (nomadic home). There is a frequently quoted traditional expression: 'Never allow a woman to own anything of value: if she brings a clay pot with her to the matrimonial home, break it.'

This attitude is gradually changing as more and more women earn and control their own cash. In Somaliland today one hears of men's appreciation for women's indispensable economic role in the country. However, many female interviewees said that men tend to feel threatened by women's increasing acquisition of cash and the freedom of movement associated with trade. A successful women entrepreneur made this point:

> I started trading 40 years ago at the age of 25. My mother was a grain seller and I experienced how earning an income enhanced her position. I took after her, and since then I have been a trader in different commodities. Through the years I also realised that owning economic resources helps women to make important decisions in their families. This could be one reason why men don't like women having economic resources. A friend of mine who is a trader had problems with her husband over her economic activities. Whenever there was an important decision to be made her husband felt his authority was being undermined by his wife. He could, for instance, say: 'Who is the man of the family, you or me?' or: 'Don't be deceived by your money, you are still a woman.'

The economic resources acquired by women, however, have not translated into political power, nor any meaningful economic power beyond the family level. Somali women continue to be absent from decision-making at the wider societal level.

The revival of traditional clan politics, in which only men can participate in decision-making, is a determining factor for Somali women's role in the political arena. It is true that women have taken initiatives in peace-building in Somaliland; however, they have been excluded from the peace conferences that took place in the country. (See for example Chapter 6, 'Women and peace-making in Somaliland') Moreover, they are absent from both houses of authority (the Upper House, or *guurti*, and the House of Representatives) and they are not represented in the Council of Ministers in Somaliland.

Until now the allocation of all these positions has been based on clan representation, which excludes women from formal authority and governance. Before August 2002, when Somaliland's first woman minister was appointed, only one woman had been appointed to a senior position in the administration and that appointment was short-lived. However, the local council elections that took place in Somaliland at the end of 2002 gave women an opportunity to become candidates. Although only two women secured seats from more than 300 seats, their victory can be counted as a groundbreaking move towards women's involvement in the decision-making process. (See also Chapter 9, and 'Afterword'.)

The rise of certain groups that might like to curtail women's movements in the name of religion is to be reckoned with. In Islam there is no verse that directly bars women from earning income as long as they follow the Islamic code of wearing clothes that do not expose their bodies, avoid close contact with men and are not involved in illegal economic activities. Nevertheless, there are many men who would prefer to see women back in their homes. Many Somali women fear this threat. Most women are not aware of the specific rights that Islam has given them, but it seems there is high awareness of the right to be gainfully employed. Many women, especially those whose income is relatively high, are exercising that right.

In addition, women's income is used nowadays in solving problems that could otherwise escalate into conflicts. A case in point is the payment of blood money (or *diya*) which used to be paid for by men. Today, when women are the sole breadwinners, they pay their family's share of that money.

TESTIMONY 5: HALIMO ELMI

Editors' note

Within a few months of Mogadishu's collapse into inter-clan warfare, in 1991, it became clear to many of the city's inhabitants that the fighting was not going to be over soon and they were likely to suffer terrible consequences if they remained. But to leave was not an easy undertaking – it required planning, resources, cooperation, weapons and personal connections. For by then transport and fuel was scarce, captured by militia fighters, and in every direction in the surrounding countryside heavily armed militia groups manned checkpoints and carried out ambushes to control movement, kill their enemy, and plunder whatever resources they could find. To pass through the checkpoints was extremely hazardous unless they were manned by members of your own or your related clan group or you were travelling with members of their clan-group, in which case you could hope for, but not necessarily be guaranteed, some protection.

For those seeking the relative safety in the far north of the country the only realistic option was to join others and travel in convoy. Finding a place on a convoy depended on your connections and what you could contribute in terms of transport, fuel, weapons, money, combat power, or skills. For the many people who did not own or have access to a vehicle, money to pay for a space, or medical skills for example, being taken on board would be down to luck or another's pity. One man who will be remembered for the number of people he helped to escape by convoy to the north is the late Ali Warsame, one of Somalia's biggest building contractors. It is said that one convoy he organised consisted of more than 1,000 people. Many vehicles ran out of fuel and had to be roped together and towed. It took more than six months for the convoy to reach the north west – a distance of about 1,000 km, covered in 80 minutes by aeroplane.[8]

Halimo Elmi travelled north on such a convoy with her four children and her mother. Unlike Halimo's husband they were not from the north but sought refuge there. Halimo's testimony describes how the war affected her extended family, which cross-cuts three of the main clan groups: Hawiye, Marehan (Darod) and Isaq. Like the many other families with links to more than one clan, Halimo's family was split apart by the war which made it too dangerous for her husband to remain in Mogadishu with her and the children. Halimo explains how she and her urban family coped with displacement to a remote, arid, pastoral area in order to escape from the violence and be reunited with her husband. Halimo used her skills as a midwife to help other women and to maintain her family.

Halimo's story

We were living in Mogadishu when the civil war broke out there. We were living in Karan, which was the first place the artillery targeted. We had to leave the area in such a rush that it was impossible for us to take anything with us. We had only one flask and a lantern, we did not even have shoes. We were rushing too fast to think about anything. Everywhere there was war. We just wanted to find some safety so we headed out of Mogadishu in a convoy of vehicles with about 100 other people. We had left Mogadishu in the morning and by the afternoon we had reached an isolated place and could proceed no further because we could not travel at night as our vehicle lights would attract attention.

This first night there were 15 women in our group who went into labour, brought on by the stress and shock of the war and our journey. Of the 15 only eight were full-term pregnancies; the rest were between five and seven months. Seven of the women were in one car and the other eight were in two cars. I and another woman, who I found out about later, were the only health professionals – I a midwife, she an assistant midwife.

That night we had no light, not even a torch. My husband heard men shouting, 'There are women in labour – we don't have anyone to help, please come and help us!' He came to me as I was cooking white rice in an oil tin. He said: 'I heard there are some women in labour. Please can you go and help them?' I said: 'How can I go at this time?' I was afraid of the snakes. Finally I was persuaded and they brought three women to me who said they were full term. I took them under a tree. I asked the driver to put on the car headlights and then we covered the space between the car and the tree with a sheet to make a shelter and so that the light would not be too visible from afar. I put the three women inside this shelter. Luckily for me they were not delivering spontaneously so I could deliver them one at a time with Allah helping me because I am alone. The first delivery was of a stillborn baby full term, nine months – a daughter. As I finished the first delivery the second and the third women started to push. I called two of the husbands and said: 'Please, I need assistance. I am alone and the two women are pushing at the same time.' One of the husbands came to me and helped me. He was not feeling shy. You feel shy when you have some privacy but without it everybody needs to help and there is no differentiation between men and women.

When we finished delivering the first three we heard shouting: 'Please we need assistance!' There turned out to be 12 other women in labour! So we collected them together in the same place under the small tree in the dark. By the end, the area near the tree was covered in membranes, placenta, blood so that when you stood on it you would slip on it. Only three of the newly delivered babies survived, one daughter and two boys out of 15 deliveries. Seven were premature and five were stillborn. We put them in separate graves. For the mothers there was no tea or water to drink – nothing. Some of the men had special pots containing water which they gave to them, but that was all. The morning came and everyone saw the 15 women lying like this. In our society people are kind in such situations and they went to try to find them some milk or tea but we could not find anything. We collected the women together and put them in one car that had shelter. Then the whole day we drove on, turning to one side and then another to prevent being attacked and when we came close to a village we would avoid it. The whole day we advanced slowly – but with nothing by mouth – no food. By the night-time we found somewhere to sleep and eventually some food and drink.

We travelled in this way for several weeks before returning to Mogadishu, expecting things to have improved there. When Siad Barre's forces left we returned to our home in Karan [a district of Mogadishu] but everything in our house had been looted. We were left with nothing. We had to borrow cooking utensils and mattresses from relatives and neighbours. We hoped that the war would soon stop. My husband who is from Somaliland wanted us to go to Hargeisa but I only knew Mogadishu and when he left in our car I refused to go with him. I hoped that security would return to Mogadishu so that we wouldn't have to travel to remote places such as Hargeisa.

But then there was another war between the sub-clans of the Hawiye tribe and we had to leave Karan again, eventually moving to the Hodan area of the city. We had not expected the Hawiye clans to start a war. We had thought that, once Siad Barre had gone, everything would be settled. But insecurity worsened after the demise of Siad Barre.

At the time the civil war broke out, although there was a government the health services were very poor, especially women's care, or Mother and Child Health services, and hospital services. So women were among the most vulnerable groups when the fighting started. During my displacement in Mogadishu there was a woman who was due to deliver living in a small hut near my home. Early one morning I took her to my home to deliver. My children had found her in need when they had rushed outside after some bomb attack to see who had been the victims – they were always curious and had become very brave whereas I didn't even like to open the door. I put her in a small corridor of the house and I delivered the baby. I cut the cord, which was asphyxiating the baby. As I tried to revive the baby a large artillery bomb landed in our sitting room. The roof was cracked and there was so much smoke that we could see nothing. I was still holding the baby boy but the mother, in her shock, had jumped up and run away still carrying the placenta inside her. We couldn't find each other in the chaos. I held onto the baby, who was alive, but we didn't find his mother until the evening – by which time she was nearly dead.

While she had been running the placenta had separated causing a post-partum haemorrhage. She had fainted in the street, in an isolated area where people were all running away from the shelling. A family living near our home identified her. They said: 'We know this woman, she is called Hawa. She lives here. What has happened?' When you see someone lying on the floor the first thing that comes to your mind is that they have been shot. Everybody thinks she is dead. It was around sunset when a small boy said to me: 'Please Halimo, there is a woman lying in the street.' She was lying about 50 steps away. We took a wheelbarrow to fetch her and I attempted to soothe her. Because she had a spontaneous delivery and didn't have an incision the procedure is to check the placenta. By this time there was no placenta, everything had separated, there had been too much bleeding and she had fallen into a coma. We had no alternative, we just did the Somali way of treating someone in shock – we wrap them up in a wet blanket and wait until they come to. After three hours she regained consciousness.

Finally I took her into our home as she didn't have any family nearby. All her family had run away but because she was in labour she had not been able to go with them. So she was alone. We stayed together for a week. Eventually she was reunited with her husband who had feared that she had died.

Hawa's mother was an old widow whose husband had died when the children were very small. They used a donkey to carry water to sell. Then the donkey was injured by shelling, its thigh was cut to the bone and the mother said: 'Please Halimo, can you try to stop the donkey bleeding?' The donkey was more important to them than a son because they depended on it. I said: 'I cannot suture a donkey because he is not tame.' She said: 'I will call some men to hold him.' So they held his two legs in front while I sutured him. I tried to stop the bleeding as best I could. When I had finished I was about to go home when there was another artillery bombardment and the donkey and the woman were blown to pieces in front of me. One could not tell the donkey's body parts from those of the old woman. I was in shock for four hours. I lost all my sense and feelings. I could not speak. I just looked at things.

Hundreds of things like this were happening everywhere. Day by day we got experience. I got used to such things so that when I heard bombing I was not so scared because it had become part of normality. There is a Somali proverb: 'You will learn from difficulties.'

Finally, though, I had to accept that the war was not going to end soon and that for the safety of my children we had no alternatives other than to follow my husband to Hargeisa. If we had had our own car we could have taken many things with us that we needed but as our car had already gone north with my husband we could only take a minimum and the priority was to find space for the children. I was not thinking of anything else at that time.

When we left Mogadishu we were about 35 vehicles with a minimum of 100 people – so overcrowded. Seventy per cent were children and women. We could not go alone. There was always a need to have gunmen for protection when we were passing from one clan area to another. We would travel with gunmen from one area who were responsible for our protection until we reached the next area, when we needed new gunmen responsible for security in that area. Altogether we had around four gun vehicles ('technicals'). My husband's clan had no power in Mogadishu at that time. So we had to get some of my family to look after us – not only us but also others, for example Isaq, who were with us. Through my family relations with the gunmen I was responsible for all these Isaq people travelling with me.

If a convoy encountered checkpoints or militias that suspected you had anything valuable, and if they were not related to your family they might kill you. My immediate family and I are the luckiest people, as we did not face any victimisation. We didn't mind about not having money or material possessions as at least we had our lives. Other people in our convoy were not so lucky – some had lost their children, their husbands. We were the only family who were untouched; the other families in our convoy all suffered – some from gunshot wounds sustained at the checkpoints. Once our convoy was attacked and we lost at least 15 per cent of the convoy in one go. People living in villages along the route were afraid when they saw a convoy coming from Mogadishu because they believed that gunmen must be coming. So they would arm themselves and there would be a clash between the village gunmen and the convoy gunmen. Even among our bodyguards there were some who were with us and some who were against us so there would be in-fighting. Others wanted to loot from the vehicles and when they were opposed they would start shooting.

By accident we found my husband when we reached Beletweyne [a town in Hiran region, about 300 km from Mogadishu]. He was on his way back to Mogadishu to find us. At that time it was so risky for him to stay with us that I asked him to go ahead with some of my male relatives to look after him.

When our convoy reached Abudwaak [about 200 km north of Beletweyne] we felt safer, as my mother's family lives there and we were able to get care from them. Travelling from that area to Burao we felt very secure. A month after leaving Mogadishu[9] we arrived in the morning at a place called Berka near Burao [the second largest town in the north west] and we decided to stop there for a rest.

While we were cooking our lunch fighting broke out in Burao causing many 'refugees' to flee from the town. We were shocked – why were all these people fleeing? They said that there was a civil war between Habr

Ja'lo and Habr Yunis [two sub-clans of the Isaq] in Burao. It was 1991. On the way from Abudwaak to Las Anod and to Burao we had felt very close to reaching our friends and relatives and safety. But when we found refugees fleeing from Burao we felt totally demoralised.

Reconciliation between the sub-clans was achieved after some time and we were eventually able to settle in Burao where we stayed more than two years. During this time I ran a private maternity hospital. I acted as a gynae-obstetrician because they had only one gynaecologist and when the conflict came he left with his tribe. Every afternoon I visited about 20 women and I learned the conditions caused by the war really affected women's lives. One of the commonest complications among women is secondary sterility. This is sterility resulting from infection, often after a woman has given birth or miscarried then become infected and had no treatment or inadequate treatment. Sometimes they suffer from infection of the fallopian tube. It is common to see a woman who had two children before the war but is unable to conceive afterwards because of secondary sterility.

The problem displaced women face is the lack of medicines and health services but also the lack of water and soap to wash. In the rural areas it is very difficult for a woman during menstruation; she has to find cloths to use and if you don't have any you have to stay isolated the whole day because you cannot walk around. It is difficult to clean your body. The water well may be three hours' walk away. Even if you can get clean water the priority is not to wash because you need to drink. Sometimes your skin feels smelly. The problem of infection for women is very serious. They are vulnerable to infection, miscarriage, tetanus. Women died like animals. And even though many have now moved into urban centres they have problems accessing health centres and they don't have money to buy the drugs they need; nor do they have specialist doctors. There is a need for specialist women who can provide women with advice and treatment on secondary sterility because if they get the right diagnosis and treatment they can be treated [successfully].

An outbreak of war in 1995 forced us to flee Burao. This time we fled into the dry, rural pastoral area where my husband's family live. We were among 700 families to flee to the area, coming from different places as refugees. Later on some people were not happy with the situation so they moved on to other areas to survive. I chose not to leave as I didn't have any money and was dependent on my husband's family. We were to live here for one and a half years.

It was a remote, isolated area. You might see a car once every three months. The first year was really hard. I was so unhappy. We were all

3 These women and children fled the southern regions of the country for Berbera, in the far north. The war displaced hundreds of thousands of people within the boundaries of Somalia. Many were women and children whose men were killed or had to flee the country. Making long and hazardous journeys, those who survived shared nightmarish memories of seeking a way through warring clan territories where bandits and militia preyed on the convoys of terrified citizens. (Betty Press/Panos Pictures)

[feeling] negative and unhappy. The biggest problem at first was the children because it was their first experience of rural life. But when there is no alternative you have to adapt to the situation. My husband and I lived in the settlement close to the wells but after a while the four children would go far afield tending the animals with their grandparents, uncles or aunts so at times we didn't see them for a week or two at a time. They were learning to be pastoralists, and learned and sang about camels and goats.

Because there was nothing else to do I developed a small bush clinic to support the people, many of whom were not used to nomadic life but like ourselves were refugees from the city. I set up under a small tree with a shelter made of leaves. I used it as a ward. Although it was a nomadic area there were many refugees from the towns who were not nomadic. There were no health services or transport. I started this thing from scratch and all the women (though not often nomadic women) came when they heard there was a midwife. They would come 500 km. Women would be brought to me on camels, for example those in prolonged or obstructed labour. At first only the most difficult cases were brought to me. It was so remote and isolated – I was the only midwife for hundreds of miles. The nearest place with a health centre was Las Anod or Erigavo. Then people started to bring all kinds of cases and to call me out to them for help. Sometimes they would come from six to seven hours' walk away. To reach them I used to ride a camel because I can not walk these long distances. Sometimes I rode a donkey but it is uncomfortable.

It was a very difficult experience. I would be brought pregnant women with eclampsia but I didn't have anything to use to assist them. If the case is prolonged labour, obstructed labour or placenta praevia or toxaemia such as eclampsia there is no solution, the woman will die in front of you – you cannot do anything. You pray or you go to the place where she is and you look at her and are able to do nothing. Your mind fills with great sadness and really it is better not to see the case. They call for help and when you see an eclampsic woman in a coma and you just only have your hands and nothing else, it is very difficult.

I kept a record of the cases I attended and people who helped me. Within one year it was 250 women. Fifty per cent of these died. Towards the end of the first year when the health demand increased I tried to buy some emergency materials such as IV [intravenous] fluids in case of eclampsia. I tried to do something to save the situation.

It took a year to adapt to this situation. We drank the same water as the camels and goats. After a year I forgot to worry. I tried my best to do something for women. We formed a committee and I said I myself am ready to support the community that I am in but I have no money to buy drugs or essential materials that we need for emergencies – at least for transferring the patient to somewhere where they can receive help. We developed a community taxi for emergency cases and we collected money. For example, there would be men buying camels or livestock and we would write to them to contribute money for emergencies. We were successful. We collected money and I would go to Yerowe to buy IV fluids, emergency treatments, dressing materials, suture kits, local anaesthesia for small emergencies.

I trained three women to be traditional birth attendants and during the last year they were doing the deliveries and they were doing the emergency calls and if any of them couldn't manage I would go with them. The second year I felt a little freer because I had support. Through these actions we were able to save the lives of 10 women with eclampsia. We bought diazepam injections to stop the convulsions and we gave them drips. We would take the old car, which was repaired by the community to be used only for medical emergencies, to the patient from the remote areas to Las Anod or El Afweyne or Erigavo the town where my husband's family is from. So during the last year I was able to save many more patients. When the security situation improved in Erigavo and I decided to leave the rural area they all cried. My husband's family is still there.

Has my marriage changed as a result of the war? For me marriage is about supporting each other. Everyone has his time. Over the past 10 years I have been the family breadwinner. I even bought his cigarettes to give him confidence. I have been responsible for the family's food, housing, shelter, everything. Now it is his time, so I give him his chance and respect him. When we go to the pastoral area they say that we are fantastic people; we look strange because the way we behave is different from the way they behave. My husband used to cook, to collect materials. Sometimes when he saw people coming, he would stop washing because he did not want to be teased. Eventually he did these things in the daytime when we were alone so that he would not be seen. We looked a very strange family!

Of all the difficulties I faced during the war, the only one that really affected me was the situation between my mother and me. It was so sad. My mother is from Siad Barre's clan. I am from Aideed's side and my husband is a Somalilander. So my mother feels insecure among us, her family. This is a very big problem. Our family is divided. We cannot speak openly with my mother, we whisper. She feels that my husband and my children are against her. To try to gain her confidence, a male member of the family and I decided we would not listen to the BBC as she got distressed when she heard bad words about Siad Barre and news of

Aideed's effectiveness. She was not happy to live with us, so finally I sent her to live with my sister in Saudi Arabia. She had said: 'I am not happy in this situation. I don't like it. There is no difference between living with the Hawiye in Mogadishu if they kill me, or if I die here. I don't want to live here with you. Send me to my children outside the country or I will go back immediately to Mogadishu. I don't care whether it is insecure or not – everywhere is insecure for me.'

She was with us in the rural area and then for about six months in the town. I could not sleep at night because I would see my mum sitting outside alone, thinking, worrying. She couldn't see that we are her supporters; she was convinced that we were her enemies so it was a very difficult situation. She didn't trust anyone. She became isolated. She refused to eat or to drink. I felt sorry and unhappy. My mother did not trust her daughter or grandchildren. Now she is happy, she has been back to Mogadishu. She said: 'I had to see Mogadishu to see what was going on. It's horrible when your children are looking like Aideed [in other words they are from their father's clan which is the same as Aideed's] so you are my enemies. I don't want to tell you anything.'

As a result of this experience – and many women I know have suffered the same experience – I have advised my 16-year-old daughter not to marry a man outside her clan otherwise she will face the same problem as I have faced if there is a conflict. We don't know what tomorrow will bring so it is better to marry a man from among her relatives. My daughter is not thinking about that yet but it is important. Relatives will have the same objectives, the same ideas, the same enemy. But if you marry into a different clan you will suffer. I didn't believe in this before – that is why I married an Isaq man. But I do not want my daughter to suffer the same problem that I faced.

NOTES

1. The research was supported by the Dutch development organisation NOVIB.
2. I.e. they don't have the money to invest.
3. In 1941 Allied Forces under British command defeated the Italians, liberating Ethiopia and the Italian Somaliland colony and reinstating British rule in its Somaliland Protectorate which had been temporarily occupied by Italy. Maria Brons (2001) *Security, Sovereignty and the State in Somalia: From Statelessness to Statelessness*? (The Netherlands: International Books).
4. Known as the *franco valuta* system, this method of sending money home to family members through clan connections without going through the state banking system was a reaction to deteriorating economic conditions

in the country and government economic policies which increasingly favoured certain clans and discriminated against others. The SNM was financed through monetary transactions processed in this way. (Brons 2001)

5. Amina M. Warsame (1987) 'Moving to the Cities: Somali Women's Quest for Economic Independence', unpublished MA thesis (The Hague: Institute of Social Studies).
6. Save the Children Fund (1993) *First Steps to Recovery: Somaliland Household Survey* (Hargeisa: SCF).
7. Reported in United Nations Children's Fund (1998) *Somalia. Situation of Women and Children Report 1997/8* (Nairobi: UNICEF Somalia).
8. Information from Zeinab Aideed Yusuf who travelled on this convoy.
9. Most convoys took longer, some as long as nine months, to cover the same distance.

Section 2
Women Mobilise for Peace

Hadaba Deeqay dagaalkanu muxuu ahaa?
Degelba degelkuu ku xigay daabcad kula kacyey,
Shisheeye haduu is dilo waaba kala durkaa,
Marada labadeeda dacal buu dab ii qabsaday.
Hadaba Deeqay, dagaalkanu muxuu ahaa?
muxuu daankaani daankaa ku diidanyahay?
Intaan dacar leefay waabay durduurtayey,
Dabaasha anoon aqoon daad I qaadayey,
Agoonkii daalanaa dib uga caymadyey,
Hooyadii weerku daashaday diboydayey,
Dadkii iyo Hargeisaba is diidnayey,
Berberadaan soo day idhi dib uga roorayey,
Hadabaa Deeqay, dagaalkanu muxuu ahaa?
Maxaa daankani daankaa ku didanyahay?

O, Deeqa, I am truly at a loss
As to the real intentions of this war.
Unlike unrelated people who can drift apart.
My own people are fighting one another,
Neighbours are fiercely at each other's throat,
My plight has no match.
My clothes have caught fire at both ends,[1]
Knowing nothing of swimming,
Was I taken away by a current.
From the bitter *da'ar* tree [aloe],
And fatal poison had I my fill.
Why do people from this bank,
Despise people on the other?[2]
Why must weary orphans flee again?
Must grieving mothers suffer afresh?
Deeqa, I am truly at a loss.

Editors' introduction

The above is an excerpt from one of the most famous peace poems composed by Saado Abdi Amare which she first recited publicly, in the form of a woman crying in protest (*baror*), in 1994 during the conflict in Somaliland. It expresses the poet's sadness and surprise at the renewal of conflict when people had thought the civil war was over.[3]

Traditionally women in Somali pastoral society play an indirect but important part in conflict resolution. In the early stages of a conflict they can act as peace envoys for their clans and are sometimes the 'first messengers sent between disputing clans to break the ice'. As Sadia Musse Ahmed notes in Chapter 2, when final peace agreements are reached they can be sealed with the exchange of a woman (or women) to be brides to their clan's former enemy. (See Chapter 6)

In the past decade women across Somalia have been deeply involved in peace promotion and peace-making. As well as exerting influence in private over their husbands, sons, brothers and uncles, the traditional means women could use to influence political decision-making, they have organised themselves and exerted collective influence at the community and wider level. Women's important contributions to ending violence and promoting peace have included formal presentations to warring parties, demonstrations, direct action, petitioning of politicians and elders, and provision of logistical and financial support to peace processes. Many have used the country's most popular form of expression, poetry, composing influential poems and songs for peace – and for war.

Yet when it comes to policy level peace consultations, or the documentation of events, women are still excluded and their contributions to peace overlooked; perhaps because their contribution has not been considered important enough to be recorded or perhaps because it is taken for granted that women will be against war. Justice Africa points out:

> In most societies women are seen as a force for peace and harmony, as nurturers and carers. This may be a myth, a cultural construct, that actually originates in sexist values ... The fact that women participate in war and atrocity shows that women have a choice: when women advocate for peace, it is not because they are naturally programmed to do so, but because they have made a moral choice to do so. This should make their contribution all the more valuable.[4, 5]

Women across Somalia have expressed their choice – mobilising others within their local communities, and beyond, to promote peace. For example, in 1994 women prevented a collapse of the Muduug peace accord; in 1993 women in Bossaso publicly demonstrated to promote a stable peace and this resulted in the creation of a peace enforcement police force; in Kismayo district women provided financial support and played key, informal roles at reconciliation meetings.[6]

Women peace activists in Somalia have been at the forefront of initiatives to demobilise combatants and to address peace-building and human rights needs. Based in Mogadishu, the women's umbrella organisation Coalition for Grassroots Women's Organisations (COGWO) is a leading peace and women's rights promoter, chaired by Mariam Abdulle Qaawane. Also in Mogadishu is the Dr Ismail Juma'le Human Rights Centre established by Mariam Hussein Mohamed, and among the many individual women who have worked to restore security to their communities, the achievements in Merca of the late Starlin Abdi Arush will be among the most remembered. A tribute to her is presented on page 215.

This section consists of three chapters. Chapter 6, 'Women and peace-making in Somaliland', details women's actions in Somaliland where local peace processes in the early 1990s re-established national stability and law and order, bringing to an end periods of violent conflict which affected areas of the country between 1991 and 1996. (See Chronology on page 228 for the pattern of conflict in Somaliland and Somalia) Chapter 7, 'Women, clan identity and peace-building', explores the view that unlike men whose sense of self is intimately bound up with their clan membership, women lack an exclusive clan identity. Sometimes referred to by women as women's 'dual identity', it is argued here that this position enables them to go beyond clan interests, and hence be strong advocates in the search for peace. Chapter 7 also explains why, within a clan-based system, women continue to be excluded from power. Chapter 8, 'Women's roles in peace-making in the Somali community in north eastern Kenya', is a study of how women have intervened to try to end years of violent inter-clan conflict in Wajir, a district in the Somali-speaking region of north eastern Kenya. Although this conflict was not rooted in the war in neighbouring Somalia, what was happening in Somalia affected Wajir and exacerbated the fighting.

6
Women and Peace-making in Somaliland

Compiled by the editors from an original paper by Zeynab Mohammed Hassan with additional information provided through interviews with Noreen Michael Mariano, Shukri Hariir Ismail and Amina Yusuf

Background

War affected the north west of Somalia from the early 1980s. The armed struggle against the Siad Barre regime ended in 1991 when the dictator was forced from power and the Somali state collapsed. As civil war expanded in the south, in May 1991 the SNM called a conference of clans in the north west. Held in Burao and attended by the clan elders this conference ended hostilities, established a framework for peaceful co-existence and resulted in the declaration of independence of Somaliland from the south.

This chapter presents first-hand accounts by women peace activists of their attempts to end the intra-clan conflicts that subsequently broke out in Somaliland within the major clan group, the Isaq. This was a period of great insecurity: the outbreak of wars between members of the same clan family came as a huge shock to many who had imagined that the fighting was over.

The Burao conflict, 1992

The initial euphoria surrounding Somaliland's independence was shattered by the outbreak of fighting between sub-clans in Burao in January 1992 and in Berbera in March 1992. Many of the people caught up in the fighting had only just arrived in Somaliland, having endured often terrifying and arduous journeys of many weeks as they fled from the horror of the inter-clan conflict in southern Somalia. (See Halimo Elmi's testimony, for example) Expecting to have found sanctuary within Somaliland many people were now once again forced to flee for their lives. This period of violence was brought to an end in October 1992 through a political settlement and peace conference, held in the town of Sheikh, brokered by the Somaliland clan elders. What is not documented about this sequence of events is the role women played in bringing an end to the conflicts, promoting the Sheikh Conference, and their role in subsequent peace processes in Somaliland.

Although Zeynab Mohamed Hassan had lived in Mogadishu, her husband's home, for many years, she is originally from Somaliland. In 1991, as a result of the fierce fighting in Mogadishu, she was forced to leave her husband behind and flee to Somaliland where she would be safer, in her clan's territory. Shortly after her arrival in Burao the town erupted in fierce fighting. She recalls how women responded:

> In January 1992 the divisions within the SNM led to armed confrontation between the two sub-clans in Burao. Women led in denouncing this civil war. The majority of women in Hargeisa and Burao could not fathom the situation in which the SNM fighters were killing each other and innocent civilians were being caught in the crossfire. Most women were emotionally at the end of their tether and tired of war. I and other women came together to see what we could do collectively to stop the fighting. We urged the traditional leaders to resolve this armed conflict, but without waiting for the elders to act, we also took action. Some women left Hargeisa and other settlements, towns and cities, and came to Burao. There were about 300 of us and we tied white bands around our heads – a sign of mourning [white symbolises anger or sorrow in Somali culture]. We marched up and down between the two groups demonstrating[7] and singing moving *buraanbur* or women's poems and songs,[8] urging: 'SNM fighters, remember the bad times you and your families have been through; this is not the day for killing one another!'
>
> As we did this the men stopped firing. They were shamed by the sorrowful songs directed towards them by their female partners, sisters and in-laws. Within a matter of days a ceasefire had been agreed.
>
> We composed a number of songs, the most important being one that begins: 'Oh Dahir! [a man's name] You have spent a long time in the bush'. This addresses the armed militias and points out that their dispute serves no purpose but only adds to the suffering of people who have already suffered much and just want to rebuild their lives:

Hayga dumin qalbiga,
Durba ii bugsaday
Hay saarin debedii,
Diilaalyadii ka raystoo,
Dugsi baaban seexdee.
Hayga dilin halyey,
Dabkii hore ka hadhay.
Ha duqaynin naafada,
Dirqii bay ku kabantee.
Dabka wiilka ridayow,
Cidi kuma duljoogtee,
Maanaad I dilaysaa?
Aaway danabyadeenii?
Daarihii maxaa helay?

Oh Dahir! Shatter not my newly mended heart,
Force me not to the refugee life,
where cold, hunger and misery resides.
For I have tasted the comfort of home. Oh Dahir!

Oh Dahir! Kill not the surviving heroes
Who miraculously escaped death.
Crush not the handicapped ones,
For they have barely recovered. Oh Dahir!

Oh Dahir! Young man with the gun,
Whom are you shooting? Me?
For there is no enemy in sight.
Have you ever seriously wondered?
What became of our brave comrades?
Whatever happened to all our buildings? Oh Dahir!
(Translation from the Somali by Amina M. Warsame)

What really made the fighters throw down their weapons was the wailing and crying songs sung by the women as we ran to and fro between the two units until a ceasefire was achieved. Poetry and songs are very powerful means of communication in Somali society. Many of the ones used or created by women contained messages like:

Why is this section of the town not speaking to the other section?
Why is my left arm not talking to my right?
Why is my brother fighting my son?
Why is my son fighting with my brother?
Why is my husband fighting with my brother?

Prayer meetings for peace: Allabari

Allabari are a traditional form of collective prayer meeting which used to occur all over Somalia and other Somali speaking regions such as Djibouti. They are traditionally held at times of common need such as drought. During an *allabari* people come together to share food and to pray to Allah to help them overcome their difficulty. *Allabari* can also be held to give thanks to God when something good has happened. Traditionally they were a way of sealing trust and forging friendships.

During the recurrent conflict in Somaliland between 1991 and 1996 women used the tradition of *allabari* but gave it a new meaning – they held prayer meetings for peace. Peace activist Noreen Michael Mariano recalled one of the occasions when women mobilised others in the community to take part in an *allabari:*

> I am searching all the time to stop the recurrence of the civil war and fighting. In 1992 a group of concerned women who were tired of the conflict in Berbera and keen to promote peace, organised an *allabari* in an attempt to get people to stop fighting each other. A group of about 300–600, mainly women but also some men and boys, gathered to cook, eat and recite prayers for peace. Our prayers called for Allah to intervene to stop the troubles. We asked for three things: peace, rain (because there was drought), and economic improvement (because there was rampant inflation).
>
> Remarkably, three days later the rains came! This gave encouragement to all of those who had participated in the *allabari*. The women went home from the *allabari* and took it on themselves to attempt to put pressure on their menfolk to stop the conflict. They called themselves 'peace workers' and wrote to the newspapers saying that they wanted to live in peace. Women who were able to recite poetry and sing came together to meet and reason with members of the militia and with the elders, in order to persuade them to end the conflict and enter into talks about peace with their enemies.
>
> They succeeded in getting the elders to sit down together.

The Berbera conflict, 1992

In March 1992 a major clan war erupted between two neighbouring clan groups of the same clan family in Berbera (the conflict mentioned by Noreen Michael Mariano, above). The conflict was further complicated by the involvement of the recently established national army, composed of ex-combatants but which the majority of the population saw as being a clan army by another name. Zeynab Mohamed Hassan described how women reacted to this new conflict:

> Women did everything we could to stop the bloodletting that dragged on for a considerable time. To begin with we addressed demands to the government, asking for it to use all means at its disposal to bring an end to the war. This effort came to nothing. Finally we wrote a declaration to the National Council of Elders and the government, copying it to the press and both sides of the warring factions, basically saying that:
>
> - the clan war in Berbera must be immediately brought to an end
> - there should not be international military intervention[9]
> - there needed to be a clean water supply established
> - there needed to be a police force established.
>
> On 5 October 1992 hundreds of women with banners and slogans marched to the presidency and parliament building urging men to stop the war and solve the disputes peacefully. At the end of the demonstration the women presented their declaration to the National Council of Elders. The demonstrators stood outside the presidency while inside the declaration was read out on behalf of all women by Noreen Michael Mariano, Shukri Hariir Ismail and Anab Omer Leye. Those of us presenting the declaration refused to leave the building until a peace process had been agreed and signed. By 2.30pm a tripartite (government representatives and the two warring sub-clan representatives) reconciliation committee had been formed with the task of coming up with a final peace proposal. We left the building.
>
> There were no women members of this committee, as traditionally formal mediation between two warring parties is a male affair. So the women's organisations sent two of us – Shukri Hariir Ismail and Noreen Michael Mariano – to represent women's views.
>
> The committee was being slow to act and women could not stand this foot-dragging attitude; in response we organised a major peace demonstration demanding that the reconciliation activities be effected immediately. We gave the committee an ultimatum that

if agreement on the date and place of the reconciliation meeting was not reached that same day, the demonstrators would force the doors of the meeting hall open and pelt the members with stones. The threat worked: the agreement was signed and the council of elders started preparations for the reconciliation meeting.

Sheikh reconciliation and peace conference, October 1992

A reconciliation and peace conference attended by elders and clan members of the warring sub-clans was held in October 1992, in Sheikh, a town between Berbera and Burao. In accordance with custom, women were not present as participants or mediators but as one man put it:

> Women were the wind behind the peace conference from A–Z in terms of mobilising the elders, in preparing the venue, the food, and in encouraging the participants to keep going until the final peace accord was reached. So they have all the credit in making that peace possible. (Dr Adan Yousuf Abokor, personal communication)

The conference, known as the *Sheikh tawfiq*, was a turning point for the establishment of peace and stability in Somaliland as it paved the way for a milestone in Somaliland's modern history, the Grand Conference on National Reconciliation held in Boroma.

During the Sheikh conference the two parties agreed to exchange 30 young women, equally representing their two sub-clans, as brides, thereby re-establishing kinship bonds between the former warring parties. The agreement was in this case symbolic rather than real, as it is said that no actual exchange took place. The meaning behind this tradition is summed up in the saying, '*meel xinijir lagu bururiyay xab baa lagu bururiya*', which translates as 'Birth fluids should be spilt [i.e. a baby born] on the spot where blood has been spilt'. Exchange carries an expectation that once wed the girls would soon give birth to children by their new husbands, preferably boys, who take the clan identity of their father – thereby replacing the men lost by the clan in the war. The exchange, known as *godob reeb* in the north and *godob tir* in the south (meaning to erase an injustice or injury), symbolised that grievances and human loss on both sides were wiped out never to return.

Women interviewed hold different opinions about the traditional practice of exchanging women to seal a peace agreement. One view, said to be held more widely by men than women, is that the tradition is not harmful to the women concerned as a girl cannot be exchanged without her consent. Some explain that most of the girls who put themselves forward to be exchanged on such occasions feel this is an opportunity to find a husband. According to this view, marriage is the right and ultimate wish of every Somali girl; thus the requirements of conciliation on the one hand, and the girl's rights and wish for marriage on the other, enhance each other. Others take a human rights perspective and see peace-offering marriage as a violation of a girl's right to choose whether to marry and whom, because the young girls are not self-selected and have no choice except to elope with someone as a means of avoiding the exchange.

Boroma Grand Conference on National Reconciliation, 1993

The Boroma Grand Conference on Reconciliation was described as a make-or-break event in the creation of the Somaliland state. Opened on 24 January 1993, it was attended by representatives of all Somaliland's clan families. It had an open time frame and in the event lasted nearly four months. The main items on the agenda were reconciliation and security between parties in conflict, and state formation. The open time frame allowed issues to be exhaustively debated and for flashpoints to be dealt with so that consensus, an essential ingredient in traditional Somali political processes, could be achieved. A national committee of 150 Somaliland elders comprised the official voting delegates at the conference. This committee was later to become the upper house in the Somaliland National Parliament. During the four months, however, an estimated 2,000 men took part in the meeting in some way. Compared with the internationally sponsored peace conferences convened to resolve the civil war in the south, the Boroma conference was an indigenous process and the costs were mostly met by Somalis, a major factor in its success. Some funding was provided by a very few foreign donors including the Life and Peace Institute, but no support came from the United Nations Operation in Somalia (UNOSOM).[10]

Just ten women, representing two organisations (Somaliland Women's Development Association and Somaliland Women's Organisation – see Chapter 9), were allowed to take part in the conference; and this was only after petitioning by women. This was an historic win as traditionally women are excluded from such clan meetings. Tradition still ensured that none of the women representatives had voting rights. Women's interests, if they were considered separately at all, were still decided on by the elders, all of them men.

Although excluded from the formal decision-making, the ten women presented their views in front of the conference delegates and they worked hard to ensure that they influenced the conference. Advocating for peace and lobbying their male clan representatives on the need to reconcile their major differences with the other clans, for the sake of the country, the ten women with support from others, created and delivered speeches, pamphlets, songs and poems, *buraanbur*. Below is an extract from one of the many poems they composed for the occasion:

> Men had been our shelter
> but they have thrown us outside.
> We are now buffeted by winds and rain,
> being thrown here and there.
> You have made us flee from Mogadishu;
> you have made us flee from Burao;
> you have made us flee from Berbera,
> we will not allow you to move us from Hargeisa.

Below is an example of the messages women were communicating, comprising a speech delivered to the male delegates by Zeynab Mohamed Hassan on behalf of the women's groups:

> Chairman, *guurti* members, Honorary members, clan delegates and observers, Good Morning. I greet you on behalf of Somaliland women's organisations.
>
> According to Somali traditions, you may be surprised to find a woman speaking in this male congregation. You may also wonder what compelled them to perform this untraditional act.
>
> Traditionally men served as a defensive umbrella for women and children. Today men have failed in this responsibility; and women and children are subject to all kinds of hazards, social, economic and environmental. As a result of this, women have to fend for themselves. That is the reason for our breach of the traditional code.
>
> Over the past ten years men, through their violent actions, displaced women, children and old people from Hargeisa, Mogadishu, Burao and Berbera. Today you intend to drive us from Hargeisa.
>
> Somaliland women demand that their partners, brothers, uncles and sons, give this tired population a rest from armed conflicts.

4 Hundreds of clan elders exercise the traditional voting powers of men and select a president during the 1993 Boroma Grand Conference on National Reconciliation. After intense lobbying, 10 representatives of two women's organisations were permitted to attend the conference. They could speak and lobby, but they were not given voting rights. (Hamish Wilson/Panos Pictures)

In conclusion, women demand that:
i. Peace and peaceful coexistence must be achieved among Somaliland clans
ii. This conference shall be in session until all suspicions that may create conflicts are resolved
iii. A solid foundation must be laid for a better future for Somaliland's population.

The women who attended the conference say that it was they who suggested that the committee of 150 elders which presided over the Boroma Grand Conference should become a House of Elders, or *guurti*, within a bicameral national parliament; and the elders' mandate should be to bring peace and reconciliation – a suggestion, based on the structure of the SNM, which was subsequently taken up.

As with the Sheikh conference in October 1992, numerous women played crucial roles behind the scenes, as food providers as well as logistical and financial supporters for the hundreds of men from all over Somaliland who were taking part.

By the time the participants of the Boroma conference had concluded their debates all but one of the existing clan grievances had been settled and inter-clan reconciliation had been achieved.[11] A new president had been chosen and the Somaliland Communities Security and Peace Charter developed. This charter established a national security framework, detailed mechanisms for demobilisation of former combatants, the formation of local police forces and judicial institutions and the securing of roads. The charter defined the responsibilities of elders in mediating and settling outstanding disputes and future conflicts; and it set out a code of conduct for the people of Somaliland, in accordance with their traditions and with the principles of Islam.

Discussions on state formation produced a National Charter to act as the constitution for Somaliland for two years. The incoming government was to be charged with drafting a national constitution to be ratified by a national referendum within two years.[12] The National Charter established a government structure with a bicameral legislature. This comprises an Upper House of Elders (*guurti*), and a Lower House of Representatives. Members of both houses were selected by the clans rather than standing for election. All the members are men. Together these two houses make up parliament.

Although later generally seen as a token gesture, the appointment of Mrs Deeqa Ol-u-Joog as a Minister of the Presidency (but not a parliamentarian) was appreciated by women's rights and peace activists.[13]

NOTES

1. An expression used when one is related to both warring parties.
2. The city of Hargeisa is divided by a dry riverbed. The two sides are referred to as the two banks and roughly divide the city on a clan basis.
3. Amina M. Warsame 2002.
4. Alex de Waal (ed.) (2002) *Demilitarizing the Mind: African Agendas for Peace and Security* (Trenton NJ: Justice Africa/Africa World Press).
5. On 31 October 2001 Resolution 1325 was passed unanimously by the UN Security Council. This is the first ever passed by the Secuirty Council that specifically addresses the impact of war on women, and women's contribution to conflict resolution and sustainable peace.
6. UNIFEM (1998) *Somalia Between Peace and War: Somali Women on the Eve of the 21st Century.*
7. The first mass demonstration by women in Somaliland had been in 1991. It was spontaneous and occurred as a response by women to the proliferation of arms in the country. Thousands of women and children walked in the streets of Hargeisa shouting anti-arms slogans and attacking any man they saw carrying a gun. Eye-witnesses reported that women were angry and emotional and that many men who were carrying arms fled for their lives (reported by Amina M. Warsame in *The Impact of the Civil War on Somaliland Pastoralists, Especially Women and Children,* The Hague: NOVIB/Institute of Social Studies, 1997).
8. *Buraanbur* is the name given to the poetic form used by women. For more information on women's use of poetry as a means of resistance see: 'Somalia: Poetry as Resistance Against Colonialism and Patriarchy' by Dahabo Farah Hassan, Amina H. Adan & Amina M. Warsame in Saskia Wieringa (ed.) (1995) *Subversive Women: Historical Experiences of Gender and Resistance* (London: Zed Books) pp 165–82.
9. This warning against international military intervention came at the time when the US was preparing to send troops to Mogadishu in Operation Restore Hope. Some people in Somaliland believed that the US wanted to send troops into Somaliland as well.
10. For more, see Mark Bradbury (1997) *Somaliland Country Report* (London: CIIR).
11. In June 1993 the National Guurti appointed Mohamed Haji Ibrahim Egal – Somaliland's first prime minister in 1960 and Somalia's last civilian prime minister in 1969 – as the new president of Somaliland, replacing Abdulrachman Ahmed Ali 'Tuur', the interim president since 1991 and former chairman of the SNM. This outcome left the Garxajis sub-clan of the Isaq with grievances about the treatment of their clansman 'Tuur', and with their share of seats in the two Houses of Parliament. These grievances were to lead to Somaliland's next internal conflict in 1994.
12. Although much later than originally intended, a national constitutional framework was drafted by January 1997, and the constitution itself by 1999; a national referendum took place in May 2001 which returned a vote of more than 90 per cent in favour. Women's organisations played an important role in mobilising women to seize their first voting opportunity in more than a decade.
13. Deeqa Ol-u-Joog lost her job after a year and a half and no other woman held a ministerial office until the appointment in August 2002 of Edna Adan.

7
Women, Clan Identity and Peace-building

Judith Gardner with Amina Mohamoud Warsame

'Only a fool will not consult his wife and seek her opinion.'[1]

This chapter was compiled largely from material generated during a workshop held with the book's contributors in October 1997. The participants whose viewpoints and analysis this chapter represents are: Noreen Michael Mariano, Zeynab Mohammed Hassan, Rhoda M. Ibrahim, Fowzia Musse, Sadia Musse Ahmed, Habiba Osman, Amina Sayid, Sara Haid, and Ladan Affi.

During the workshop participants, who had not previously met, shared their personal experiences of the war and its impact on women. They frequently referred to the fact that, unlike men, women have a dual clan identity and that this is why women have been at the 'centre of suffering' – a phrase several used to describe their position in the middle of conflict between their birth relatives and their family through marriage. At the same time they said women were also at the forefront of grassroots peace-building. (As the accounts in Chapter 9 testify, this dual clan identity also represents a major barrier to women's full participation in a male-dominated clan-based political system.)

This chapter sheds light on what participants meant by women's dual clan identity. It also describes how the Somali system of kinship, or clan, operates differently for men and woman, which is fundamental to the way the war and its aftermath have affected men and women differently.

The Somali clan-based system

All people of Somali ethnicity[2] will belong through patrilineal descent to one of the six kin-based clan families that make up a confederation of genealogically related clans (Lewis 1961). A clan is thus a group of people who claim descent from a common ancestor and who trace their blood relationships through the male line.[3] The six principal lineages or clan families are Dir, Isaq, Darod, Hawiye, Digil and Mirifle (the latter two are collectively known as Rahanweyne). Each of these clan families breaks down into a number of clans (e.g. the main clans in the Darod case are, Ogadeni, Marehan, Majeerteen, Dulbahunte, Warsengeli) and each of these segments into smaller sub-clans (each known by the name of the common ancestor). Some clans are sub-divided into as many as ten smaller sub-clans. Sub-clans are composed of primary lineage groups and within each of these are the *diya*-paying groups, each of which can act as a corporate unit and as such are the most meaningful and binding level of the clan system for most people. 'These extended families are normally composed of people as widely related as tenth cousins in the lineage tree; together they are bound to pay and receive blood compensation to and from other *diya*-paying groups'[4] (see below). The uterine family (i.e. mother with her children and their father) is the smallest unit of social organisation and usually corresponds to the household.

Lewis stresses that 'the lineage system is an on-going structure, continually developing by segmentation over the generation as the population expands' (Lewis 1961: 158). In other words, the number of *diya*-paying groups, primary lineages, sub-clans and even clans can increase over the generations; what is needed for this growth is an increase in the number of male members. Hence the political importance of marriage and social celebration of a boy's birth.

Typically every child at an early age will learn his or her sub-clan kinship genealogy and will be able to name as many as 20–30 patrilineal ancestors over generations. This is information usually imparted by the child's mother. The purpose of memorising this information is so that any two individuals can quickly establish what relationship, if any, they may have with one another and their corresponding obligations or sanctions. Under normal circumstances, however, it would be considered rude and provocative for people to refer explicitly to their own or others' clan identity; or openly to treat people of one's own lineage differently from others.[5]

Within the clan structure there is no hierarchy of political power, although power is differentiated along gender and age lines with women subjugated to men, and young to old. Hereditary positions with symbolic authority approximating to chief or leader, sometimes called *Sultan*, are found at the level of clan division (i.e. below the widest level of clan family) within some, but not all, clans.[6] On the other hand, the position of 'elder' is common to all clans. The term 'elder' can be applied to all adult males at every level of the clan family, from the nuclear family upwards. And all elders, thus all men, have the right to speak in an open council (*shir)* which can be called for at every level of segmentation, as required. *Shir* are 'called to discuss relations between groups, to settle disputes, or to decide upon war or peace'. (Bradbury 1994) As the accounts of women given in Chapters 6 and 9 testify, *shir* exclude women. Amina Warsame points out, however:

> Since all decision-making at the lineage, sub-clan and clan level was regarded as the domain of men, women were never called to give their opinions publicly. However, there are indications that women were consulted privately on the matters under discussion. But in order not to undermine men's decision-making powers, women's 'invisible' role of contributing to decision-making was never publicly acknowledged. (Amina Warsame 2001)

Clan identity and personal security during conflict

Traditionally the collective and individual obligations and responsibilities under the clan system provide protection against random killings or attacks by one group against another in relation to war or conflict. If a man or woman is killed or injured by another, revenge or compensation will be sought. Other than in acts of individually motivated violence, therefore, the decision to kill or attack will be taken collectively by the group having weighed up the arguments for and against and the risks entailed, including: What clan or sub-clan is the target identified with? What relationship are they to my clan or sub-clan identity? If a member of this other clan is killed what are the consequences for the killer's clan or sub-clan? What relationships will be jeopardised? The more closely related a potential target is in clan terms the more difficult it would be to make a decision to kill them.

In the context of domestic conflict, when a woman is the victim of a violent or abusive husband, her male family relatives should intervene and act in the interests of their daughter, sister, niece or cousin. She is 'one of their clan' and an injury to her can be interpreted as an offence against the clan and could bring retribution and sanctions against the husband.[7] However, this intervention is contingent on an exogamous marriage relationship. Male relatives are unlikely to intervene when the marriage is endogamous or between people from the same clan lineage. Thus a woman in an exogamous marriage is more protected against domestic violence occurring. (Testimony 5 and Chapter 4 discuss some of the impacts the war has had on this aspect of marriage relations.)

When there is armed conflict, both women and men can find personal protection in the conventions of the clan system. However, this is contingent on factors such as their whereabouts at the time; and women have more options for protection than men do.

Spatially Somalia itself can be mapped in terms of traditional clan grazing territories or areas of predominance.[8] In the context of a war in which clan identity plays a part, men will enjoy greater safety and protection in the space controlled by their clan kinship group. Outside of this area they are vulnerable though if they are staying among their wife's lineage group they should be physically protected by her male relatives.[9] If the conflict is between the husband and the wife's clan families this protection may be difficult to sustain. For women the situation is slightly different. A married woman who is not from her husband's clan should nevertheless be physically safe within his clan area as his clansmen will protect her. If she is childless and the conflict is between her and her husband's clan she is likely to seek to go back to her father's home, where she will feel safest. If she is a mother of a dependent male child or children she will almost always seek security for them and herself among her husband's/their father's clans-people rather than her own. Staying within their own clan area keeps them under the protection of their paternal male relatives and particularly protects them, as males, from being targets of revenge killings. Whilst she might be physically secure among her husband's clans-people, however, she is likely to feel emotionally insecure – particularly if the conflict is between her own clan and her husband's. From gossip and conversation she will be all too aware of the hostility towards her clans-people. If her dependent children are girls they are not at risk from revenge killings and she will probably take them to stay with her father's family where she will feel safest.

Similarly, a man's mother-in-law may also be offered similar protection within his clan area but whether or not she feels completely safe under this arrangement will depend on the individual and her circumstances. (For example, see Halimo Elmi's testimony, which describes how her mother felt unsafe among her son-in-law's people.)

According to the inter-clan conventions on protection and security in times of war fighters were expected to observe strict rules during a battle, including on the treatment of captured and wounded opponents. Conventions delimited who could and could not be attacked. Those who were immune from attack (known as *biri-ma-geydo* or 'spared from the spear') include women, children, the sick and elderly, men of God (*wadaad*), poets, honoured guests and community leaders.[10]

As the accounts in this book testify the civil war has been largely fought with a widespread disregard for these conventions, making it highly risky for anyone, man or woman, to live outside their own clan's territory. For this reason there are many women in Somalia and the diaspora who separated from their husbands to seek security among their father's kin or outside the country.

The *diya*-paying group

From birth all males will be members of a *diya* group. For men it is at this level that collective action takes place and the political and social implications of clan membership are most clearly defined. A man's security, and that of his property, depends on his *diya* group membership. A single *diya* group may contain from a few hundred to several thousand members. (Lewis 1961)

Diya group members are linked through kinship. A son will belong to his father's group, and their membership of the group unites them through a contractual alliance to collectively receive or pay blood compensation (*diya*) for homicide or injury committed by or to members of the *diya*-paying group. Put simply, if a member of your *diya*-paying group needs help you are obliged to provide it. In the case of intentional homicide, if one of your group is injured or killed it is as if the whole group has been wronged and thus the whole group is obliged to seek justice. Justice may be to forgive the killer, or to demand the execution of the killer, or to request *diya* payment. Traditionally, compensation for loss of a man's life is normally measured in camels and is usually worth 100 camels (preferably young she-camels because they can reproduce).

Women are not members of *diya*-paying groups in the same way as men. They are not regarded as paying or receiving members when it comes to the group paying out compensation or sharing compensation received. In other words the amount to be paid or received is divided by the number of men in the group not the number of men plus the number of women. A family which has only girl children will thus have less to pay in *diya* contributions but will also receive less.

The *diya* group functions in the same way for women in terms of demanding compensation for death or injury either of or by a woman and the male *diya* group members share the responsibility for payment and share the benefit. An unmarried woman is the responsibility of her father's *diya* group. A married woman will still be their responsibility but less so; with variations across the different clan families, responsibility will be apportioned between the father's and the husband's *diya* group. (Lewis 1961)

Compensation for the loss of a woman's life is usually 50 camels, half that of a man.[11]

When the victim of a killing is a woman the general rules may be interpreted in favour of *diya* payment rather than execution of the killer, in the belief that 'a man worth 100 (camels) cannot be executed for a woman worth 50' (reported in Faiza A. Warsame 2001). In the same way, if the killer is a woman and her victim a man, the clan will seek *diya*, not a revenge killing.

Lewis notes that as long as the sex of the foetus was identifiable so that the correct compensation could be demanded, *diya* was claimable for a miscarriage caused by violence.[12]

With the war and the widespread financial dependency of men on women, it is now common for women to provide their husbands, brothers, uncles the resources they need to pay their *diya* group liabilities. Time will tell whether this new role for women will change the relative 'worth' of women or alter the *diya* system.

A family, and through it, the *diya* group members, expands its access to grazing and water areas by inter-marrying with families from different clans or sub-clans, as Sadia Ahmed explains in Chapter 2. Clans gain political and fighting strength from increased numbers and membership expands when a new child is born. In the case of a boy child who takes his father's clan identity and will become a member of the same *diya* group, the gain to the clan is obvious. In the case of a girl child, who also takes her clan identity from her father, the value to the clan is ambivalent as she is expected to marry into and bear sons for another clan. Thus, although she may facilitate potentially important alliances for her father's clan, her offspring may become their enemy.

Clan identity and loyalty

Clan identity is patrilineal and it is for life; you belong to your father's clan and this does not change when you marry, for either a man or a woman. Having said this, there are differences for men and women.

For a man the paramount clan relationship, sense of identity and loyalty is with brothers and male relatives on the father's side, and with his own sons. All are from the same clan and lineage and this represents his political affiliation. (Lewis 1961) Together with his female relatives of the same clan, these are the people whom he must protect and be protected by in times of conflict, for example. 'When dealing with the paternal family (*reer adeer*), he will always have to show that he is strong, virile, ready to do anything to defend his clan.'[13]

His links with his mother, who may or may not be from the same clan as his father and himself, will be emotionally strong, but in terms of clan solidarity and loyalty will be relatively weak. A man's relationship with his mother's relatives (*reer abti*) is different from that with his father's relatives. Due to the exogamous marriage principle and cross-cousin marriage, he has a special relationship with his maternal uncle – his mother's brother – with whom 'he will be able to let himself go, express his feelings and his doubts, or ask for advice. As far as his in-laws are concerned he shows them respect and never reveals his problems'. (*Ibid*)

The strong relationship with his maternal uncle means that if his clan and his mother's are in conflict, a man 'will seek to protect his mother's immediate relatives but, if it comes to a choice in battle, he is expected to forsake his mother's relatives to protect his father's'. (Faiza A. Warsame 2001) He is not seen as a possible bridge between the two. Likewise, if a man marries, in clan terms he will have a weak relationship with his wife's relatives. In *A Pastoral Democracy* Lewis notes a Somali saying, 'xayn iyo xiniin', meaning the cloth (worn by a woman) and the testicles. He explains that this is a description used to distinguish a man's relationship traced through women (e.g. a mother or wife) from that traced through men (father, brother, paternal uncles). What is expressed is that paternal relations are like the testicles, they are essential to a man, whereas links through women are like a cloth which can be thrown off without diminishing the whole. (Lewis 1961)

Figures 1 and 2 illustrate how contributors to this book interpret the relationships available to men and women. They were constructed by Somali women at a workshop in London in 1997. Figure 1 shows that for a man within the clan system the network of social relationships that he can draw on, and which determine responsibilities, is dominated by those traced through his father's line. Figure 2 shows that the network of relationships and social responsibilities available to women through the clan system is different.

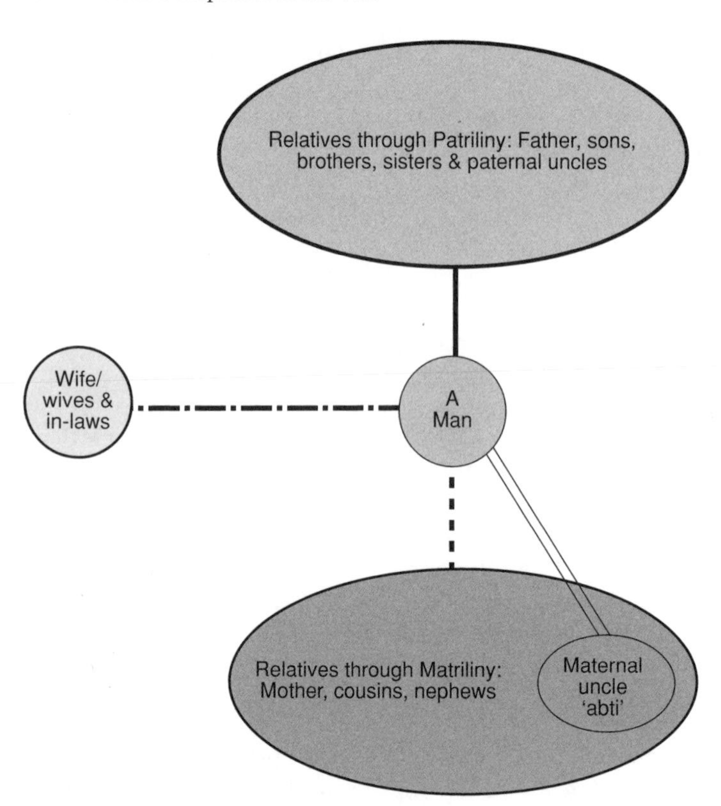

Figure 1 A man's key relationships within his kinship network
Shading represents the different possible clan or lineage relationships; width of circle border represents political affiliation and thickness of linking lines indicates strength of loyalty and identity.

A woman is like her brothers in that her primary clan identity comes from her father and is shared with paternal relatives; and like her brothers she has a special relationship with her maternal uncle. However, unlike a man whose maternal family relationships are weak (with the exception of his maternal uncle), a woman has strong relationships with her mother's clan and her maternal relatives. There is a popular saying, 'A woman has ten very close relations in society: her mother, mother-in-law, father, father-in-law, daughter, daughter-in-law, son, son-in-law, paternal uncle and maternal uncle.' (Faiza A. Warsame 2001)

Depending on the situation, in terms of clan loyalty she can be identified with either her maternal or paternal clan. This affords her

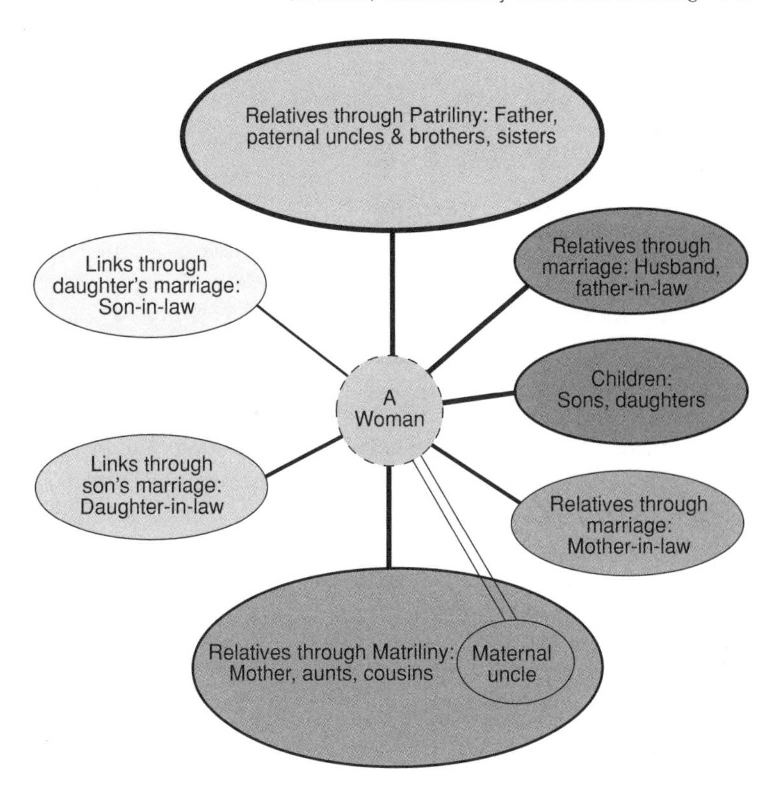

Figure 2 A woman's key relationships within her kinship network
Shading represents the different possible clan or lineage relationships; width of circle border represents political affiliation and thickness of linking lines indicates strength of loyalty and identity.

protection, support and influence not available to men. At the same time, this 'dual' identity of a woman means women are perceived to present a risky ambivalence at times when clan loyalty may be put to the test. (See Chapter 9 for the reasons elders gave for excluding women from voting during the Somaliland inter-clan peace conferences.) Whilst a man can be relied on to be loyal to his clan, whose clan will a woman be loyal to – her father's? Her mother's? Or perhaps her husband's – because it will be the clan of her children and she will have a strong tie with her sons' clan. And any grandchildren by her daughters will belong to her sons-in-law's clans, thereby opening yet another set of relationships.

Being at the centre of multiple and potentially conflicting loyalties is precisely what put women at the 'centre of suffering' during the post-1991 inter-clan wars. By the same token, being mobile within this network, and traditionally valued as a bridge between clans, women were at the centre of promoting peace at the grassroots and an end to inter-clan warfare.

'Women at the centre of suffering'

Because war-makers from Siad Barre onwards have used the clan system as a weapon and a shield, a person's fate has largely been determined by his or her clan identity. Numerous Somali women, including many of the contributors to this book, are partners in exogamous marriages and therefore do not belong to the clan of their husbands, the fathers of their children, nor to the clan of their sons and daughters. By implication their fathers and brothers also belong to different clans from that of their husbands, their children's uncles, their son-in-laws. The impact of the war on such families has been immense and cruel. Clan and family have been brought into opposition, forcing apart individuals despite their love and loyalty for one another. One of the most common tragedies has been the prolonged separation of wives and husbands, children and their parents as the family members seek survival by fleeing to the traditional 'safe areas' of their clan groups or abroad. For some the escape is from a situation where clan-fuelled conflict has turned their neighbours, friends and even their own relatives into potential enemies.

Women interviewed in Erigavo in 1994 recounted an experience shared by many women: having escaped from the main inter-clan conflict of 1991–92 in Mogadishu, and reached the relative safety of the rural clan territory, they faced another outbreak of war but this time it was between sub-clans of the same clan and there was no where left to run to. Women described their distress at a war in which husbands were fighting against fathers-in-law, sons against maternal uncles. To bring an end to this conflict in which their closest kin were killing one another in acts of sub-clan loyalty and *diya* group revenge, the women of Erigavo, representing different clans and sub-clans, collectively exploited their extensive network of male relatives spanning the clan and sub-clan structure. By persuading and reasoning with male relatives, they managed to influence attitudes enough whereby the clan elders agreed to sit together and discuss a way of ending the conflict. Eventually a peace agreement was reached.

Women at the centre of peace

What occurred in Erigavo demonstrates that women can be an important channel for communication between conflicting parties. They can act to influence both sides in a conflict and may be used as emissaries, whereas a man's influence will tend to be limited to his patrilineal relatives.

A woman's network of significant relationships is likely to span several lineage and clan divisions in the clan system. Women said this cross-clan network of relations was important to their attempts to bring an end to conflict, and it was one that they exploited collectively. Another factor was that Somali society has few class distinctions and people mix freely together without feeling self-conscious about their differences. 'Within one family you may come across a senior academic and an illiterate, a successful businessman or woman and a small stall owner, a nomad and a city dweller, an ambassador or a highly placed government official and a non-governmental employee.' (Hassan *et al* 1995). Thus, acting collectively, women representing a range of income and livelihood groups had been able to 'reach' all levels of society from the grassroots to religious leaders, business people, politicians and warlords as well as all sides of the war.

Traditional peace-making and conflict reduction

Establishing a communication bridge between warring parties to help bring reconciliation and peace can be a vital stage in the process of transition from war to peace. It is a role women are well positioned to take on due to their position within the clan structure, and for which women are politically valued.[14]

Women are however excluded from the other stages and traditional mechanisms involved in securing an end to a war in a Somali pastoral setting. These include dialogue and mediation by elders chosen for their specific qualities or skills relevant to the situation, such as wisdom, knowledge of genealogy, clan contracts or *xeer*, and politics; religious sanctions and intervention by men of religion, *wadaad*, who traditionally do not take part in and are protected in war; compensation demands and if necessary, the use of military strength convening of open councils or *shir* attended by elders from both sides to discuss grievances and agree the grounds and means for reconciliation. Thus traditionally it is men, the elders, who have the means to make peace a reality and women who have a significant role in making it a possibility.[15]

NOTES

1. A saying used by men to confirm that Somali men sought the advice of female relatives in issues of importance. Quoted by Amina M. Warsame in *Queens Without Crowns: Somaliland Women's Changing Roles and Peace Building*, Horn of Africa series 4, Life & Peace Institute/Somaliland Women's Research and Action Group, 2002.
2. See Introduction to this book for definition of Somali ethnicity.
3. Christine Choi Ahmed notes how some historical linguistics research has pointed to the possibility of Somali pastoral society having been matrilineal/matriarchal focused in an earlier age. Christine Choi Ahmed (1995) *Finely Etched Chattel: The Invention of a Somali Woman* (Trenton NJ: Red Sea Press).
4. Faiza A. Warsame (2001) 'The Role of Women in Rebuilding Puntland', in *Rebuilding Somalia: Issues and Possibilities for Puntland* (London: War Torn Societies Project/Haan).
5. Contributors to this book felt that referring to clan names, including their own, could be divisive. Where they refer to specific clans they do so in order to describe aspects of their experiences relating to clan identity.
6. *Sultan* (among the Isaq), *Garad* (meaning 'wisdom', among the Darod) and *Malaq* (among the Rahanweyne). Where they exist they are a symbol of the unity of the clan over its constituent lineages and enjoy respect but not reverence. Their position above sectoral lineage differences enables them to function as arbiters and peace-makers. Mark Bradbury (1994) 'The Politics of Vulnerability, Development and Conflict: Exploring the Issues with Reference to Somalia and Somaliland', unpublished thesis for the School of Public Policy, University of Birmingham.
7. Faiza Warsame, personal communication.
8. Maps attempting to define clan territories or *deegaan* are often disputed by Somalis for there is little consensus about boundaries, which are by necessity fluid, depending on seasonal grazing availability and the movements of nomadic pastoralists. Nevertheless, as the war has clearly shown, and reinforced, a concept of clan territories and boundaries does exist and if anything they have been hardened by the conflict.
9. I.M. Lewis (1961) *A Pastoral Democracy: A Study of Pastoralism and Politics Among the Northern Somali of the Horn of Africa* (Oxford: OUP). Lewis's ethnography provides detail of the different forms of household location a man may adopt and their corresponding levels of protectiveness and responsibility.
10. For a full explanation of traditional codes and conventions of warfare in Somali society, see *Spared from the Spear – Traditional Somali Behaviour in Warfare*, Somali Delegation of the International Committee of the Red Cross, February 1997.
11. Faiza Warsame points out that 'in the case of inheritance a woman also receives half the share of a man. The reason is based on the ideal practice that a man's share must be shared among the whole family, including his sisters who he is expected to protect and provide for until they marry, a

woman's share of an inheritance is for her alone. This is the ideal; in practice men do what they want.' (personal communication)

12. I.M. Lewis (1962) *Marriage and Family in Northern Somaliland* (Kampala: University of Glasgow and East African Institute of Social research).
13. Mohamed-Abdi Mohamed, 'Somali Kinship and Relations Derived from it' in Adam & Ford 1997: 153.
14. Lewis (1962) refers to men being able to play this role when their wife is from the opponent's clan. He refers to married men having 'dual status' in both their own kin group and that of their wife's male relatives.
15. Mark Bradbury (1993) *The Somali Conflict: Prospects for Peace*, Oxfam Research Paper No.9.

8
Women's Roles in Peace-making in the Somali Community in North Eastern Kenya

Dekha Ibrahim

Introduction

In the town of Wajir, in north eastern Kenya in 1993, a young Somali woman hid her first child under the bed to protect the infant from bullets that flew through the town each day in a fierce local inter-clan war. When she discovered that she had been hidden under a bed by her own mother during the unsuccessful war for Somali secession from Kenya in the 1960s, she was galvanised into action. 'I decided that my daughter was not going to hide my grandchildren under beds to protect them from bullets 20 years from now', she recalls. Her work mobilising other women, and later men, to work to end the violence in Wajir District, led to a citizen's movement for peace, which was instrumental in almost completely stopping the inter-clan violence.

The roles played by Somali women in reducing violence and transforming conflict in north eastern Kenya is the subject of this chapter. I examine traditional conflict resolution roles that Somali women have played and the part that Somali women are playing in conflicts engulfing their societies today. It is hoped that documenting the peace-building roles of Somali women may stimulate other more in-depth research and analysis of this subject. This chapter flows from my own commitment to peace and to women, and to the contributions, often unrecognised, that women make to building peaceful communities and societies.

Traditional roles for Somali women in peace-making and conflict resolution

To date no systematic account of local conflict-resolution systems has been described in the literature concerning the Somali people. The roles of women in either promoting conflict or promoting peace have been even less documented. It is clear, however, that women did historically and do today play a role in promoting both war and peace.

Women are usually not part of formal peace negotiation and reconciliation meetings. There are several other ways in which they contribute to formal processes, however. Anthropologists have described a number of roles for women in conflict resolution, including the exchange of nubile girls in marriage and the solidifying of peace agreements and relationships between clans by intermarriage. These are indeed important in maintaining peaceful relationships in Somali society. Yet this is only one aspect of the roles that Somali women have played in building peace in their communities.

Since Somali marriages tend to be inter-clan (according to a Somali proverb, 'We do not marry our friends'), women are frequently messengers between clans in peacetime and war. Women born into one disputing clan and married into the other often feel loyalty for both, and work hard to lower tensions between them. At such times, women with dual connections to opposing clans are often the only persons who have freedom of movement between hostile camps. They may be sent to state grievances and requests, and to carry responses back, often allowing the conflict to be resolved without violence. The importance of women as messengers has been underestimated in most literature.

Research carried out by a colleague and I in Kenya and Somalia has revealed other traditional roles of Somali women in peacemaking. A woman may resolve disputes at the family and extended family level, preserving harmony between herself and her husband, and ensuring good relationships between her daughters and their husbands. Somali society values hospitality and sociability very highly. It is a woman's role to provide for guests to her household, and her skilful performance of this role is the backdrop against which clan deliberation and negotiation are set.

Somali society is an oral society, and good orators, both men and women, are highly regarded. Women's opinions are heard and valued, although not often in public meetings. Women may also lend their weight to attempts at reconciliation by influencing formal proceedings, for example by organising prayer meetings seeking a return to peace.

The inclusion of elderly women in elders' meetings may not be as rare as portrayed in much of the literature. At least in north eastern

Kenya women past child-bearing age attend councils of elders and may help settle disputes, although they cannot participate in all the activities of elders. These women 'come to the tree' where the elders meet, without specific invitation from the elders. They stay silent unless they disagree with the elders, in which case they interject their opinions, which are then considered by the elders in their ensuing discussions.

Wajir Women for Peace

Somali society is modernising, with a small but growing minority of women receiving education and entering professional occupations. These women are increasingly being recognised as vital to current conflict resolution and peace-building. Wajir Women for Peace is an organisation that illustrates this trend.

Between 1992 and 1998 a violent inter-clan conflict raged in Wajir District, in the north eastern province of Kenya. Although exacerbated by the concurrent conflict in neighbouring Somalia and Ethiopia, with refugees, arms and mercenary soldiers flowing into the district, the Wajir conflict was rooted in local and national issues, including grazing and water rights, parliamentary political representation, and the impoverishment and displacement of thousands of families caused by several cycles of severe drought. Unlike the war in Somalia, this conflict, though devastating to the local population, was limited in area and hardly noticed by the rest of Kenya let alone the international community.

Wajir is one of the largest and driest districts in Kenya. Its population, excepting civil servants and military personnel, is almost entirely ethnic Somali. More than 80 per cent of the population are nomadic pastoralists, with livestock herds of camels, cattle and goats. A 'closed district' during the colonial era, Wajir remained under a state of emergency from Kenya's independence in 1963 until 1992. The Somali people of North Eastern Province, including Wajir District, fought an unsuccessful war for secession from Kenya in the mid to late 1960s.

At the height of the fighting in Wajir District in 1993, all public transport to the district had stopped, lorry traffic (including vehicles bringing food and relief supplies) was disrupted, herd movement for water and pasture was curtailed, most schools and health centres closed, and normal life, for both pastoral and urban Somalis, was impossible.

By 1993 the entire district, pastoral areas as well as trading centres, were insecure. Wajir town was divided into clan zones, and people avoided areas of the town not controlled by their own clan. In the market, women refused to buy or sell to members of other clans, which often included their husbands' relatives. Fights broke out, resulting in injuries to several women, and further heightening tension in the market place.

At this time several educated Somali women attending a wedding observed that they could go to the wedding together but not visit each other's homes because of inter-clan disputes. Three women decided to begin work to restore peace and security to their community. They began by spending a week visiting the educated women in Wajir town, representing all clans. The 16 women initially contacted agreed to invite more from their clans to a general meeting of 'all women in Wajir who love peace'. The first meeting, in July 1993, was attended by more than 60 women, both urban and pastoral. This meeting was very emotional, and focused on the power the women had either to cause the violence to continue or to bring peace to the district.

In that meeting the women agreed to work together for peace in Wajir. The first step was the formation of a committee to monitor the market and mediate in the case of violence, and to bring the market women into the new group, called Wajir Women for Peace (WWP). The committee met every day for over a month with the market women, focusing on the causes of violence and hatred, and the women's responsibilities. The market women's theme was that 'the men start the violence, but it is we and our children who suffer'. Soon many of the women joined the new peace group: fighting at the market stopped and trading normalised.

The initial goals for WWP were to restore peace in Wajir, to reconcile women in conflict and to mobilise the rest of the community toward peace. Membership was, from the beginning, open to any woman in Wajir committed to peace, with no registration or dues. An effort was made to involve women from all clans and social strata. Initially, the group functioned as a grassroots effort mobilising women at family and village levels towards peace rather than violence. Later on, the women realised that the work of peace is not only for women, and that the issues were too complex to handle on their own. They approached concerned men and the District Administration to enlist them in the cause of peace, and in 1995 they together formed a coalition of groups (women, elders, youth, business people, religious leaders, NGO representatives and government representatives) which came to be called the Wajir Peace and Development Committee (WPDC). In 1995 the WPDC became a member of the Kenya Peace and Development Network, linking the local efforts to a national organisation.

WWP, as a member of the coalition, took a leading role in the WPDC, occupying committee positions and acting as trainers and mediators. Women travelled around the district, visiting trading centres and nomadic encampments, and appealing to women to stop the violence. This was done especially by three women elders, well respected for their integrity and wisdom. Training was an important part of their work, and the women organised a series of workshops throughout the district for elders, chiefs and councillors, religious leaders, youth and the District Security Committee. Each of these workshops focused on the violence, and appealed to members to stop encouraging violence and work for peace.

In 1995 and 1996 district-wide peace festivals were held celebrating the return of security and decrease of violence. The women of Wajir were involved in all stages of organising the festival, and took part with poetry and songs that had messages of reconciliation. The guest of honour at the celebration commended the women of Wajir for their efforts in bringing peace back to the district.

Fundraising has been an important part of WWP's work, since many of the activities involve extensive travel and food and accommodation costs for workshops and other activities. Early on the women collected funds from local business people to facilitate their own activities as well as the activities of the Elders for Peace group. Later, representatives of the women's group (by then also representing the other peace groups) approached NGOs and others for funding. The main external funding for peace work in Wajir has come from Oxfam (UK/I), Quaker Peace and Service, and Mennonite Central Committee.

A recent activity of the women's group is to help with the rehabilitation of ex-militia. Through conversation with these men, the women recognised that the basis of their fighting was their economic need. Therefore, the women's groups have begun making small loans (about US$35) to wives of ex-militia members to enable them to start small businesses. The women are required to repay the loan at 35 cents per day. This project seems promising in assisting in the prevention of recurrent problems.

WWP members have been part of direct inter-clan mediation to stop violent incidents. Again it has been mostly older women who have travelled throughout the district, and have intervened in specific situations of violence. In the following example, women were involved in direct mediation with elders and government officials.

Inter-clan mediation by the Rapid Response Team of WPDC

In July 1998 WPDC received a report that there was a conflict between the Degodia Fai clan and the Murrulle. The Fai clan had refused the Murrulle access to a water pan. On receiving this information the WPDC put together a rapid response team consisting of three elders, two women, and two government representatives, to visit the area and investigate, with the intention of mediating and finding a solution to the problem. There had previously been fighting between these two clans, so any small dispute report was taken seriously by the committee because it could escalate into bigger conflict and lead to violence.

The team travelled east about 90 miles from Wajir town. On reaching the village they met the area chief and community leaders. The meeting started with a prayer, after which the leader of the WPDC delegation explained the purpose of the visit. Community leaders explained that the problem had arisen because a Murrulle family had sick camels which had been refused access to water by the water management committee, requesting that they move to an area set aside for sick animals. The family was unwilling to accede to this request. The Rapid Response Team, asking the local Ber Janai elders to join them, visited the family concerned.

Two Rapid Response Team members – both women – were veterinarians by profession; they checked for the disease the community had described and found that the camels were healthy. They reported their findings to the community representatives and to the family of the allegedly sick animals. The community representatives were not satisfied. The WDPC chairman asked each of the three groups – the family owning the camels, the Fai clan representatives, and the Rapid Response Team – to discuss the matter separately and propose solutions.

The family with the 'sick' camels proposed that, in the interests of peace, they would move away, since there was no scarcity of water and pasture. But they would do this on condition that they be given time to prepare for their journey, that all their livestock be given water while in transit, and that the Ber Janai elders should take responsibility for ensuring that they encounter no problems while leaving the area. The Rapid Response Team proposed that in addition, for the sake of the future peace, a member of the minority Murrulle clan be added to the water committee, so that they would feel part and parcel of Ber Janai. The clan representatives agreed to these proposals. At the suggestion of the Rapid Response Team a public meeting was called in which the resolution was made known to everyone in Ber Janai.

The conflict in Wajir is far from over. Although there is relative peace between the clans, there has been fresh conflict between one clan in Wajir and the neighbouring Boran tribe, and this has entailed large-scale human and material losses. WWP has again teamed up with the Wajir Peace and Development Committee to work on the problem with the neighbouring district.

Ten years ago, when the women's peace group began in Wajir, peace was exclusively the concern of elders and government forces. Women were relegated to minor roles, and attempts were made to exclude them from the process. At one early meeting with elders from various clans, the question was asked: 'What do these children have to do with peace? Why are they telling us what to do?' Today, any mediation, dialogue or discussion concerning peace in Wajir District includes women as important and respected participants in the work for peace.

Conclusions

The wars affecting Somali societies appear to have fundamentally changed the perception of women's roles in ending violent conflict and building a peaceful society. Current writing no longer completely ignores the contributions of Somali women, although a number of different explanations are given for their involvement in peace and development activities. Some writers see what has happened as nothing less than a profound reversal in gender roles and power relations. Others say the economic changes brought about by the wars, and subsequent increase in female-headed households, have led to the emergence of women's voices in Somali society. Still others see this as the organic outgrowth of the roles that Somali women have always played. The truth is probably a complex interaction of all of these and more.

Women's experience of peace-building has enabled them to develop their own perspectives on what peace means. They have come to believe that individuals involved in a conflict situation have a responsibility to work towards non-violent resolution: peace-building cannot and should not be left solely to leaders or outside intervenors. They have learned that peace and development are linked; without peace, development and economic stability cannot occur, and without underlying economic security, peace becomes impossible. As a testimony to this, the Somali women's delegation to the 1995 Beijing Women's Summit stated: 'There is a strong predominance of women-led NGOs active in and for their communities. They have all seen that there can be no development in their communities and country without peace, and conversely, there can be no peace without development.'

To fulfil their potential in peace-building and development Somali women have learned to counter the passive, victim role often ascribed to them by people in their own society and by western scholars and media. They have come to recognise – almost intuitively – the importance of their place in a clan system in which patrilineal descent (based on the male line of descent) forms vertical divisions, while marriage ties create horizontal integration and have unifying potential.

Furthermore they have acknowledged that local initiatives must be the main instrument of peace work, with donor money and advice or training being an adjunct to the work, not the major push. And they have joined with wider peace efforts outside their own conflict, thus placing the conflicts that they are addressing within a wider framework. They take a broad view of a peaceful society, where children can be fed and educated, and where people can live in right relationships with each other. While supporting the work of (mostly) men in negotiating the fine points of settlements, they have themselves been less involved in the details of these settlements than in advocating for a just and peaceful community in which to live and raise their children.

It would be naive to ignore the problems Somali women face in peace-making. Their role has not been accepted easily, either within the local or international community. Gender bias does not disappear during violent conflict, and while women's roles are often expanded during situations of crisis, they are pressured to return to the status quo after it ends. Women active in peace work have been threatened, both by their own clans and by others. (Of course, neither women nor Somalis are alone in this; working for peaceful solutions in the midst of a violent conflict is often a dangerous occupation.) The peace processes in Somali society, both internationally and locally, continue to be male-dominated, and women's contributions are often dismissed or ignored. Some fear a backlash against women active in peace and development, which may push women out of the roles that they currently occupy. The way forward is not an easy one; but it is a road that many women must take in order to restore their societies, live out their lives, and raise their children and grandchildren.

Conflict resolution theory and practice have relied on top-level negotiations between leaders of the opposing parties, often with the intervention of powerful third-party negotiators. However, theorists increasingly recognise the importance of an integrated and multi-faceted approach to peace-making, encompassing a variety of roles and activities. They acknowledge the role of mid-level players who can connect the top-level leaders with society's grassroots, as well as connect horizontally through the dividing lines in the society. In Somali society women such as those involved in Wajir Women for Peace are ideally placed to function as these connecting points, serving as bridges both vertically and horizontally in Somali society. Recognising and supporting these women's groups is important in helping to build sustainable peace in Somali communities.

It is our hope that this initial discussion of women's roles in peace-making and conflict resolution in Somali society will validate the important roles that Somali women have played, and continue to play in forging a just and peaceful society, and will stimulate further work and research in this area.

I would like finally to end with a quote from an elder who was attending a peace meeting in Wajir:

> I was taught by my grandfather that a woman has no brains, but the Wajir workshop has changed my attitude. Women can have breasts and brains. That will be my message to my sons and grandsons.

Section 3
Women's Rights, Leadership and Political Empowerment

Editors' Introduction

Sisters, you sold your jewellery

Depriving yourselves,
Enriching the struggle.

Sisters, you stayed as one,
United, even when your brothers
Divided and deceived our nation.

Sisters, you joined the fight –
Remember the beautiful one,
Hawa – stabbed through the heart.

But, sisters, we were forgotten!
We did not taste the fruits of success
Even the lowest positions
Were not offered
And our degrees were cast aside as dirt.

Sisters, was this what we struggled for?

The above poem, by the woman poet Hawo Jibril, was composed shortly after Somalia's independence in 1960.[1] Recalling how women had financially supported and even physically sacrificed themselves in the struggle for Somalia's independence, she expresses women's grievances with the corruption of the new leaders and their failure to meet the aspirations of women, such as equal access to education and employment and political participation. (Hassan *et al* 1995) Although written more than 30 years ago, the sentiments conveyed in Hawo Jibril's poem would resonate with many women in Somalia today.

Somalia's women's movement up to 1991

Somalia's women's movement emerged during the struggle for independence in the 1940s and 1950s when Somalis actively organised against colonial domination. Large numbers of women participated in the struggle. As their experience of the independence movement grew 'they began to feel increasingly conscious of their subordinate position in the society and at home. As a result, they began a struggle against their oppression as women within their own political environments.' (*Ibid*) The first women's organisation, Somali Women's Association (SWA), was set up in 1959. Led by the female relatives of the political parties' leaders, 'although SWA voiced women's rights, most of its activities were in the area of social welfare'. (*Ibid*)

Chronology of the pre-war women's movement in Somalia

1959 Somali Women's Association established: its main focus was welfare.

1960 Somali Women's Movement (SWM) established: radical but short-lived organisation set up by middle-class women with the aim of fighting for women's social, political, cultural and economic rights.

1969 Siad Barre comes to power and bans all political parties and social organisations – ending the first phase of the women's movement.

1970 Founding of a Women's Section under the Political Office in the Presidency of the Supreme Revolutionary Council (SRC): membership came from the banned SWM. Tasked with mobilising women and raising their political consciousness, the Women's Section of the SRC established a committee in each village, district and region of the country.

1977 Somali Women's Democratic Organisation (SWDO) founded by the government as the women's branch of the Somali Revolutionary Socialist Party (which at its formation in 1976 had a female membership of 66 per cent.[2] Its Chairwoman was Kadija Ma'alin (wife of Siad Barre) and its mandate to 'propose, promote and initiate progressive policies and programs for the advancement of the Somali women'.[3]

Pro-women's rights national legislation included:

- Article 55 of the Workers Statute: ensuring the right of equal salary for equal work (it was never fully implemented)
- Family Law amendments 1975: giving equal rights to women and men in matters of marriage, divorce and inheritance (though not prohibiting polygamy)

- Labour Code of 1972: promoted equality of women in the workplace
- Law No. 173 of 1975: made all land state property whereby women could obtain land leases or inherit leaseholds
- Constitution of 1978: established equal rights and duties for women and men alike.

SWA, and the Somali Women's Movement (SWM) which developed shortly after, were dismantled when Siad Barre took power in 1969 and all but government-linked social organisations were banned. The promotion of women's rights was integral to Siad Barre's socialist vision for Somalia; progressive legislation was introduced (but not always enforced) in the 1970s and in 1977 the SWDO, the women's branch of the party, was founded. Throughout the mid-1970s to 1980s the proportion of women in government posts did increase sharply.[4] It is worth noting, however, that throughout Siad Barre's era the number of women in parliament did not rise above 10 per cent of the 176-member total, only one member of the 76-member Central Committee was a woman, only two out of 51 ministerial positions were held by women and all five members of the Politburo were men. (Bryden 1998)

In relation to SWDO, Maria Brons writes:

> The SWDO was an integral part of the socialist one-party system. In all government ministries it had a representative whose responsibility was to safeguard women's rights and see that no discrimination was practised. SWDO had branches from the national to the local level; weekly meetings were held to build awareness of women's rights. SWDO representatives were involved as voluntary lawyers or advocates in courts on issues such as domestic violence or divorce. The organisation campaigned for an increase of the number of girls in education, pressed for an increase in the number of women judges and high political functionaries, and recommended a change in the land law with regard to women's ownership ... However, members of SWDO were not politically free; the party and other open and secret control mechanisms within the state framework strictly controlled them. In fact, it was not only subject to political control, it, itself, was and (sic) instrument of control. (Brons 2001)[5]

Thus SWDO raised the discourse on women's rights and proved a useful vehicle for policy change where issues concerning women converged with government policy, such as participation in public office and the campaign to abolish female genital mutilation (FGM). (See Part 1, Chapter 3) However, it was fundamentally flawed by being part of the controlling apparatus of Siad Barre's corrupt and highly repressive regime. Moreover, the principal beneficiaries of Siad Barre's state feminism[6] were middle-class urban-based women; for the majority of rural women little changed. The credibility of SWDO grew increasingly tarnished by the late 1980s as, along with the rest of the heavily centralised government structure, it was infected by clan patronage, corruption and inefficiency. Given the extent of grievance, hatred and bitterness the regime evoked, it is not hard to imagine that for some Somali sceptics on women's rights and equality, both men and women, 'women's rights' is a concept (conveniently for some) too tainted by its association with Siad Barre to be easily embraced in the new era of statelessness.

Whether or not this is the case, what progress in women's rights SWDO had contributed to at the public and political level was quickly reversed when the civil war erupted. The different forms of administration to have emerged in different parts of Somalia since 1991 have almost all been clan-based with all or majority male membership; women's rights have for the most part been a non-existent or marginal item on their agendas. Across Somalia women have had to begin again the struggle for their rights to be recognised and respected.

This is the subject of Chapter 9, 'Post-war recovery and political participation', which explores how women have collectively organised to tackle war-related community based problems, and in the process are laying foundations for a new women's rights movement. The chapter presents experiences of women from around the country in relation to their struggle for equal participation in the political decision-making structures established since 1991.

Women's involvement in peace-building and their striving for political empowerment are linked to the significant community-based leadership and organisational roles that women assume. Throughout Somalia women have been at the forefront of actions to assist vulnerable groups affected by the war, including the wounded, the starving and the displaced. Testimonies in this section, by Dahabo Isse and the late Noreen Michael Mariano, provide insights into some of the challenges and personal danger faced by those who took actions chiefly to prevent more death and suffering. A further testimony to the leadership and bravery that some women have demonstrated is provided in the obituary to the late Starlin Abdi Arush, community leader from Merca.

The following poem, composed in the 1960s by Hawo Jibril, explains why women joined the struggle for Somalia's independence in the 1940s and 1950s. It is an apposite message for today's generation of Somali women working to improve their communities and to empower women:

> We wanted to break away from our seclusion.
> We wanted to have the responsibility
> To express our feelings and our views.
> We wanted to show our concern for our country. (Hassan *et al* 1995)

TESTIMONY 6: DAHABO ISSE

Editors' note

The violent inter-clan warfare in southern Somalia convulsed the southern region into a state of anarchy; creating a man-made famine and causing the displacement of many thousands of people. Although the United Nations was slow to respond to the disaster in the country, the International Committee of the Red Cross (ICRC) and non-governmental humanitarian organisations such as Save the Children, SOS Kinderdorf, CARE, Concern, Médecins Sans Frontières responded early. Their employees worked under difficult and dangerous conditions. Amid looting, kidnapping and armed extortion and in the absence of any formal security or police force, humanitarian agencies hired armed guards to protect themselves.[7]

By the time the UN responded, in April 1992, an estimated 300,000 people had died of starvation and hunger-related diseases, and as many as 3,000 people – mainly women, children and the old – were dying daily.[8] A former administrator in USAID said:

> By the middle of 1992 food had become the medium of exchange and a principal source of wealth in Somalia. Because food was so scarce – as a result of both drought and civil conflict – its absolute value had risen to an extraordinary high level ... Thus food imported through relief effort became an enormously attractive objective of plunder by merchants, by common working people without a source of income, by organised gangs of young men and by militia leaders in need of the

> wealth represented by food aid, which they would use to purchase more weapons and to ensure the loyalty of their followers. (Natsios 1997)

Dahabo Isse worked with the ICRC as its Feeding Programme Coordinator from 1991 to 1993, becoming a well-known figure in Mogadishu and beyond. She was influential in ICRC's decision to open soup kitchens whilst thwarting those who were intent on 'diverting' food aid to fund the war. ICRC reported that 980 open-air soup kitchens were in operation by November 1992, feeding 1.17 million people a day. The system involved transporting food in small quantities so as not to draw attention to it, and cooking it immediately; cooked food being unmarketable by the thieves and warlords. Estimates conclude that the soup-kitchen programme saved the lives of as many as 1 million people between 1991 and 1993. (*Ibid*)

There were drawbacks with the programme. Many of the kitchens were located in areas held by General Aideed because that is where the affected populations were. This was of significant benefit to Aideed, drawing people into his area of political influence and control in their search for food. (*Ibid*)

Dahabo's testimony illustrates the kind of intimidation a person with control of sought-after resources would have been under in Somalia at this time. She came from Aideed's own sub-clan family and was seen to be involved in actions that undermined the diversion of food aid so that it reached the hungry not the warlords. These were two factors which Dahabo believes placed her in an untenable position vis-a-vis her own clan and the US-led UN operation in Somalia.

Dahabo's testimony begins in late 1990. She had come under surveillance because she worked with a Somali non-governmental organisation involved in assisting people displaced from the civil war in the north west, and for associating with westerners. When she did not heed the warnings to end her activities and associations, supporters of the Siad Barre regime tried to assassinate her.

Dahabo's story

My work in Mogadishu in 1989–90 involved me working with a local charitable organisation, Aadamiga ('humanity'), which was helping displaced women from Somaliland [the north west region] and the central areas.[9] The government's attitude towards Aadamiga was hostile. Siad Barre did not want any non-governmental humanitarian initiatives in Somalia.[10] Aadamiga's director, my cousin, had been threatened in 1989 and had left the country for a long time without warning. I had stepped in to help in her place. Because of the work I was doing with Aadamiga, helping disadvantaged people, and because of my relations with international people I became a target and four attempts were made on my life.

My work involved me in getting to know many international people. My neighbours saw me coming and going with foreigners and threatened me, telling me to stop my activities. I told them there was nothing wrong with what I was doing – that I only socialised or discussed humanitarian and development issues, not politics with white people.

One day in late 1990 one of my neighbours asked me if I had heard the warning that I was targeted and would be shot? I felt angry because she and other neighbours clearly didn't want me to stay in the neighbourhood. 'This is my *gof* [land]', I told her. In other words I intended to stay put. Later that day I saw a neighbour's boys behaving suspiciously and overheard them say: 'Is she still here?' Some time after, a vehicle went past and someone shot at my house.

It was some days after the shots were fired at my house that a friend of mine, a Marehan girl, told me to be very careful because she had heard the Marehan military say they would 'clean' the town in the next three days.[11] By 'clean' she meant that they would kill or force everyone they opposed to leave. She encouraged me to ask protection from the Italian Embassy. Being Hawiye, my family was from one of those groups opposing the regime so on hearing her warning I contacted members of my family to warn them to store food and water enough for three days and I asked my brother to come and stay with me. This was when the war was starting [December 1990]. During this time whenever I went out I wondered if I would come back.

On 31 December, despite the insecurity in the city [war had broken out the day before] I decided to go to buy charcoal for the family as we desperately needed fuel to cook with. As I was going to the market I noticed some men following me and some people were looking at me and at each other. When I reached the man who was selling charcoal I asked him how much it was. He told me and I thought it was expensive and he was taking advantage of the war. Just as I bent down to say 'This is expensive' I was hit in the head by a bullet.

My skull was broken, fractured. They had aimed at my face but luckily I bent and escaped with just the top of my head hit – you can see the hole! I don't remember everything that happened next; I just thought my head was divided into two, and remember blood all over my body. But someone put ground charcoal on the wound to stop infection and bleeding. Four women carried me to my home and I was eventually taken to hospital. After two to three hours my brother comes looking for me and took me to my German friends to treat me and for an X-ray to check if the bullet was still inside. Luckily it wasn't.

I was helped to get back to my family's house just at the time when Siad Barre was ousted from Mogadishu on 26 January 1991. The situation in Mogadishu was terrible. At first I had felt happy for the war as it meant something would change, but then I became disappointed as the fighting continued after Siad Barre had gone, and many people were suffering far more.

I was starting to recover, meanwhile. Around me I saw the terrible situation developing in Mogadishu. I saw in the street a child suck from its mother though she'd died the night before. I saw destitute women and I thought what's the difference between her and me? God will see us as the same. That's when I decided 'I can only die once and I've missed that day. God has saved me so I must be brave and help the people.'

Some food aid was being provided by the International Committee for the Red Cross (ICRC) but I saw that the dry food rations donated to help the hungry were instead mostly being looted and some sold in the market – the poor people were not getting it. It seemed to me that the answer was to cook the food for those who needed it as it would be less attractive to looters. I discussed the situation with the director of the ICRC and suggested the wet feeding programme could use just some of the dry rations, leaving the rest for other means of distribution. Even some of my own people [people from the same clan family] said they would kill me because they saw my idea as a threat to their income – as they had been exploiting the food aid system.[12]

I started with one 'kitchen' supported by the ICRC as a pilot initiative. When it started, there was an old man who had come for food but lay on the floor because he was too weak to stand. After a month getting cooked meals he was standing again. Nobody wanted to help in the beginning. It was hard to find people to cook the meals but we expanded to seven kitchens and then 50. Later on everyone wanted to run a kitchen as it become a source of food to eat [volunteers received food in return for work]. Both public and private sectors had collapsed. By the end of 1991 there were 100 kitchens in Mogadishu and about 600 altogether as the programme expanded to Merca and then Baidoa – it wasn't possible to go beyond Baidoa because of fighting in the Lower Juba area.

Most people who came to the kitchens were displaced or receiving food for work.[13] People were desperate. Some people I saw had walked for 30 days from Kismayo to try to find food and safety. They had survived by eating wetted animal skins and green grass, like the animals, until they reached the kitchen camps in Mogadishu.

The camps of displaced people were mainly in public buildings such as schools, often in existing residential areas. We put kitchens in the same location as the displaced. Some people, who were residents rather than displaced, complained that the kitchens were creating epidemic diseases. They felt that the kitchens should be moved to encourage the displaced people to stay outside the residential area. I told them it wasn't the kitchens causing disease but the fighters who were causing the people to be displaced.

5 Women prepare food in one of the International Committee of the Red Cross' soup kitchens in Baidoa, which was the epicentre of the war-created famine of 1992 in which several hundred thousand people died. The testimony in this book by Dahabo Isse describes the soup-kitchen programme that was set up in response, and which reportedly kept 1.7 million people alive each day. (Heldur Netocny/Panos Pictures)

There were many threats and complaints, and much jealousy and suspicion about the kitchens, particularly coming from other women. Of the first 50 kitchens established, I was accused of giving 47 to my own 'tribe' – meaning the people working in them were from my clan. I said: 'I care about who will eat the food, not who will cook it.' I was accused of hiring illiterates to work in the kitchens but I explained: 'This is an emergency – we need people to cook, we don't need qualifications.' One shipload of rations was looted. A 'minister' of one warlord came to me and said that if I expanded the programme to Afgoi [about 30 km outside Mogadishu], 'you dig your own grave and the Red Cross won't come and get you out of it.' [This threat meant the militia controlling Afgoi did not want their power over the population diminished by the arrival of the soup kitchen programme.]

One day in February 1993 American troops came to my house in Mogadishu. They came in the afternoon when I was resting. They had their helicopters circling over my house. They kicked every door down and broke them. I had cars parked at my compound by workers for the kitchen programme. The UN had agreed that each relief worker with a vehicle should have four guns for protection and had given us ID cards. I don't know who told the soldiers. Maybe someone told them I was a stronghold for Aideed.

My brother was there at the time. There was a big gun at my house, known as a 'Zu' [an anti-aircraft gun]. It wasn't working but it was on show to protect us from thieves – it belonged to a neighbour's boy whose belongings had all been looted. The American soldiers confiscated the four guns and the broken anti-aircraft gun. My brother told me to explain about the guns but the soldiers didn't want to listen. I showed them that the guns were for the relief car and I showed my identity card and told them I was a relief worker – which was why I needed the guns. They didn't listen to me. They confiscated the guns. They took my identity card, which proved I was a relief worker, and said: 'You don't deserve to have this!'

While I was speaking the Somali interpreter kept winking at them as if to say 'Don't believe her'. I asked him to help me make them understand my situation but he replied: 'You talk in English and they can understand you if they want to.' This was typical of the time – the different groups [clans and sub-clans] were revenge-killing the intellectuals and important people in each other's groups. The US troops were used by some of their informants as a means of 'getting' those people their clan group was against. I was important in Mogadishu at the time so I was a target for my sub-clan's enemies, and for jealous people in my own sub-clan. I believe these enemies led the American soldiers to me to do their work for them.

Even though you don't want to believe in tribal or clan things, you have to. It is like a passport. I am from the general tribe [clan] of Hawiye and from Aideed's sub-tribe [sub-clan]. Those who hate Hawiye will hate me because the Hawiye ousted Siad Barre's people, and those who see Aideed as an enemy also see me as an enemy because I belong to the same tribe as him. Aideed was being hunted by the Americans, so I was considered their enemy too.

Some Somali people working for the UN were jealous of my work and were planning to use any means to stop me. To the UN they said I was supporting the USC [Aideed's party], and to the warlords they said I was 'breaking the backbone' of the USC [weakening it] by using illiterate women for the kitchen programme and young militia for food escorts. I was taking warriors away from fighting for the USC.

One day a woman who was close to the warlords came to me and told me that it was agreed that one person from each of the sub-clans from my main tribe would organise to kill me[14] because: 'You undermine the motives USC fight for and also you breached the religion.' This last part I didn't understand but I think she meant because of my close relation with foreigners. The rest meant that in giving work to women and young militia I was offering them an alternative to supporting Aideed. A senior relief worker also warned me that Aideed was angry with me and wanted to stop me working with the ICRC.

I was cowed because of my tribe and sub-clan and because of people's belief that my relief work made me a 'backbone breaker' of the USC. I felt powerless to deal with what had happened. And the American soldiers had taken away my only source of protection – the guns my brothers used to protect me and my work vehicle. My brothers had never taken part in the civil war. They went everywhere with me as my bodyguards. Without the guns who would protect me? Life really was insecure for me now.

The invasion of my house by the American forces was a big shock for me. I was one of the people who had publicly asked for international military intervention for Somalia through the BBC World Service in 1991 to save lives. Now I was being seen as the enemy.

By March 1993 the number of kitchens operating in Mogadishu was 600 [less than the November 1992 total of 980]. They had been keeping many hundreds of thousands of people alive throughout the most awful period of Somalia's war. The situation of the displaced had improved.

When I left Somalia at the end of March I hadn't intended to leave for good – just to participate in the peace conference in Addis and then get a visa to the UK for a training course. I reached the UK in April 1993. In June 1993 there was the clash between Aideed and the American-

UNOSOM which left 24 Pakistani peace-keepers dead [the event that placed the UN at war with Aideed]. I learnt that two of the kitchen managers were killed when their vehicle was targeted by US helicopter gunfire. I was advised that it would not be safe for me to return to Mogadishu. In my heart I wanted to be there – I didn't want to be a refugee. But I was scared to go back. I was scared of what had happened to me that day in my house when the American soldiers came, and of being defenceless. I decided I should stay in the UK.

UN operation in Somalia, 1992–95

It is now more than 10 years since US marines landed on the beaches of Mogadishu in December 1992 to lead Operation Restore Hope but the ensuing events have gained new significance since the terrorist attacks in America on 11 September 2001. Some have suggested that Osama bin Laden, incensed by the US intervention, saw Somalia as a battleground between Islam and the west. It has been argued that he gave support to General Aideed's forces that brought down two US Black Hawk military helicopters in 1993.

The ostensible purpose of US intervention was to support the UN operation in Somalia (UNOSOM) to end the famine and rebuild a state torn apart by war. Initially welcomed by many Somalis, the operation was to leave many feeling betrayed. In June 1993, after 24 Pakistani UN peace-keepers and 35 Somalis were killed during a weapons search of Radio Mogadishu, the UN found itself at war with General Aideed. The US Admiral Howe, Special Representative of the UN Secretary General, head of UNOSOM II, ordered Aideed's arrest and offered a reward for his capture. By mid-September 1993 at least 56 UN soldiers and several hundred Somalis had died in clashes between the UN and Aideed's forces. The UN's approach was widely condemned and it was accused of human rights violations. Meanwhile, Aideed was accused of using a human shield of women and children to protect himself and his forces. In October 1993 two US Black Hawk helicopters were shot down in Mogadishu whilst on a mission to capture Aideed. Eighteen US soldiers died and more than 70 were injured in the ensuing fighting. More than 500 Somalis were killed and more than 1,000 injured. This event signalled the beginning of the end of the US military mission in Somalia and the international community's disengagement from the country.[15]

The three years of UN international intervention cost an estimated US$2–3 billion.[16] While the massive humanitarian aid it brought did help stem the tide of famine in Somalia, it also distorted grain markets and local productivity. UNOSOM's military and political efforts to mediate an end to hostilities or engender a process of national reconciliation failed. Instead UNOSOM became embroiled in the conflict and, its critics argue, deepened the crisis by conferring a measure of legitimacy on the warlords, thus shoring up the power structures of the warring factions (UNDP 2001). This was despite pursuing a two-track approach to nation-building which involved an attempt to form district councils at grassroots level, with compulsory seats for women representatives, and a top-down approach through international peace conferences with the warlords, held in Addis Ababa in 1993. (Bradbury 1997)

NOTES

1. The Somali original of this poem, which was recorded on audio cassette and stored in the Women's Documentation Unit of the Somali Academy of Arts and Culture, has been lost in the destruction of Mogadishu.
2. Elisabetta Forni (1981) 'Women's Role in the Economic, Social and Political Development of Somalia', in M. Bryden & M. Steiner (1998) *Somalia Between Peace and War: Somali Women on the Eve of the 21st Century* (Nairobi: UNIFEM).
3. SWDO quoted in Brons 2001.
4. SWDO figures for the proportion of women in the public administration, ministries and autonomous agencies for the period 1975–84 show an average annual increase of 40.6 per cent. (SWDO, quoted in Brons 2001)
5. That SWDO itself was part of the coercive machinery of the state perhaps helps explain some men's view (and maybe that of women too) that 'men were seen as the enemy of the revolution' and the organisation of women was a means to control them.
6. Lidwien Kapteijns, 'Women in the Crisis of Communal Identity: The Cultural Construction of Gender in Somali History', in Ahmed I. Samatar (ed.) (1994) *The Somali Challenge* (Boulder, London: Westview Press) p 229.
7. In this way, and through the food they provided, the humanitarian effort unintentionally provided resources to the warlords. It is reported that the ICRC had 15,000–20,000 local armed guards on its staff at the height of the violence. Andrew S. Natsios, 'Humanitarian Relief in Somalia: The Economics of Chaos', in Walter Clarke and Jeffrey Herbst (eds) (1997) *Learning from Somalia – The Lessons of Armed Humanitarian Intervention* (Boulder: Westview Press).
8. Mohamed Sahnoun (1994) *Somalia – The Missed Opportunities*, (Washington DC: US Institute of Peace Press).
9. They were displaced from Somaliland and the Central Regions as a result of the fighting in these areas between opposition and government forces.
10. In Aadamiga's case it was not only outside 'the Party' but it was providing welfare assistance to those groups who were in opposition to the regime and hence the target of state-controlled violence.

11. Marehan, a clan group of the Darod family, is the same clan group as Siad Barre and had become the group where power and resources were concentrated.
12. The threat to those working in the food distribution programme was real. When the kitchens which Dahabo initiated expanded, reducing the amount of dry rations available for looting, one Red Cross worker was killed, reportedly in revenge for the impact the kitchens had had on militia income.
13. Food for work is an emergency food aid model that provides food rations in return for participation in some organised labour-intensive projects. Those working in the kitchens were themselves recipients of food rations in return for their labour.
14. Agreeing for one person from each sub-clan, or *diya* group, to be involved in killing a person of the same clan is the way to avoid incurring a revenge-killing for that person's death – it shows that every part of the clan, or *diya* group shared responsibility for the killing. No one can exact revenge. During the past decade, in the absence of a state legal system for prosecution or protection there has been a revival of this traditional way of dealing with those who come to be seen as a threat to the collective security of the clan, sub-clan or *diya* group.
15. Mark Bradbury (2002) 'Somalia: The Aftermath of September 11th and the War on Terrorism', unpublished paper for Oxfam GB.
16. UNOSOM's headquarters cost US$160 million to build; by early 1994 UNOSOM was paying US$40 million in salaries and contracts. Mark Bradbury (1997) *Somaliland Country Report* (London: CIIR).

9
Post-war Recovery and Political Participation

Compiled from information provided by Shukri Hariir and Zeynab Mohamed Hassan with additional material from documents by and interviews with Zakia Alin, Faiza Warsame, Amina M. Warsame and Maria Brons, and Sacda Abdi.

Editors' note

> 'Whilst I myself felt helpless I realised there were others in greater need and I felt moved to help them.'[1]

This chapter is concerned with how Somali women have shaped post-war recovery and relief activities and how they are now striving to shape a future for Somali society in which political power is shared with women.

The war has changed much in the lives of Somali women and men. Women have played a leading role in trying to save their families by whatever means available to them. Many more women are now the family breadwinners than was previously the case, often with men as their dependants. With their increased economic role has come an increased decision-making role over aspects of family life such as marriage, divorce and property ownership. For some women, their family and community's survival, and concern with the longer-term consequences of continued violence and warfare, has led them to become peace activists. And countless women have become involved in action outside their immediate family through women's groups. For many, this is their first experience of a decision-making role in the public domain.

The contributors to this chapter draw attention to the fact that, despite women's increased economic importance, their leadership in responding to war-related emergencies and community welfare needs, and their significant role in peace-building, women in Somalia and Somaliland have yet to be treated as equal to men when it comes to political power and leadership.

The chapter is concerned with how women have fared in gaining participation in the political administrations which have been established in Mogadishu, Puntland and Somaliland. A first-hand account by Zakia Alin from Mogadishu describes how women 'beat the [clan] system' in order to have representation in Somalia's Transitional National Assembly. Zakia describes what they achieved by their ingenious strategy as well as the unexpected and disappointing aftermath. A summary of the experience of women in Puntland is provided by Faiza Warsame and the War Torn Society Project in Somalia. This is followed by a case study from Somaliland compiled from the contributions of more than one woman; it includes detail of the 2002 multi-party local government elections, and traces the efforts women have made to gain representation in the Somaliland government, and the nature of the opposition they have faced.

A theme running through the chapter is how today's Somali women's organisations, like their antecedents in the women's movement of the 1940s and 1950s,[2] perceive the struggle to restore security and well-being to their communities as an opportunity for the long-term structural improvement of women's lives. The Somaliland case shows how a renascent women's rights movement is evolving from the legacy of women's self-help groups that formed during the civil war. Founders of these groups describe their struggle to overcome a lack of basic skills and experience in organisational development – problems resulting from the exodus of the majority of educated women at the start of the war, and the lack of opportunity to develop civil society organisations under Siad Barre's regime.[3] Resonating with the experiences of women in Somaliland, Zakia Alin's interview highlights the empowering experience women in Somalia have gained from their involvement in the civil society organisations which have mushroomed since 1991. (See opposite) Both contributions mention the formation of women's coalitions and umbrella organisations such as Coalition for Grassroots Women's Organisations (COGWO) in Mogadishu and Negaad[4] in Hargeisa.

The concessions to women's representation that have already been made are far outweighed by the remaining barriers, many of them the same ones that faced the women's movement prior to and during the Siad Barre era:[5]

- A cultural bias against female leadership in government (voiced by women as well as men), based on cultural perceptions that women are created to bear children and do household work and are incapable of being leaders. One of the many Somali sayings illustrating this view describes women as 'children with big feet'[6] – a view often reinforced, incorrectly, through reference to Islam.
- Patrilineal clan-based governance, which has prevailed since the war and by definition excludes women on the basis of their 'ambiguous' clan loyalty.
- Many more women now work as full-time, subsistence level breadwinners with no spare time to engage in self-development or politics because of the war's impact on the family livelihood system and the loss of male breadwinners.
- Women's low self-esteem regarding their role in politics and other public decision-making roles which comes from years of socialisation as subordinates to men. As the 2002 local government elections in Somaliland showed, often women are unwilling to stand for political or public positions.
- Gender-based inequalities of domestic responsibility and child-care leave women, particularly poor women, overburdened and with little time to become involved in public or political work.
- Gender-based inequalities in education result in high levels of female illiteracy and few educated women available to stand for public office (a problem compounded by the fact that most educated women with any experience in public life have fled the country and are now living in the diaspora).

Civil society organisations

During the socialist period of the Siad Barre era all but government-linked social organisations were banned. Change came in the early 1980s when international NGOs rushed to assist with the influx of refugees created by the 1977–78 Ogaden war, and to alleviate hardships arising from the World Bank-imposed structural adjustment programme. In their wake a few indigenous Somali organisations emerged and like their international counterparts these Somali organisations mainly focused on health and income-generation.[7] Although no longer banned, NGOs operated under constant and oppressive scrutiny by the regime.

Since the collapse of the regime in 1991 and the loss of formal employment opportunities possibly thousands of people across the country have set up organisations or group responses related to the social, employment and infrastructure needs resulting from the years of conflict. Widely varying in purpose, power structure, membership or personnel characteristics and motivation, target groups, sources of funding and quality of activities, the collection of organisations defy a single definition. Some could be classified as welfare or charity groups perhaps engaged with a specific need such as education, literacy or health; others are employment or profit-seeking self-interest groups searching for opportunities to gain a livelihood from their activities; others are common-interest groups such as people with disabilities, youth or minority groups; there are credit and income-generation self-help group and others that are issue-based pressure groups. There is also the phenomenon of 'briefcase NGOs' – a term Somalis have coined for a bogus organisation which exists only in its representative's briefcase, which he or she gets out to impress a potential sponsor.

Perhaps the most widespread characteristic among these new groups and organisations is the tendency for many, but by no means all, of them to be clan or sub-clan specific.

Within this diverse range of organisations are those that distinguish themselves as 'women's groups/organisations' of which there are many in all regions of the country. Many, but not all, of the women's groups which have formed since 1991 came about when women joined together to plan and undertake collective activities to promote peace and security in their localities. For many, this involved addressing the basic welfare needs of the community and its most vulnerable members, such as shelter, water, landmine clearance and help for the wounded, orphaned and widowed.

Women's participation in Somalia's Transitional National Assembly

(For information about the formation of the TNG, see page 6)

Zakia Alin, who works for Save Somali Women and Children, recounts how women managed to overcome male objections to their 'dual clan' identity (see Chapter 7), so as to be included in the internationally sponsored Somali National Peace Conference, held in Djibouti in 2000. As she describes, they made sure that women were represented in a national governing body that emerged from the conference but then found unexpected problems within their own movement.

Zakia's account begins by describing her organisation's involvement in promoting what was to be Somalia's 13th international peace and reconciliation conference to attempt to put together a new form of governance for the country:

> We [about 120 women] wrote a petition-letter to the UN Secretary-General, Kofi Annan, informing him of the problems we have in Somalia in general and how women are suffering. And he responded and put in his report that Save Somali Women was among those who give him advice. And soon after, the president of Djibouti Republic, His Excellency Ismael Omar Guelleh, also said in the Security Council in September 1999, that we have to interfere, we have to make a reconciliation [and peace conference]. At that time there were about 60 intellectuals [from Somalia] in Djibouti and among them were about five women including the chair of Save Somali Women, Asha Haji Ilmi. They told him that women should participate as equal partners, not as observers. And he accepted. We have also to thank President Omar Guelleh.
>
> So we got that delegation of 100 women and we tried hard to mobilise ourselves and then got also 50 observers out of the 100 delegates. [But] people fight because of clan and they wanted to reconcile according to their clan – every clan wants to get a share. We as women refuse to rally behind the clan, and said, for example, if you are married to another clan, you are 50–50 – nobody wants to give you a share, and according to traditional clan structure, women have no role. So we said why don't we form our own clan which is the 'Women's clan'? We lobbied to get one clan [of women included in the conference], and we succeeded in having our own clan.[8] [There were] two people co-chairing, and three vice-chairs who were representing the five main clans of Somalia [represented at the conference]. So we also tried hard to get also somebody who [was] representing our 'Women's clan'. And we selected the same Honourable Asha [Haji Ilmi] to represent the 'Women's clan'. She is a member of the African Women's Committee on Peace and Development. So she is a very articulate woman, and she really sacrifices, because she left her six-month-old girl behind and stayed there for six months. All of us stayed there but for her it was very difficult because she left a six-month-old baby.
>
> During the conference we [the conference delegates] decided to draft a national charter and we [put] five women in the drafting

committee [of] about 14–16 [members]. And we put our perspectives [in the draft]. With a lot of struggle and sleepless nights we got 25 [seats reserved for] women in the parliament [the Transitional National Assembly] out of 245. It was really very good.

We were thinking that at least the seats would be there. We were not thinking about the quality of women [who would take them]. After all it's the elders who would give us the names of the women [who would be given seats]. So we are not very happy now about the composition of our parliament because you may see people who do not have a good educational background.

But we say if you give them a lot of skills they can make it. The plan was [that the TNG] had to come up with a national constitution. We are ready to put women there and put our own gender perspectives there and affirmative actions. We were also planning to get about 12.5 per cent [female representation] to the parliament. We were thinking [women] should also be in the cabinet [a 25-member all-male body], in the district level, in the village level, but this is not happening. [Since being elected the TNG has not succeeded in gaining control over the country and its influence remains confined to an area of Mogadishu.]

The problem is that it is a male-dominated society and it is now saying 'we belong to our [kinship] clan, we don't belong to this [clan of women] you are talking about'.

Some people in the top leadership used women to destroy the spirit of our innovative initiative. We got about five women in the parliament from our organisation Save Somali Women.

So now our problem is that there has not been reconciliation yet. So we are hoping [for] women to represent the 'Women's clan' and to come [to further talks] as men's equal partners. We want to participate in these peace talks. We are looking for women to participate in these peace talks as women [not as kinship clan members].

(This is an edited version of an interview between Zakia Alin and International Alert, conducted in Kampala, Uganda on 26 March 2003 and transcribed by International Alert.)

Women's participation in the Puntland administration[9]

When the Puntland administration was established in 1998 five out of 66 seats in the House of Representatives were reserved for women.

And, as in the case of the TNG, the seats were given to women who were hand-picked by men rather than the selected through consultation or voting by women or the wider community. So some women criticised the allocations as tokenism although they were enshrined in the constitution and had some male support. (Faiza A. Warsame 2001)

Like elsewhere in Somalia and Somaliland, in Puntland women seeking political rights and power face opposition from conservatives. To have succeeded in obtaining 7.5 per cent female representation in the administration is therefore a significant step towards greater political equity with men. But according to participatory research conducted in Puntland by the War Torn Societies Project (WSP) in Somalia, 'the question of women's participation in the political process in Puntland remains a deeply divisive topic'. In consultations with a broad section of the modern and traditional male leadership WSP found that it is recognised that it is desirable to involve women in the process of governance and that 'women should play a major role in decision-making'. Yet the research found no broad-based support for the 'notion that women should be represented in the *shir* [an organised meeting of elders to discuss matters of agreed importance] or other political forums – whether traditional or modern'.[10]

The Puntland Administration was the outcome of an indigenous consultation process lead by civic and political leaders from across the north east region which started in February 1998 and culminated in the Constitutional Conference of 15 May to 11 August 1998. Reportedly, the elders (all of them male) had eventually agreed to the allocation of seats for women in the administration after hearing Anab Xasan, frustrated by what she called 'male power-grabbing and selfishness', recite a powerful poem. It is said that many men had tears in their eyes. In this translated extract from Anab's poem 'we' refers to women:

Dalka haystaa aan idiin-ka haajirnee
Haween waa duul jannaa oo dakana magalo
Nin doorka ma dilaan iyo wiilkii ay dhaleen
Daban intay kuu dhigaan ruuxna kuma dagaan
Dulmi ma qaataan oo xaaraan ma dadabsadaan
Ee ragow dabkaad shiddaan baan ku daadanaa ...

Xiliga aan joogno ragu waa inuu hubsado
Ama dalkii haysta aan idinka haarjirnee
Dadaalku markuu habsaamoo waanu hiilnaa
Kama harnee nimanka hareertan kataaganahay
Heshiiska iyo nabada horay bann utaagannahay
Hannaankii dawladnimo heegan baan unnahay
Wixii aan hubino haan baad ku aaburtaan
Dheeftii aan helilahaa baad hamboobsataan
Haween baad-tahaye hoos u foorarso baad dhahdaan
Hadaynnaan hubin hawshaan ku aadannahay
Heshiiska iyo xeerka aan haatan lagu salaysnayn
Raggow waan kaahurudnayee waa inoo hadaba

Keep the land, we emigrate
Women are heavenly folk and rarely commit cruelty and injustice,
They do not massacre heroes and sons they breastfed,
They do not deliberately plot or set up traps for a soul to fall into,
They neither condone exploitation nor indulge in forbidden bread.
But oh men, we succumb to the fires you ignite ...

Oh men, why don't you realise the difficult circumstances that we are now facing?
Or keep the land and we will emigrate.
When the rhythm for rebuilding slows down, we rally and mobilise
For the purpose. We are always beside men, never behind them.
We are at the forefront for peace and reconciliation,
We are ready with what it takes to resurrect good government.
But you men [ignore] our advice and inspirations,
You suffocate our intellect, so it never sees the daylight,
You grab and swallow all benefits due to us.
If you don't rethink and vividly acknowledge the role women play,
And institutionalise it in modern and customary laws,
Be warned, we are now awakening after a long sleep and passivity.

(Translated by Faiza A. Warsame 2001)

Women's participation in the governance of Somaliland

From papers by Shukri Hariir and Zeynab M. Hassan, and interviews with Noreen Michael Mariano.

> Just as Somali women were absent from decision-making [in] the public domain in the past, so are they also absent now. Women are not represented in any of the formal and informal institutions of decision-making whether at the village, district, regional and national levels of Somaliland. They are also absent from top economic leadership positions in the private sector. (Amina M. Warsame 2002)

> Women have no chance of competing with men while clan remains the main basis for political life in Somaliland. Male candidates are supported by their clans but women are not. (Member of the Women's Political Forum in Somaliland[11])

Shukri Hariir and Zeynab Mohamed Hassan, who have been at the forefront of the campaign for women's equal political status in Somaliland, describe how the campaign emerged from women's experiences of organising to put their country back on its feet after the war. They reflect on their experience of helping to bring about peace and reconciliation between warring clans, and the many challenges women face:

> In April 1991, when the population began returning from the refugee camps in Ethiopia to their original places of residence, they were distressed at the level of destruction they found in the main towns, caused by large-scale shelling. They found the settlements plundered and the destruction of even piped water supplies and electric power lines, the wholesale looting of furniture, equipment, medicines and appliances from dwellings, offices, hospitals, schools, banks, post offices, shops and factories. Women had to make homes from discarded cardboard boxes and scrap metal when they found their own homes roofless, without doors or windows [men were also involved but partly because women are traditionally responsible for building the family's shelter and some men were reluctant to use the poor materials available, many left this task to women].
>
> The civil war in Somaliland, at its height between1988 and 1991, weakened political institutions in the country. The unexpected

defeat of Siad Barre's troops caught the SNM leadership and the communities they represented totally unprepared for the immediate aftermath of war. They had neither the authority to deal with large-scale unrest nor the capacity to cope with the devastation of public institutions and infrastructure. A large influx of returnees overburdened the devastated cities that were without the most basic amenities. There was no running water, 90 per cent of the buildings had been destroyed, there was no communication system, food was in critically short supply, and all public infrastructure (factories, schools, hospitals and government offices) had been ransacked. More than 1 million anti-tank and anti-personnel mines were either littered around or buried below ground.

Life was made more precarious by the general instability ... During the civil war, almost all male Somalilanders possessed an automatic rifle, and some had even heavier weapons. The existence of enormous arsenals of heavy weapons and personal arms that now fell into the hands of hundreds of thousands of largely 'traumatised' male youth paved the way for lawlessness. Senseless acts of looting and indiscriminate killing terrorised the population, and also disrupted the flow of trade, while the economy was in shambles and the service infrastructure in ruins.

Emergency assistance and recovery – the role played by women's groups

Many people, especially those who had previously worked in social and welfare roles such as teachers or health workers, found themselves taking a leading role in the relief and reconstruction needed to make towns habitable and safe once more. A large number of these spontaneous activists were women. While some worked in the community as individuals, others got together, usually with women from their clan or sub-clan, to form groups or associations or to revive self-help groups and organisations that they had established in the refugee camps in Ethiopia.[12]

The leading women's organisations operating in Hargeisa by 1992 were the Somaliland Women's Development Association (SOWDA, originally called Alla-Aamin, meaning 'Faith in Allah') and the Somaliland Women's Organisation (SOLWO) established in Hargeisa in 1992. Alla-Aamin had been founded in 1988 by displaced women in Balli Gubadle, an area south of Hargeisa next to the Ethiopian border, and later transferred with the population to the refugee camps in Ethiopia. One of the group's founding members recalls how Alla-Aamin came about:[13]

> After we were uprooted from our homes by the military regime ... nearly every able-bodied man joined the fighters [the SNM]. It was then that a group of women decided to contribute to the struggle ... by direct assistance. Every day we saw how the wounded fighters were brought back and laid down under makeshift shelters. There was a shortage of everything that the wounded needed ... We couldn't stand to see the suffering of the wounded so we women organised ourselves into different committees. Some women did the washing for the wounded, others cooked for them, some collected contributions and still other women took the responsibility of awareness raising so that people who did not know about the situation [the destruction of Hargeisa] could get information. The committee responsible for collecting contributions would walk to remote areas in the bush to collect milk from the pastoralists ... We even sent women to Mogadishu [over 1,000 km away] ... to buy medicines ... That is how we started the women's self-help groups. (Brons & Warsame 2003)

Once it was possible to return to Somaliland, in 1991, Alla-Aamin transferred its head office to Hargeisa where it renamed itself the Somaliland Women's Development Association (SOWDA). The difficulty of shifting from an informal to a formal institutional set-up is expressed in the following account:

> We wanted to form our own women's organisations, but unlike the informal self-help groups, which we formed when we were in the refugee camps, we didn't know what to do with formal organisations. For instance, what are the different bodies in the organisation supposed to do and how are such organisations run? We went to the men for assistance and asked them to give us directions regarding the structures and legal procedures. Gradually we learned through trial and error. (*Ibid*)

Inspired by experiences in mobilising for peace in 1991–92 (see Chapter 6), their priority became establishing sustainable peace and stability. Along with other women's organisations such as SOLWO, SOWDA lobbied the interim government for the establishment of a police force and judiciary. SOWDA promised that women would contribute to a police programme. It kept its promise and when the police force was eventually established in 1992, SOWDA donated 500 police uniforms, bedding and utensils to different police stations.

Demobilisation of combatants

Through lobbying and training initiatives, women's organisations also played an important role in the demobilisation campaign to disarm and rehabilitate former SNM fighters. At the end of the war, in 1991, many SNM fighters laid down their arms and returned to civilian life. Some stayed together as military units linked to their sub-clan group. Others turned to banditry and lawlessness. During the first half of the 1990s well armed, sometimes traumatised, and badly disciplined gang members – known as *dey-dey*[14] – caused widespread insecurity and violence, especially along the roads.

With agreement from the clan elders and material support from business people and local organisations such as SOWDA, in 1995 the government finally completed the demobilisation and reintegration of up to 5,000 militiamen. Using the campaign slogan, 'Put down the gun and take up the pen', SOWDA alone claims to have demobilised more than 400 former fighters, receiving from them 1,500 items of weaponry and ammunition which SOWDA in turn handed over to the government.

Political participation

Until the reconciliation and governance processes established at the Boroma Conference of 1993 (see Chapter 6) women activists' overriding concern was how to achieve peace and reconciliation. From late 1993 the focus was women's rights, particularly their right to take part in government. A revival of traditional forms of governance and reconciliation[15] was the means by which the leaders in Somaliland transformed clan-based conflict into a sustainable peace. There was significant input from women peace activists, who themselves advocated the revival and use of traditional means of conflict resolution and peace-building. Yet within the traditional form of governance based on the patrilineal clan system, women are excluded from direct participation and decision-making. So began a struggle by women in Somaliland to assert their human right to equal political status – a right legislated for under the Siad Barre regime but not attained by the vast majority of women.

Women lobbied for political inclusion from the start of their involvement in peace-building in 1991. Their 1992 letter demanding an end to the clan war in Berbera (see Chapter 6) demanded that a third of the national parliament be women – they had decided to postpone demanding their right to half the parliament until later. The inclusion of 10 women observers at the National Peace and Reconciliation Conference in Boroma in October 1993 fell short of women's ambition but was seen by many to be an historic precedent as it allowed women some measure of participation in what was otherwise a traditional clan *shir*. It represented a step towards achieving full political status. Below is a translated copy of the letter presented by women's organisations at the Boroma Conference:

> The Republic of Somaliland
> To: Chairman of the National Reconciliation Conference
> To: Secretariat, delegations and observers at the National Conference
> Subject: Request for women's membership in the National Conference
> On behalf of the Somaliland women's groups which we represent here at the National Conference, we first of all wish to express our support for the *guurti* (assembly of elders) for the bold and democratic decision they have taken by offering us membership with observer status at the Conference. We are very much obliged to you for taking this unprecedented step. Secondly, and in relation to peace and reconciliation, we would like you to take into consideration this application for women to be included [with voting rights].
>
> Somaliland women are the backbone of the country. We are also the majority of the population, about 63 per cent. We are human beings dignified by God and our rights cannot be undermined.
>
> Brothers, given all that, we have the right to share in decisions about the destiny of our own country. Also, as Muslim people, we claim the fundamental rights that our holy religion gives us. Therefore, we request full membership in the National Conference, with voting rights, as women's representatives.
>
> Brothers, blame not, nor indeed ignore us. For God created us as women. Women are not clan members but should be taken into consideration as members of the nation.
>
> Lastly, if the National Conference concerns Somaliland and all its people, women should play their part. But if the conference is

only for men and only they have voting rights, we may feel that we have nothing to share in this event.

With many thanks
Fadumo Warsame Hirsi, Shukri Hariir Ismail, Fadumo Mohammed Ibrahim, Faisa Haj Abdillahi, Asha Haji Yusuf

In 1994 a conflict developed between the government and a sub-clan in Hargeisa. Fearful of a descent into violence, women's organisations demonstrated for a peaceful resolution to be found. The demonstrators, exclusively women and children, protested: 'Enough with war! Enough with armed fools! Enough killing of children! And enough fleeing of women!'[16] Women took the lead in setting up a committee consisting of women and youth organisations, to mediate between the two sides. Chaired by a woman, Shukri Hariir Ismail,[17] the committee held talks with the government on the one side and with the clan elders and armed young men of the clan on the other. The committee undertook reconciliation discussions with the president, elders from both sides and clan militia, in an attempt to diagnose their differences. Despite the committee's efforts, on 15 November 1994 civil war broke out in Hargeisa and lasted into 1996 when peace and reconciliation were finally brokered.

Around this time some women's organisations such as the Women (sic) Advocacy and Progressive Organisation (WAPO) and Dulmar moved away from their social and welfare role and began focusing their energies on 'advocacy for women's rights to be acknowledged and respected and for women to be allowed to participate in politics'. Shukri Hariir Ismail, founder of WAPO and its successor, Women's Advocacy and Development Association (WADA), recalls the efforts made by women and the responses from elders and politicians at the time of the *Shir Beleleedka* (Congress of Clans – a national congress held in Hargeisa from October 1996 to January 1997 that brought together all Somaliland's clans for reconciliation and the selection of a new president and vice president):[18]

The women's organisations in Hargeisa wrote letters to the House of Elders demanding that women should be able to participate at the conference. The Elders response was that there could be 11 women attending the conference but their role would be restricted to that of observers and they would not have the right to vote.

6 Women bearing a banner reading 'There is No Life Without Peace' participate in a protest with tens of thousands of people in Hargeisa, Somaliland, in 1994. Twenty-five thousand militia had been demobilised, peace and stability were returning to Somaliland, yet warmongering by opponents of the Somaliland government was threatening to spark civil war. Not long after the protest, war broke out. (Hamish Wilson/Panos Pictures)

This offer, although not satisfying women's demands, was accepted for the following two reasons: 1. The offer would allow women to contribute their peace-making ideas to the conference, 2. Women attending the conference would be able to raise the agenda of the right of women to share in the decision-making bodies of government.

At the conference's opening ceremony women presented songs which sent the message of the new mutual understanding and wholeheartedness of the Somaliland community. Meanwhile I was chosen to articulate the women observers' demands, which included the recognition of the women observers as full participants with voting rights. The chair of the conference responded that the first phase of the conference would address solely the issue of tackling clan conflicts. The women's agenda would be addressed during the second phase when the national constitution was on the agenda.

During the conference the government and opposing sub-clan who had been fighting (since 1994) eventually reconciled. The militia was demobilised and joined the government forces. Being motivated by this, women tried to forward their agenda to the conference of 500 male representatives – but without success. Again the chair of the conference responded with the excuse that the women's agenda would be discussed once the National Constitution had been approved by conference. Whenever women came near to a hope of having the issue of women's agenda discussed it was shattered ...

The draft Nation Constitution was introduced to the conference and was discussed ... This draft Constitution actually enshrined articles ensuring women's rights. The draft was approved by a majority vote.

Being energised by the fact that the draft National Constitution clarified the recognition of women's rights, women again submitted their appeal for gender equity in the House of Parliament and called for the recognition of the 11 women observers as full participants in the forthcoming parliament. In addition six observers from minority clans[19] submitted an appeal similar to ours. We politicised the agenda, questioning the chair of the conference on every aspect.

The conference chair finally stated that both the observers from the minority clans and the women observers were to be comprised of six participants each and that they would be made full voting members of the conference. The six participants from the minority clans were approved by the conference. As for the six women observers, when introduced for approval, the conference started quarrelling ... Some were saying: 'Which clan do they belong to?' ... 'the conference consists of clan representatives'. Eventually the conference did debate whether or not women would be allowed to participate at the conference and join the parliament and the house of elders. The debate concluded that it should be first clarified whether the Islamic *shari'a* law[20] allows women to participate in national conferences and at national assemblies.

It seemed clear to us that the men did not want us but were avoiding giving a direct objection. Whenever we overcame one obstacle men would present us with yet more difficult ones.

Sheikhs [respected authorities on religion] were assigned to clarify whether Islamic *shari'a* law allows women to participate at such conferences or not. After three days the Sheikhs clarified that yes, *shari'a* law does allow for women to take part in national assemblies and conferences. They further defined that during the period of Prophet Mohamed (peace be upon him) women used to take part in all community activities. Sheikh Abdillahi Sheikh Ali Jowhar, a participant, read the clarification on behalf of the other participants and sheikhs. Sheikh Omer, a participant, also gave details of women's rights as prescribed by *shari'a*. The positive response of the Sheikhs was a relief – but only for a few minutes. Whenever one obstacle had been overcome a more irksome one appeared. The conference had conditioned women's participation on *shari'a* Islamic law permitting it. But as soon as [the Sheikhs] found out that *shari'a* would allow women's participation they presented another story.

Contrary to our expectation, on the day when the women's agenda was introduced to the conference, the conference had to be halted as a result of the confusion and disorder made by the [male] representatives when our agenda was introduced for approval. We felt the atmosphere was anti-women judging from the words of some of the male representatives who were saying 'the conference is only for the male representatives of the clans'.

The next day the chairman declared that conference-chairing committee had withdrawn the agenda for women's participation from the conference, on the basis that the clans sent only men representatives to the conference. The chairman further stated that this issue had brought about a great deal quarrelling and argument which showed that it would be rejected if put to a vote. He further directed that women would have to wait until the end of the next term of government [in other words, 2000 at the earliest], when a multi-party system would be introduced. Then, with the formation of independent political parties instead of clan representation, women could stand to become elected as members of parliament.

To add to our disappointment, the only woman candidate for the post of the president, Radiya Roda Haj Ali, was ignored by the Chairing Committee, which chose neither to respond positively or negatively to her candidacy, whereas they gave a reply to all the male candidates.

The conference's objection to our long-sought aspiration of sharing decision-making bodies with men coincided with International Women's day on 8 March. We arranged the festival ceremonies and celebrations both in the morning and in the evening of this day. We invited members from the House of Elders, the Parliament and the Cabinet of Ministers. In her speech for the occasion, women's leader, Faiza H. Abdillahi, said that whilst this day was a celebration for the women of the world it was a black day for the women of Somaliland for on this day the rights of the Somaliland women were rejected by the national conference.

The Somaliland Constitution

Article 57 of the Somaliland Constitution, referring to the rights of women:

- Women and men are equals as far as the rights, freedom and responsibilities outlined in the Somaliland Constitution are concerned.
- The Government should promote the rights of women to be liberated from customs and traditions which are against the *shari'a* and which affect their body physically and psychologically [a reference in particular to the practice of female genital mutilation].
- Women have the right to own, manage, supervise, use and donate their assets in accordance with *shari'a*.
- To enhance knowledge and income, women have the right to education including skills training and adult education

---

Angry but undeterred, women in Somaliland continue to campaign for their rights, turning the challenges that confront them into opportunities to develop further organisational and planning skills. A welcome decision by the transitional president[21] was the appointment of a woman to be Minister of Family and Social Welfare.

Somaliland's first multi-party district council elections, December 2002

Although later than planned, following a referendum on the draft constitution in 2001 the government duly paved the way for a multi-party political system to replace the clan-based form of governance which had been in place since 1991. For the entire voting population this heralded the first multi-party political election since 1969 when Siad Barre took over power. For women, this shift away from clan-based politics provides a major opportunity not only to vote as men's equals for the first time in more than a decade but also to field candidates and gain representation in the political parties competing for election.

In October 2000 a group of leading women within Somaliland's civil society came together to form the Women's Political Forum (WPF). Forming two years before the December 2002 multi-party district council elections were due, WPF's original aim was to promote women's political participation at every level.

Within a few months of being formed WPF decided to create its own political party, Qoys, meaning 'Family', to represent women's concerns. But they could not find women willing to stand as political candidates for their party. All those they approached were either not prepared to stand, felt they could not give up their jobs or did not feel they had sufficient education. So WPF changed its strategy, concentrating instead on persuading the other (male-dominated) political parties to include women candidates and to give greater priority to women's issues in their party manifestos. Women candidates did come forward and were encouraged by WPF to seek positions in the parties' hierarchies. In the end two parties did nominate women as co-vice chairs.

WPF also selected one party, Hormood, to align with on the basis that its manifesto was pro-women's rights and being aligned with Qoys would attract women voters. The understanding of this alignment was that Hormood would offer the position of vice chair to a woman but in the event they did not do so: 'They finally said "It won't work" – in addition they delayed making the list of candidates and when the list came forward there were not enough women included.'[22]

Undefeated, WPF joined other civil society groups in conducting voter-education training and awareness raising. WPF's aim was to encourage women to come out and use their vote on election days and for both voters and candidates to prioritise women's issues.

When election day came on 15 December more than 400,000 women and men over the age of 16 turned out to vote. In the absence of census data no one is certain what proportion of the eligible voters this turn-out represented, and there is no figure for the number of women although women were reported to have voted in large numbers. There were six parties competing in an electoral process based on proportional representation whereby votes were not for individuals but parties and the party which received the most votes at the district level won the most seats on the council. Each party submitted a list of candidates drawn up in priority order; names on the list would qualify for a seat on the council depending on the number of votes won by their party. Between the lists of the six parties there was a total of approximately 2,760 candidates for 332 seats across 23 local councils. Of these 2,760 candidates just six were women. When votes were counted, two of the six women came through the process qualifying for seats and now hold elected positions in their local councils (in Erigavo and Gebiley).

For WPF, the experience of this first multi-party election in Somaliland has proven that with democratic electoral processes the lack of educated women to promote women's interests at the political level remains a major constraint on efforts to improve women's lives. Educated Somali women are a minority in Somaliland (and in Somalia as a whole), the majority being in the diaspora. As noted in the UNDP *Somalia Human Development Report 2001*, 'Tradition and lack of education mean that few women are fully aware of their rights and in their efforts to hold communities together, they often accept violations of their rights as being consistent with *shari'a* and customary law.' (UNDP 2002)

Women in the diaspora

The renascent women's movement in Somalia and Somaliland is severely constrained by the lack of educated women in the country. There are few women who feel sufficiently confident about their skills and experience to stand for political positions, for example – not that inadequate skills and experience ever seems to prevent large numbers of men standing for, and attaining, such positions. Somali women have always had limited access to education but from the

1980s onwards the educated women in Somalia largely left the country to seek asylum in the diaspora. The war resulted in the complete collapse of the state education system across the country. As a result many young women (and men) who are now in their late teens and twenties have had no educational opportunities.

One potential source of energy and skills that may have the capacity to transform the future of women's rights in Somalia and Somaliland are the women and girls currently in the diaspora.

Living in the diaspora as a refugee is usually a difficult and stressful experience but one which has enabled many thousands of girls and women to access educational and training opportunities which would not have otherwise been available to them. As long as violent insecurity and high unemployment persist in Somalia there will be little to attract women back from the diaspora, where many are earning a living and supporting their dependants through school as well as remitting money to relatives back home.

In Somaliland at least, the pattern seems to be that those women who choose to return are older women whose children have completed school and remain independently in the diaspora; those who are younger and still have children at school stay in the diaspora. Not surprisingly perhaps, few educated young Somali women appear to be opting for a return to 'traditional' life in Somalia or Somaliland.[23]

Women who have returned from the diaspora to Somaliland, sometimes intending to stay just a few months, are proving invaluable sources of inspiration and leadership in many sectors, from commerce to community development. Sharing and combining their skills and experience with those of other women together they create a powerful challenge to the status quo in Somali society.

TESTIMONY 7: NOREEN MICHAEL MARIANO

THE REHABILITATION OF HARGEISA GROUP HOSPITAL

Editors' note

In 1988 the population of Somalia's north west region was estimated at between 1.78 and 2.05 million, excluding Ethiopian refugees who had been there since the 1978 Ogaden War. Following the massive aerial bombardment and destruction of Hargeisa and Burao by Siad Barre's forces in May 1988, up to 1 million people had sought refuge in Ethiopia and elsewhere, including the south of the country.

In January 1991 as the United Somali Congress (USC) took Mogadishu, and Siad Barre and his supporters fled, the Somali National Movement (SNM) captured the northern cities of Hargeisa, Berbera and Burao, bringing an end to the civil war in the region. Refugees and displaced people began cautiously returning to the towns and cities which they had run from three years before. Throughout 1991 and 1992 those arriving in Somaliland included people who had never previously lived there. By January 1992 Somaliland's population was estimated to be 1.35 million. (Bradbury 1997)

The people arriving in cities like Hargeisa and Burao in 1991 found little left standing. In Hargeisa more than 90 per cent of buildings had been destroyed. The only part of the city left relatively unscathed was the area that had been held by government troops. People returning did so at considerable risk of being injured by the 1 million or more landmines laid in the region during the civil war – many of them scattered in and around ruined buildings. Water sources had been systematically blown up, contaminated or booby-trapped; airstrips, bridges and communication routes had been destroyed or badly damaged, and all public services, like health care and education, had collapsed. By the end of 1992 a foreign professional mines-clearance company had arrived to train Somalis but until then mines were cleared by whatever means were available. A group of volunteer men organised themselves into 'the Pioneers' and showed courage in clearing mines with nothing but their ingenuity and bare hands.

At the same time as having to negotiate the lethal hazards left by the former regime the men, women and children returning to the country confronted gangs of gun-carrying, trigger-happy and *qaad*-chewing bandits or *dey-dey*. Such bandits tended to be young former SNM fighters, many traumatised by the war and with no vision of a future except to survive on illegal gains. Usually operating in gangs, and equipped with heavy artillery including tanks and gun-mounted vehicles known as 'technicals', they survived through looting, intimidation and extortion and the very real threat of violence. At the same time as being aggressors, many groups functioned as the protectors and military vanguards of the clan or sub-clan they represented; as militias they were under the control of the clan elders. Clan elders sometimes took action against their own militia members, including executions, in order to ensure the clan abided by traditional codes of conduct and reparation or to curb their violent tendencies.

Probably there is no one who lived in Hargeisa between 1991 and 1995 who did not experience a violent or threatening confrontation. Faced with the need to get on with rebuilding their lives, everyone took risks and showed courage. But motivated by a determination to prevent further death and suffering, some women and men exposed themselves to additional risks and showed extraordinary courage. The late Noreen Michael Mariano was one such person.

Noreen was a founder member of the Committee of Concerned Somalis (CCS), a volunteer group of 10 men and women set up in 1992. One of CCS's first goals was to address the high maternal mortality in Hargeisa by re-establishing the Hargeisa Hospital which had been badly damaged in the war and had become home to a variety of squatters including former militiamen.

Noreen's story

In 1991 when people returned to Hargeisa and other parts of Somaliland such as Burao, Gebiley, or Arabseyo, they found little left standing. This was particularly the case in Hargeisa where so many houses and building had been destroyed. The mass destruction of homesteads meant that many people found themselves homeless. Amidst the destruction, Hargeisa Hospital remained intact. Consequently the hospital became a place for homeless people to set up home. Whilst the hospital wards were left for sick patients, other areas such as the doctors' room and the nurses' room, the storage area for medicines, the kitchen, the administrative offices, were occupied by homeless people. The squatters were ex-hospital staff members, disabled people, SNM veterans, and returnees from Ethiopia whose homes had been destroyed. Some people even set up the traditional Somali homestead known as the *aqal* inside the hospital, while others constructed their homes within the hospital using corrugated-iron sheeting.

In 1992 my friend Amina and I had started working to try to improve the health situation in the town. We had developed a dispensary for the SNM Veteran's Widows. One of the medical staff who helped at the dispensary regularly referred people to the hospital, thinking that it was at least standing. So Amina and I decided to go and visit the hospital to see for ourselves. Human beings were living everywhere and there were even *qaad*-chewing sessions going on – one room was just a *qaad*-chewing venue! People, young men and young women, would say: 'Oh, we're meeting at the hospital (for a *qaad* chew).' Secondly, people were using the medications to sell or to use for themselves – there were some drugs, tranquillisers, that could be sold and other drugs that would make you spaced out. But worst of all we found that the maternal mortality level at the hospital was incredibly high. At one point, in one night there were 10 maternal deaths. This was horrendous. A child and a mother would die. A child and a mother! There was no professional screening of staff. People were operating and working without necessarily being qualified to do so. It was a terrible situation.

A doctor at the hospital who was disgusted by what was happening came and asked us if we could do something to help sort the place out. We realised that it was too big a thing for us alone so we set about getting others involved. In the end we managed to get a team of 18 together – four members of the Committee for Concerned Somalis, three doctors and 11 businessmen.

Our first task was to clean the place. Cleaning the place meant removing the squatters. We counted 53 families living in the hospital. After some negotiation a few agreed to leave but 47 families simply refused. So we talked to them, we brought SNM people to talk with the SNM veterans, we tried our best to persuade them to leave. We kept visiting them, spending time with them. They didn't like it. The group was willing to help the squatters to entice them to leave the hospital. Each squatter family was offered a truck to take them and their property wherever they wanted and every five family members were provided with a tent. If there were ten family members then they would be given two tents. Eventually the squatters agreed to go – all except six individuals who adamantly refused to leave. They saw me and Amina as the biggest threat because I had a car giving us the freedom to come and go to the hospital.

Some of the squatters were suffering from mental problems or trauma, which made evicting them difficult and dangerous. One day one of the remaining squatters pulled an automatic gun on me. In the belief that the further away one is from a gun the more dangerous it is, I rushed towards him and said 'Shoot!' He was shocked and said: 'I want to kill you!' 'Yes! Kill me!' I replied and stayed close to him, staring him in the eyes. He looked at me and seemed amazed. 'Now I know you must be crazy. You are a crazy Christian', he said. 'Yes, I am a crazy Christian who, like you, comes from Burao',[24] I told him. At this reference to the place we had in common, he gave up his gun to me. By then everyone was coming to see what was happening. I took the gun and gave it to someone to remove the bullets. The squatter who had pointed the gun at me was a disabled man and was using a wheel chair. I told him that if he ever threatened me again I would take the two arms of his wheelchair and throw him backwards. He asked if I was going to kill *him*? I said: 'Yes. You wanted to kill me so now I am going to kill you!' He saw the funny side of this and we settled our dispute as friends though he still refused to leave the hospital.

Another squatter who had had a leg amputated was similarly aggressive towards me. When he started threatening me I told him that there were men from my own tribe who were amputees like him but they didn't squat in the hospital preventing it being used for the care of the sick. The next day when we were alone together, he brought out a hand grenade. I had never seen one before but I guessed what it was. He told me he was going to pull the pin out if I did not give in to his demands. Without thinking, I rushed at him, taking his left hand in my right hand and taking his right hand with my left hand and I said: 'OK. Let's pull it together. Come on, after three. One, two, three.' He was really shocked and told me that it would kill us. 'Yes. We will die together', I said. 'Your body and my body will never be separated. We will be buried in one batch but then you will go to hell. On top of everything else you will go to hell.' He argued that it would be me who went to hell if I killed him. No, I told him: 'You pulled the grenade, I'm just helping you.' He was really afraid and said that he couldn't pull the pin. He asked if I really wanted to and I told him no. I asked him what he was going to do and he said he wouldn't do anything. I persuaded him to hand over the grenade to me. The thing was, I didn't know what to do with it and I didn't know if it was still safe or not. So I called for someone to come and help. They came and they told me that as long as I didn't pull the pin it would be safe. I eventually found a policeman and gave it to him. The amputee and I became friends after that. He would say: 'Ah, the crazy Mariano, the crazy Christian.'

In both situations I was lucky. It was the danger that made me quick. In such a situation your life depends on you being fast; otherwise you are gone. There's so much that could make you afraid but as my mother told me, 'You die every day if you are afraid.'

After these incidents the remaining squatters realised that my group and I were serious. With the hospital cleaned and cleared of most of the squatters the Hargeisa Hospital Group, as we were then called, arranged a selection process for doctors, nurses, paramedics and auxiliaries. It was easy to check the credentials of the nurses because they had been registered in Mogadishu and we had copies of the registers in Hargeisa. But we had to find ways of verifying the rest – the doctors, lab technicians and so on. We got verifications from the (newly established Somaliland) Ministry of Health in the end but we were afraid that tribalism would lead to dishonest claims.[25]

We set up an emergency rota system consisting of three shifts. The group would take it in turns to visit the hospital, the wards, and patients and monitor what was happening. We would check with patients: 'Did you get your medicine last night? Did you get you injection?' We would do spot checks, turning up in the middle of the night sometimes. We met with the Matron every morning at 10am and with the doctors. Many doctors were unhappy about what we were doing. They were threatened because until then they had done what they liked. The Hargeisa Hospital Group actually ran the hospital for four months and even paid salaries. The money for the salaries was collected as donations from Somali businesses and the international organisation Caritas.

We were active in trying to bring down the high levels of maternal mortality. We made a great deal of noise about it. We went to the doctors, the Ministry of Health, and then we started to campaign for attention, saying that maternal deaths were not like measles or cholera that are seasonal. Why have the high numbers of deaths been occurring? We really blasted the doctors. It was because we made such a noise that President Egal let us be responsible for the hospital temporarily.

We discovered that three or four of the doctors (one of them hadn't even completed his second year at college) were using veterinary drugs, meant to be used for livestock, on women to speed up their labour. The use of this drug was the main cause of the maternal death rate – scandalous! When we found out we told the doctors that we'd take them to court. In the face of questions the doctors kept quiet. They denied it. Then we made lists with photographs. We didn't print them in the newspapers but we had photographic evidence. We went to the court and said that we wanted to file a case. We were told that we couldn't because the medical code of ethics hadn't been drawn up.[26] (And who is going to draw them up? The very doctors who are carrying out criminal practices? If a man shoots a woman he is taken to court and very likely shot or put in prison. Why then is nothing done when he kills a child and mother through medical malpractice?) We succeeded in having the veterinary drugs taken out of the store and removed from the pharmacy. We announced in the newspapers that we would publicise the names of anyone found holding the drug because it was a criminal act. All the pharmacies subsequently destroyed their stocks.

The Hargeisa Hospital Group handed over management in April 1994 but by August the civil war had broken out [between the Somaliland government and Isaq sub-clans]. The tribal nature of the war meant some of the hospital staff had to flee for their lives. All the people we had sacked came back to the hospital[27] – this time with guns. During one of my support visits to the hospital some of these people reminded me that they were the ones I'd sent away and they threatened to shoot me. I went to the Minister to complain and to ask what he was doing allowing the hospital to be invaded.

While I was at the ministry some of my tribal cousins got to hear about what had happened to me. About ten of them went to the hospital carrying guns and demanded to know who had been threatening Noreen

Mariano? I was summoned to the hospital to prevent my tribesmen from causing trouble and I found the ones who'd threatened me had run away. We called it a truce but after that I kept away from the hospital more as I didn't want to be the cause of any trouble between the tribes.

I'm not brave. It's just that you have to live in this country. I am determined to live here and improve it. This is the most important thing. In 1992 [when an earlier conflict had broken out in Hargeisa] I decided I would not leave. I was displaced from Mogadishu, Berbera and Burao and if I get displaced from Hargeisa I will literally leave Somaliland and never come back – that's my promise. So I have to make Hargeisa liveable.

Starlin Abdi Arush – a tribute

Editors' note

It is too early to judge the impact of her work but a book about the war and women in Somalia would not be complete if it did not mention the late community activist and leader, Starlin Abdi Arush, of Merca, a town south of Mogadishu. Starlin was killed before we were able to invite her to contribute to this book. We include here an obituary by British journalist James Astill who spent some time with her in Merca.

> Whether negotiating with warlords, setting up hospitals or chairing her Somalian homeland's Olympic committee, Starlin Abdi Arush, who has been murdered in Nairobi aged 45, often seemed a lone voice of good humour and good sense. Some diplomats spoke of her as the first president of a new, democratic Somalia, but she eschewed such ideas of power.
>
> She died on her way to observe the latest peace talks between Somalia's warlords. It seems that Starlin was the victim of a robbery; an ironic end for a woman who lived through the nihilistic battle of Mogadishu in 1991, and for whom confrontations with gunmen were a daily ordeal.
>
> Starlin maintained that tribalism had no place in the workings of a nation state and saw plans to save Somalia founder around the rejection of this principle. In 1993, Starlin tried to negotiate an end to the stand-off between the warlord Mohamed Farah Aideed and the American peace-keepers who saw him as the cause of all evil. The Americans launched a disastrous attack on Aideed, and thus became just another faction in a tribal war.

In 1999 Starlin turned down a high-level job in a new, United Nations-sponsored government. She predicted that the government – elected on tribal quotas – would fail. She told clan elders who demanded their share of jobs in her projects: 'I understand your cousin needs a job. But when you have a heart attack, do you want him to treat you?'

Starlin advocated the creation of local governments, to take over aid projects such as those she ran for COSVI, an Italian charity. The projects' beneficiaries could be expected to support these administrations; and in this way the state could be rebuilt.

Starlin's childhood in Merca, a small Indian Ocean port 60 miles south of Mogadishu, prepared her for a role in Somalia's male-dominated society. Her mother – the estranged first wife of one of Somalia's first vets, and a patron of a Sufi order – expected as much of her four daughters as [of] her three sons. She taught Starlin a fierce love of Somalia's unique Islamic culture; and an equally fierce intolerance of its misinterpretation by male chauvinists. As an unmarried woman, Starlin wore neither head-scarf nor veil.

After graduating from a Catholic convent high school, Starlin lived in Italy for 13 years. She dabbled with medical school, then forged a successful career in Turin's municipal government. Italy's nepotistic institutions were familiar; but its democratic freedoms impressed her.

In 1991 Somalia erupted into war, and when Starlin's younger brother and brother-in-law were killed as fighting reached Mogadishu, she returned to support her sister, Halima. Weeks later, the battle of Mogadishu began. Their home was mortared daily and ransacked twice. Throughout the fighting, Starlin and Halima organised food deliveries. This led to her involvement with the UN's emergency relief effort when famine came. With Starlin an increasingly troublesome critic, Mohamed Aideed cited these international ties as a reason to have the Arush sisters hauled before a tribal court. He accused them of scheming with foreign agents. Standing proudly, Starlin with her head bare, the two women asked: 'If we wanted to kill Aideed, why would we need foreign help? Why would we not take a knife and do it ourselves?' The elders were won over instantly.

Shortly after, Starlin returned to Merca to negotiate the release of some Italian aid workers taken hostage by a fundamentalist militia. Here she endured a slight which was to lead her to transform the town's dire fortunes. Having assured the militia that she would not help the hostages to escape, one militiaman pointed his gun at her and asked: 'But why should we believe you?' Starlin was stunned. Only an outsider – and a thug at that – could have dared insult her in the town where her family had lived for generations. Instantly, she vowed to try putting Merca to right. It was no easy task. Its hospital had 300 employees, many of them idle militiamen, and few medical supplies. She dealt calmly with confrontation. When a thug pressed his gun to her throat, she responded: 'I am Starlin Abdi Arush of the Habir Eji clan. Put down your gun or you will be dead by tomorrow.' Starlin accepted such incidents as inevitable. Far more damaging was when her European donors listened to rumours, put about by rivals, that she was a warlady carving out a fiefdom.

Strolling around Merca with Starlin was humbling, if time-consuming – everybody flocked to pay their respects. And Starlin, gravely nodding, gently teasing or cheerfully chatting, always repaid the compliment. Then came her aid projects: the hospital, clinics for mothers and babies, schools for 3,000 children, the demobilisation camp for militiamen. For foreign correspondents, these were practically the only contemporary good-news stories in Somalia.

Starlin had hoped to hand over her aid projects and help set up a local administration in Merca. There seems little doubt that the people would have supported her. More than 1,000 of them lined the streets to receive her body home.

She is survived by her family and her fiancé, Roland Marchal, a French academic, who said: 'She never much considered her own future. She only thought of her country.'

Starlin Abdi Arush, peace activist and aid worker, born 3 March 1957; died 24 October 2002.[28]

NOTES

1. Recalled by a woman activist during a workshop held in the preparation of this book.
2. Some of the women active in the women's movement during the 1960s to 1980s remain proactive and important figures in the movement today.
3. Maria Brons & Amina M. Warsame (2003) 'Empowerment after return: Negaad women in Somaliland', unpublished paper.
4. The Somaliland national umbrella of women's organisations, Negaad, plays a central role in the campaign for women in leadership. Negaad works to advance the economic, social and political status of women in Somaliland, and to strengthen the capacity of its members to implement effective projects that facilitate the realisation of this structural change goal.

5. With thanks to Amina M. Warsame.
6. The same saying is used by women to describe men; it is said to have been coined by women.
7. Mohamed Sheik Abdillahi (1997) *Somaliland NGOs: Challenges and Opportunities* (London: CIIR).
8. Sceptics argue that women were allowed to participate in the Conference so as to build international donor confidence; Ibrahim Nur (2002) 'Somalia case study', in 'Gender Sensitive Programme Design and Planning in Conflict-affected Situations', ACORD, unpublished.
9. This section on Puntland is compiled from Faiza Warsame's 'The Role of Women in Rebuilding Puntland' in War Torn Societies Project (2001) *Rebuilding Somalia: Issues and Possibilities for Puntland* (London: Haan Associates). It is extracted with permission of the author and WSP.
10. Adam J. Bixi, 'Building From the Bottom Up: Basic institutions of Local Governance', in WSP 2001.
11. CIIR/ICD (2003) *Multiparty Local Government Elections in Somaliland, December 2002* (London: CIIR) www.ciir.org.
12. As international aid agency relief and rehabilitation programmes got under way in Somaliland in the early 1990s the formation of local non-governmental, particularly women's, organisations was encouraged. The international community wanted local organisations that could be contracted to deliver emergency relief aid and reconstruction and, more broadly, to empower women.
13. From an interview in Maria Brons and Amina M. Warsame, 2003 'Empowerment after Return: Negaad Women in Somaliland' (unpublished).
14. The term used in the south of Somalia to describe such gang members is *mooryaan* – thought to mean a group 'of hunger-driven men, with no honour and no dignity, who would eat or do anything' (Nuruddin Farah 2000), and known as *jiri* in Puntland.
15. In traditional Somali politics there is no centralised state, nor are there political offices or ranked leaders. Decision-making is conducted democratically (although formally excluding women) by segmentary groups of kinsmen meeting in general assemblies, where all adult male family heads or elders seek to reach decisions through consensus.
16. Amina M. Warsame (1997) 'The Impact of the Civil War on Pastoralists, Especially Women and Children', unpublished thesis (The Hague: Novib/Institute of Social Studies).
17. The other committee members were: the late Faiza H. Abdillahi – Vice Chairperson, Anab Omer Leye, Maryan Abdi Obsiye, Ahmed Aw Gedi, Hasan Jama, Muhamed Elmi.
18. More than 10 people put themselves forward as candidates for the presidency, including one woman. Out of those who nominations were accepted, Mohamed Haji Ibrahim Egal, the president since June 1993, achieved the greatest number of votes and was reinstated for a second term.
19. Including the Akishe and the Gabooye (composed of the Midgan, Tumal and Yibir).

20. During the civil war Somalia's legal, judicial and law enforcement system collapsed. Since then no uniform constitutional and legal rules have been applied across the country. The Somaliland government has adopted Islamic *shari'a* as the basis of all laws in combination with the pre-1969 penal code, in place prior to Siad Barre's regime. For many people the pillars of laws are a combination of Islamic *shari'a* and *xeer*, or customary law, governing clan behaviour. UNDP (2001) *Somalia Human Development Report 2001* (Nairobi: UNDP).
21. President Mohamed Ibrahim Egal died in May 2002 while undergoing surgery in South Africa. The Government of Somaliland immediately appointed the Vice-President, Daahir Rayaale Kaahin, to take over as transitional president until the multi-party presidential elections in 2003.
22. Member of WPF quoted in CIIR 2003.
23. Though some, like Sara Haid, a young Somali woman born in Britain and founder of the British-based Somali organisation Tawakal, find ways of contributing to life 'back home' through Somali organisations in the diaspora.
24. Noreen was one of Somalia's few Christians.
25. The concern Noreen refers to here is that without original documentation to prove a person's medical qualifications it was quite possible for false claims to be made and impossible to disprove; the likelihood of this happening was high given the very weak administrative systems in place and the strong clan tensions prevailing at the time.
26. Drawing up a Code of Ethics for Medical Practice was only one of the numerous legislative tasks which faced the newly formed Somaliland government.
27. Noreen is referring here to those people who had been sacked on the grounds that they had been found to be unqualified to practice as medical personnel.
28. *Guardian*, London, 4 November 2002.

Afterword: Political Update, July 2003

Judith Gardner

Somalia

At the time of writing, July 2003, Somalia's faction leaders, individuals defined as 'members of civil society', and the Transitional National Government (TNG) formed at Arta in 2000, continue to struggle in pursuit of a way forward on the future governance of Somalia. They are doing so through the 14th internationally convened Somalia National Reconciliation Process (SNRP). Designed and managed by the Inter-Governmental Agency on Development for the Horn and East Africa (IGAD), with support from the international community, including the European Union, this process began on 15 October 2002 in Eldoret, Kenya. It was expected to last three months. Almost ten months on the process is still some way from completion with the final phase, the election of 315 parliamentarians, a president and prime minister, still to be finalised. Before this can happen agreement needs to be reached on the major remaining issue of contention: whether or not Somalia should become a federal state immediately or after a transition period and public referendum. Conference delegates and most Somali observers are divided over this question. One issue over which there seems to be consensus is the call for an (African) international peace-keeping operation to begin during the post-conference transition phase when disarmament, demobilisation and reintegration will be a priority in the steps to establishing peace and reconciliation inside the country.

More than 100 women, among them supporters of various faction leaders, members of the TNG, professionals from the diaspora and individual grassroots peace activists, tried to take part in the conference. With the conference management de facto in the hands of the faction leaders and the regional powers who support them, many women (and men) who had much to contribute but were perceived as 'threats' to various powerful factions were rejected. Of those that remain, 21 are officially registered observers and 34 are official delegates allowed to vote in plenary sessions. A woman has sat on each of the six Reconciliation Committees established as part of the process. Two women are on the Leaders' Committee consisting of 22 faction leaders and five members of 'civil society'. The Leaders' Committee has come to constitute the power within the process, making many decisions without reference to the plenary.

Women are divided both by loyalty to opposing factions and clans and over the question of federation – 26 of the women are taking part as members of faction groups or the TNG. Nevertheless women have been united in pursuing an agenda for women's representation in whatever form of government is finally created. Aiming for 25 per cent representation women have had to settle for 12 per cent, just a 1 per cent increase on the Arta. UNIFEM and the IGAD Women's Desk have played a significant support and lobbying role to achieve this outcome, providing women delegates with a Resource Centre and seminars from veteran women's rights campaigners from Uganda, Sudan and Kenya. At least one woman is standing as a presidential candidate alongside more than 40 male candidates.

According to the process agreed by the Leaders' Committee, the parliamentary deputies will be selected on a clan basis, chosen by the faction leaders, in consultation with traditional clan elders.

Throughout the period of the peace process, and despite the much-publicised Declaration of the Cessation of Hostilities achieved just three weeks into the process, on 27 October 2002, serious armed conflicts have continued to affect parts of Somalia. Promulgated by the very same faction leaders and warlords who signed the Declaration, these violations have included gender-based crimes of sexual violence targeting women and girls.

Somaliland

Some people from the regions of eastern Sanaag and Sool, which are contested by Somaliland and Puntland, have participated at the SNRP, believing that their future interests will be best served by a united Somalia rather than an independent Somaliland. The majority of people in Somaliland, however, support their government's decision to stay away from the process in the belief that the time for talking will be once peace has been achieved in Somalia and an accountable government is in place.

During the 10 months that the SNRP process has been under way in Kenya, Somaliland has carried out the first democratic multi-party elections in Somalia since 1969. Multi-party elections to district councils took place in December 2002, and these were followed in April 2003 by presidential elections. The elections are 'a crucial part of the transformation of Somaliland's post-war system of government, from a clan-based power-sharing system to a constitutional government based on multi-party democracy'.[1] The process is considered 'potentially very significant for the future of Somaliland and the political entity (or entities) that emerge from the remnants of the Somali state'. (*Ibid*)

Three parties fielded candidates in the Presidential Election[2] and 488,543 votes were cast by women and men of eligible age at 782 polling stations.[3] Voting was conducted peacefully and international observers who witnessed the elections, including a large delegation from South Africa, concluded that they had been carried out in a free and transparent manner and generally in line with international standards. The party of the incumbent president, Daahir Rayaale Kaahin, won the elections, beating its closest rival, Kulmiye, by only 80 votes. The narrow margin of victory gave rise to a period of tension as Kulmiye contested the results and the government sought to prevent violence by invoking emergency laws, detaining opposition supporters and controlling the media. Civil society forums stepped in to mediate and the public made clear that the parties should follow constitutional process to resolve their differences.

On 16 May 2003, following confirmation of the result by the Supreme Court, Daahir Rayaale Kaahin was sworn in as the first elected President of Somaliland. Three weeks later a committee of *sultans* persuaded Kulmiye to concede defeat and prepare to contest parliamentary elections. (*Ibid*)

One of President Kaahin's first decisions was to appoint Edna Adan as Minister of Foreign Affairs, the most senior position yet held by a woman in any Somali government. A second woman was appointed as Minister of Family and Social Welfare.[4] Women also expect to gain seats in Somaliland's next parliament, which will be formed through multi-party elections within two years.

NOTES

1. Mark Bradbury, Dr Adan Yusouf Abokor, Haroon Ahmed Yusuf, 'Choosing Politics over Violence: Multi-party Elections in Somaliland', *Review of African Political Economy,* May 2003.
2. A woman, Fawziya Yussuf Haji Adam, tried to challenge the system by running as an independent candidate but was barred by a Supreme Court ruling.
3. Two districts in eastern Sanaag and three in Sool did not vote.
4. This post had previously been held by Edna Adan.

About the Contributors

Amina M. Warsame is a specialist researcher and writer on Somali women and development. Originally trained as a teacher, she became the Head of the Women's Documentation Unit of the Somali Academy of Arts and Culture and was responsible for supporting and undertaking some of the earliest research by Somali women on women's position in society. She went into exile in 1989 finding refuge in Sweden where she settled until March 1997, when she returned to live permanently in Hargeisa. Since returning to Hargeisa she has been at the forefront of research and advocacy on the impact of the war on women's lives, particularly within the pastoral community, and is a key activist on the issue of the political empowerment of women. A former executive committee member of the women's umbrella organisation, Negaad, Amina is the founder of the Somaliland Women's Research and Action Group (SOWRAG).

Amina Sayid had completed her training as a medical doctor shortly before the war reached Mogadishu. Originally from Brava in southern Somalia, Amina and her family fled the fighting in Brava and Mogadishu, eventually reaching Yemen in 1992. Unable to return to Somalia because of the impact of the war on her community, since leaving Somalia Amina has worked as a health specialist and social services officer supporting other Somali refugee women and children, both in Yemen and in the UK where she now lives.

Dahabo Isse was born in southern Somalia and grew up in Mogadishu. Shortly before the war erupted in the city she was working for Aadamiga, a women's non-governmental organisation. From 1991 to 1993 she was a key figure in the emergency relief wet-feeding programme (kitchen project) of the International Committee of the Red Cross. Unable to remain in Somalia she sought refuge in the UK where she continues to live. An active member of the diaspora she is the founder of Dadihiye, a Somali development organisation which responds to social service provision needs of disadvantaged Somali refugees and asylum seekers in London.

Dekha Ibrahim, a Kenyan Somali, has been a visiting trainer for the Birmingham-based organisation Responding to Conflict and is the

Kenyan representative for Coalition for Peace in Africa (COPA), a conflict transformation network.

Fowzia Musse is a social researcher and community development worker who trained in both Somalia and North America. She was involved in the first urban poverty survey of Mogadishu conducted in the late 1980s. Originally from north eastern Somalia, she was living in exile when the war reached Mogadishu. In 1993 Fowzia was recruited by the UNHCR to research the high incidence of rape occurring in the Somali refugee camps in Kenya. She went on to design and coordinate a project aimed at preventing rape and responding to the needs of survivors. She currently lives and works in the United States.

Habiba Haji Osman is a nurse-midwife and trainer from the Bay Region of Somalia who was working for the Ministry of Health and an international health organisation, AMREF, at the start of the war in southern Somalia. Bay Region was the epicentre of the war and famine in the first years of the conflict and after more than a year of trying to escape, Habiba finally reached Yemen in April 1992 where, unable to return home, she remains today. In Yemen Habiba has worked as a midwife trainer/supervisor for more than six years with a health programme which trains Yemeni women midwives and health care workers to provide locally managed mother and child health services at community level.

Halimo Elmi Weheliye, a nurse-midwife, was Principal of the Post-Basic Nursing and Midwifery School in Mogadishu until the start of the war when the services collapsed. Although from Mogadishu, Halimo was uprooted by the war and forced to seek refuge with her children among her husband's family in the north west of the country, Somaliland. Since 1997 she has been the leading health worker and driving force behind an internationally sponsored programme to support the local staff development and management of Hargeisa's primary health level services for women and children.

Ladan Affi is the youngest contributor to the book. She was a student in the United States preparing to return home when conflict broke out in Somalia. Unable to return to Somalia she settled in Ottawa, Canada and works closely with the Somali refugee community there. She is particularly concerned about Somalis' experience of living in the diaspora. Ladan was instrumental in forming a group of Somali community members that attempts to raise awareness, promote positive images about Somalia and promote Somali culture. She works for the Catholic Immigration Centre in Canada.

The late **Noreen Michael Mariano** spent all of her adult life fighting for justice and was committed to improving the lives of women and children. In the late 1950s and early 1960s as a young woman she was an active member of Somalia's first woman's organisation, the Somali Women's Association. Later, along with other women activists, Noreen personally lobbied Siad Barre to amend the Family Law to address the injustices endured by women throughout the country. Having worked for UNICEF Somalia for many years Noreen was a skilled development practitioner by the time she fled Mogadishu in December 1990. Although she could have found refuge in the west or elsewhere in the world Noreen chose to live in Hargeisa as soon as it was possible for her to return there in 1991. She was a founder member of the Committee of Concerned Somalis (CCS) a local non-governmental organisation which set up in 1992 to help restore basic services in the city. Noreen went on to establish a credit programme to develop income generation initiatives run by widowed and poor women; she was also responsible for opening Hargeisa's first restaurant run by women – herself and her close friend, Amina Yusuf. Noreen's health deteriorated in the late 1990s and she passed away in May 2000 while in Rwanda.

Rhoda Mohamoud Ibrahim has been a development practitioner for more than 18 years, working before the war with international agencies including Oxfam UK and Overseas Education Fund. She went into exile in Britain in early 1990 and worked for the Pastoral and Environmental Network for the Horn of Africa before becoming involved with the diaspora organisation SOMRA (Somali Relief and Assistance) which was set up to respond to emergency needs in Somaliland. Originally from Burao in Somaliland, she returned to Somaliland in 1995 to set up CIIR's programme to support emerging civil society organisations. In 2001 she was appointed chair of the SNM veterans organisation, Soyaal. She is currently the Somaliland representative for Coalition for Peace in Africa (COPA), a conflict transformation network.

Sadia Musse Ahmed, a social scientist and one of Somalia's only female anthropologists, was before the war Deputy Head of the Women's Documentation Unit in the Somali Academy of Arts and Culture in Mogadishu. Accused of anti-revolutionary attitudes she was arrested and imprisoned under Siad Barre's government. She sought exile in Britain in 1990 and in 1991 worked with other Somali refugees to set up the diaspora organisation Somali Relief Association (SOMRA) to raise funds and set up projects in-country for the needs of war-displaced and affected. In 1994 Sadia co-founded Hal Abuur, a Somali literary and cultural journal publishing literature to promote Somali identity. Having previously worked in Ethiopia as the Gender Officer for the Pastoral and Environmental Network in the Horn of Africa (PENHA), Sadia is now PENHA's Somaliland Programme Director, based in Hargeisa.

Shukri Hariir Ismail is a well-known radio broadcaster and also a poet and writer. Shukri had to flee her home city of Hargeisa when it was bombed in 1988 and spent the next two and a half years in a refugee camp in Ethiopia. There, along with other women, she became involved in community activities. Returning to Somaliland in 1991 she has become one of Somaliland's leading spokeswomen on peace and women's rights issues. As well as being the founder member of the Women's Advocacy and Progressive Organisation (WAPO), and a broadcaster for Radio Hargeisa, in recent years Shukri has worked on a radio-based health promotion programme run by Health Unlimited.

Zeynab Mohamed Hassan worked before the war as a teacher in primary and secondary schools, and held various posts within the Ministry of Education, including Bay Regional Coordinator for women's education, Director of income generating programmes in the Women's Education Institute, and Supervisor of women's income generating programmes in the Institute of Adult Education, Mogadishu. Between 1992 and 1994 she was the Programme Coordinator for the Somaliland Women's Development Association (SOWDA) in Hargeisa. She has written materials on adult education techniques, hand-sewing, child care and nutrition, and female genital mutilation. She is currently working in Hargeisa with the international development agency Life and Peace Institute.

The Editors

Judith Gardner is trained in anthropology and community development. A development practitioner with a special interest in gender relations and how communities cope with crisis, she has worked in Sudan, Somalia and Yemen. She is currently the Africa and Middle East Regional Manager for CIIR.

Judy El Bushra is a development practitioner who has specialised in gender and conflict since the early 1990s. Until recently Head of ACORD's Research and Policy Programme, she has worked in many contexts throughout Africa with particular focus on Sudan and Somalia. Her previous publications include *Development in Conflict: The Gender Dimension* (Oxfam UK/I, ACORD, 1993) and 'Transforming Conflict: Some Thoughts on a Gendered Understanding of Conflict Processes', in Ruth Jacobson, Susie Jacobs, Jennifer Marchbank (eds) *States of Conflict. Gender, Violence and Resistance* (Zed Press, 2000). Judy currently works as a freelance consultant.

Appendices

Appendix 1: Chronology of Somalia's civil war

Colonial and pre-Siad Barre era

1897	Colonial partition of Somali-inhabited territories between the United Kingdom, France, Italy and Ethiopia.
1890–1921	Dervish movement under the leadership of Sayid Mohamed Abdulla Hassan fought to rid Somali territories of colonialists.
1943	Creation of the independence movements the Somali Youth Club (later Somali Youth League) and the Somali National League.
1955	Western part of British Somaliland Protectorate and Reserve Area (the Ogaden) is annexed to Ethiopia.
1959	Somaliland Women's Association (SWA) established.
1960, 26 June	Former British Somaliland Protectorate gains independence.
1960, 30 June	Former Italian colony, under UN trusteeship since 1950, gains independence.
1960, 1 July	The two territories unite to form the Somali Republic.
1960	Somali Women's Movement (SWM) set up.

Siad Barre's dictatorship

1969, 21 October	Military coup led by Major General Mohamed Siad Barre overthrows the civilian government, suspends the constitution, bans all political parties and social organisations, introduces capital punishment. Measures to enforce state control of the economy including sale of livestock, are introduced over the next few years in contrast to the free-enterprise economy of the preceding nine years.
1970, 21 October	Siad Barre declares Somalia a socialist state dedicated to Scientific Socialism; himself, 'Father' of the nation whose 'Mother' was the Revolution. Clan-based tribalism is denounced and *diya* payments are officially abolished. National Security Service (NSS) set up to deal with political

	offences including tribalism and 'lack of revolutionary zeal'. (Lewis 2002). It is led by one of Barre's sons-in-law.
1970	Women's Section of the Somali Revolutionary Council formed.
1970	The Power to Detain Law (Law No. 1 of 10 January 1970) gives the NSS arbitrary powers of arrest and facilitates long-term detention without charge or trial for an unlimited period. (AfricaWatch 1990)
1971	National campaign against tribalism continues with effigies representing 'tribalism, corruption, nepotism and misrule' symbolically burnt or buried. Reference to one's 'ex-clan' is outlawed.
1972	People's vigilantes or 'Victory Pioneers' (*guulwadayal*), established as a neighbourhood uniformed paramilitary force reporting directly to Siad Barre and headed by one of his sons-in-law.
1972, 21 October	Written script for the Somali language is introduced with a modified Roman alphabet as the official orthography.
1973	Labour Code promotes equality of women in the workplace.
1974	Somalia joins the Arab League.
1973–74	*Dhabadheer* drought: one of the worst droughts and famines in Somali history in central and north eastern regions leads to massive airlift and resettlement of 300,000 nomadic pastoralists from these areas to fertile agricultural land appropriated by the state along the southern lower Shabelle river, at Jalalaqsi and Kurtanwarey.
1974–75	Urban and rural mass literacy programme involving 30,000 secondary school students sent out to 'extend instant literacy to the nomads'. (Lewis 2002) Self-sufficiency campaign starts.
1975, January	Ten religious sheikhs publicly executed and 23 others imprisoned, charged with preaching against amendments to the Family Law giving women the same inheritance rights as men.
1975	Law No. 173 introduced making all land state property. As a result women could obtain land leases.
1977	Somali Women's Democratic Organisation (SWDO) founded by the government as the women's branch of the Party.

War in the Ogaden

1977–78	Somalia launches major offensives inside the disputed Ogaden region starting war with Ethiopia but retreats after the Soviet Union switches its support to Ethiopia.

Armed opposition and civil war

1978, 9 April	Coup attempt by disaffected Majeerteen officers. The Majeerteen-based opposition movement, the Somali Salvation Democratic Front (SSDF) is created.
1978–79	The government prosecutes 'scorched earth' policy against Majeerteen civilians in the central regions of Muduug and Hiran in reprisal for the SSDF's guerrilla campaign. Thousands of civilians are killed, along with livestock, and water sources destroyed in what becomes the first stage of civil war. Between 400,000 and 800,000 refugees, mostly ethnic Somalis, from the Ogaden arrive and are settled in northern Somalia where they are given preferential treatment by the government which creates paramilitary groups among them and forcibly conscripts them into the army. (Africa Watch 1990) Their settlement creates some internal displacement and environmental damage. International aid organisations set up programmes in Somalia in response to the refugee influx, giving the government access to millions of aid dollars with which to maintain its regime at a time of economic crisis.
1979	New Constitution establishes equal rights and duties for men and women.
1980	Somalia strengthens diplomatic links with the United States and receives economic and military aid in return for US access to Berbera port.
1981, 9 April	Somali National Movement (SNM), an armed opposition group drawn largely from the Isaq population in the north west and with a base in Ethiopia, is formed to overthrow the Barre regime.
1981, December	Arrest and imprisonment of 30 prominent Hargeisa businessmen, doctors, teachers and civil servants for working to improve local public services (known as the 'Hargeisa Group') –

	indicative of increasingly repressive policies and human rights abuses including summary killings, targeting the Isaq population.
1982, February	Mass protests, particularly by intermediate and secondary school students, throughout the north west in response to the trial and sentencing of the Hargeisa Group. Curfew imposed.
1982	Under pressure from western donors the Barre government abandons socialist policies and adopts an IMF structural adjustment package. Begins a decade of substantial foreign aid from western and multilateral donors.
1983	The sale and cultivation of *qaad* is banned. This has an impact on the northern economy. (See Chapter 5)
1986	Freedom of movement restricted in the north west region. Rape, including gang-rape, by soldiers in the region has become common, especially in the countryside, fuelling SNM membership. (Africa Watch 1990) (See Testimony 3)
1988, April	Somalia and Ethiopia sign a peace agreement which will end the SNM's ability to operate out of Ethiopia.
1988, May	The SNM briefly captures the two main towns in the north west, Burao and Hargeisa. The Somali government responds with heavy shelling and aerial bombardment in heavily populated areas, killing thousands of civilians and forcing hundreds of thousands to flee to Ethiopia. Reports of human rights abuses lead to the freezing of foreign aid. (See Testimonies 3 and 4)
1989, January	United Somali Congress (USC) formed in Rome, an opposition movement drawn from the Hawiye clan family.
1989	Opposition to Siad Barre proliferates with armed movements forming including the Somali Patriotic Movement (SPM), formed by disaffected Ogadeni soldiers and other opposition groups formed by the Dolbahunte, the Gadabursi and the Rahanweyne.
1989, July	Anti-government riots in Mogadishu sparked by assassination of Catholic Bishop of Mogadishu, and subsequent arrest of several prominent religious leaders. Some 450 people killed during rioting, including in mosques, followed by mass

	arrests, looting, rape and executions of civilians, many of them Isaq.
1989, September	Constitution is changed to allow a return to a multi-party system. *Qaad* is legalised and the laws giving equal inheritance rights to women are revoked by the regime in an attempt to appease some of its opponents.
1989, October	SPM attacks Kismayo. Hawiye soldiers mutiny in the town of Galkayo. Fighting spreads through the regions of Muduug, Galgadud and Hiran. Government forces retaliate by bombing villages and massacring civilians.
1990, May	An open letter, 'Manifesto', is published signed by 114 politicians, religious leaders, professionals and business people. It condemns the regime's policies and calls for political reform through dialogue with the opposition groups. Many of the signatories are imprisoned but later released following mass demonstrations and international pressure.
1990, August	SNM, SPM and USC agree to form a united front against the Barre regime.
1990, December	Government forces lose control over most of the countryside. USC enters Mogadishu on 30 December.

Collapse of the Somali state

1991, 26 January	Siad Barre flees Mogadishu as USC forces capture the city. Reprisal killings and heavy fighting cause the mass displacement of civilians. (See Testimonies 1, 2, and 5) SNM take over Hargeisa and the rest of the towns in the region.
1991, February	Internationally sponsored peace talks in Djibouti. One section of the USC elects Ali Mahdi as interim president, but others reject the appointment. This precipitates a split within the USC which results in the ongoing conflict between the two main factions.
1991, 9 February	Brava invaded (see Testimony 2) and wave after wave of fighting, massacres, rape and looting unleashed on the unarmed communities of the southern riverine area and coastal towns.
1991, April	Siad Barre's forces attack Baidoa. (See Testimony 1) Fighting in Afgoi and continued fighting in the southern agricultural areas. Women in

	Mogadishu urge their men to fight against the return of Siad Barre's forces. (See Testimony 2)
1991, 18 May	At the Grand Conference of Northern Peoples, held in Burao, popular pressure results the SNM leadership proclaiming the secession of Somaliland from the rest of Somalia.
1991, May and June	Two internationally sponsored conferences held in Djibouti but fail to end the factional fighting in Somalia.
1991, November	Fighting again erupts in Mogadishu between General Aideed (and his Somali National Alliance, SNA) and Ali Mahdi, both from sub-clans of the Hawiye. Battle for Mogadishu lasts four months.
1991	From early 1990 until March 1992 there is almost continuous warfare in the south. (See Testimonies 1, 2 and 5)
1992	Attempt by Al-Ittihad Islamic forces to control the north east defeated by the Somali Salvation Democratic Front. Man-made famine rages through much of southern Somalia. (see Testimonies 1 and 5)

(Italics indicate chronology specific to Somaliland)

1992 January–March	*War in Burao. Reconciliation lead by elders and women. (See Chapter 6)*

UN intervention in Somalia

1992, March	United Nations brokers ceasefire in the South.
1992, April	UN Operation in Somalia (UNOSOM I) created. (See Testimony 5)
1992, April–August	*War in Berbera between Isaq sub-clans. Women mobilise for peace and conduct allaburi. (See Chapter 6)*
1992, July	Operation Provide Relief launched to airlift food aid to the famine devastated southern regions.
1992, September	War in Baidoa between two sub-clans of Rahanweyne.
1992, October	*Peace demonstration by women in Somaliland. Peace Conference held in Sheikh bringing to an end Berbera conflict. Peace sealed with symbolic exchange of 30 young women. (See Chapter 6)*
1992, December	Operation Restore Hope launched with US-led multinational peace-keeping force, UN Task Force (UNITAF); 30,000 UNITAF troops land in Somalia.

1993, January–May — *National Peace Charter for Somaliland agreed and Mohamed Ibrahim Egal selected as president of the Republic of Somaliland by an assembly of elders at the Grand Boroma Conference. The bi-cameral parliament based on clan representation effectively excludes women from holding office. (See Chapter 9)*

1993, March — Internationally sponsored Peace and Reconciliation Conference held in Addis Ababa. Fifteen factions sign an agreement that is not implemented.

1993, June — Supporters of General Aideed and the Somali National Alliance ambush UNOSOM Pakistani troops, killing 24.

1993, August — *Sanaag Region Peace and Reconciliation conference of elders in Erigavo.*

1993, October — US forces announce withdrawal of their troops following the death of 18 US Special Forces and hundreds of Somalis in clashes in Mogadishu during which two US Black Hawk helicopters were downed. (See Testimony 5)

1994, January — General Aideed and Ali Mahdi sign peace agreement. Security in Mogadishu improves.

1994, March — US military forces withdraw from Somalia.

1994, November — *Civil war between Isaq sub-clans breaks out in Somaliland, called the Hargeisa War as it divided the town's population, displacing half to camps in Ethiopia. The war extends to Burao displacing most of the population. Peace is not restored until the end of 1996.*

1994, November — Aideed's forces capture Baidoa.

1995, January — Siad Barre dies in exile in Nigeria.

1995, February — Women demonstrate for peace in Mogadishu.

1995, March — UNOSOM forces and civilian officials leave Somalia. The country still divided with no central government.

Post-UNOSOM

1995, March — Rahanweyne form the Digil-Mirifle Governing Council for Bay and Bakool regions.

1995, September — General Aideed's forces occupy Baidoa, toppling the Digil-Mirifle Governing Council and displacing civilians. Aid agencies withdraw from the region. Rahanweyne Resistance Army (RRA) formed.

1996, February–June — *Peace and reconciliation meetings held with communities displaced by the Hargeisa War.*

1996, June	*Women organise* allabari *to pray for peace in Somaliland. (See Chapter 6)*
1996, August	General Aideed dies. His son, Hussein Aideed takes over leadership of SNA.
1996, November	Internationally sponsored Peace and Reconciliation Conference in Sodere, Ethiopia, brings together most southern factions, but is boycotted by Hussein Aideed and Somaliland.
1996, November–December	*Somaliland National Conference in Hargeisa officially ends civil war in Somaliland. Displaced begin to return.*
1997, October–December	Flooding in Shabelle and Juba valleys and inter-riverine regions. International community responds with the largest relief programme since 1992.
1997, November	Internationally sponsored peace conference in Egypt where leaders of 30 factions sign a peace accord but it is not implemented.
1997	Kenya and Yemen sponsor peace meetings.
1997	Ban imposed on the import of Somali livestock by Saudi Arabia due to Rift Valley Fever; lasts 15 months and affects the northern areas of the country that rely on livestock exports for hard currency.
1998, July/August	Mogadishu-based faction leaders negotiate creation of Benadir regional authority. Hussein Aideed relinquishes claim to presidency of Somalia.
1998, August	North eastern leaders form Puntland State of Somalia, a non-secessionist state with Abdullahi Yusuf as president and a 69-member parliament (five seats reserved for women). (See Chapter 9)
1999, May	Rahanweyne Resistance Army recaptures Bay and Bakool and installs its own administration, resulting in much improved food security and increased access for aid agencies.
2000, May	Thirteenth internationally-sponsored Somali National Peace Conference convened in Arta, Djibouti.
2000, August	Transitional National Assembly composed of 245 representatives (25 seats reserved for women) elects Abdiqasim Salad Hassan as new president of a Transitional National Government (TNG) for Somalia.
2000, September	Second ban on Somali livestock imposed by Arabian peninsula

2001, May	*Somaliland holds national referendum on provisional constitution paving way for non-clan based multi-party politics. It is approved by 99 per cent of voters. Women have been allowed to vote for the first time in Somaliland's 10-year history.*
2001, June–August	Puntland constitutional crisis over contested leadership provokes clashes in Bossaso.
2001, 11 September	Terrorist attacks on America. Somalia named as a state where 'terrorists' may find safe haven.
2001, September	*Activists in Somaliland form Women's Political Forum to promote women's participation in political structures.*
2002, August	*Somaliland president, Mohamed Egal, dies during an operation in South Africa. Somaliland parliament follows constitutional process and vice-president Daahir Rayaale Kaahin sworn in.*
2002, August	Somalia's 14th internationally-sponsored peace and reconciliation conference gets underway in El Doret, Kenya.
2002, December	*Somaliland holds first local government multiparty elections. Two out of more than 350 seats go to women candidates. (See Chapter 9)*

Appendix 2: Somalia in facts and figures

Landmines

Somaliland: estimated 1 million mines laid by both sides during the civil war of the 1980s. With the present capacity for clearance the region could be declared 'mine safe' within seven years.

Demography and livelihoods

Estimated population (2001)	6.38 million (Somalia and Somaliland)
Urban based population	24 per cent
Sedentary agriculture	17 per cent
Pastoral	59 per cent
Population under 15 years	44 per cent
Internally displaced	300,000 (down from over 2 million in 1992)
Registered Somali refugees in Ethiopia, Kenya, Djibouti and Yemen	246,000 (down from more than 700,000 in 1992)
Somali refugees in wider diaspora	up to 1 million
People connected to the Internet	4,500
Number of radios per 1,000 people	72

Economy

Principal exports	livestock (sheep, goats, camels and cattle)
GNP per capita	US$200
GNP	US$1.3 billion
External debt	US$2.6 billion
Remittances	US$300–500 million per annum
Donor aid	US$115 million pledged in 2000; actually received much lower

Health

Average life expectancy (2001)	47 years (30–35 years in 1995)
Life expectancy	44.6 males, 47.8 females
Infant mortality rate	132 per 1,000 live births (pre-war 152/1,000)
Under-five mortality rate	224 per 1,000 live births (pre-war 275/1,000)
Maternal mortality rate	1,600 per 100,000 live births (same as pre-war 1990 – one of the highest maternal mortality figures in the world, representing the death of nine women every two days as a result of pregnancy and childbirth-related complications)
HIV/AIDS prevalence	<1 per cent
TB	around 300 per 100,000 (twice the number of males to females affected)
Access to health services	28 per cent
Access to clean water	23 per cent
Doctors	0.4 per 100,000
Nurses	2 per 100,000

Education

Adult literacy	17.1 per cent (24 per cent in 1985)
Of literate,	65 per cent are male
Female adult literacy	12 per cent (14 per cent in 1985)
Male adult literacy	22.1 per cent (36 per cent in 1985)
Urban adult male literacy	43 per cent

Urban adult female literacy	26.2 per cent
Rural/nomadic male literacy	13.5 per cent
Rural/nomadic femaleliteracy	6.4 per cent
Children of school-going age enrolled in primary school	13.6 per cent (9 per cent in 1998/99)

Girls represent 37 per cent of pupils enrolled in grades 1–4, but only 29 per cent grades 5–8
1.1 per cent children enrolled at secondary school (10 per cent in 1989). Of the 5,350 secondary school students attending the 20 functioning secondary schools, 10 per cent are female.
Tertiary education enrolment 0.1 per cent (3 per cent in 1989)
15 per cent of primary school teachers are women

Human development status

Somalia has a declining human development index. Ranked globally it is placed 161 out of 163 states in terms of level of human development, with only Niger and Sierra Leone having lower human development status.

Source: *Somalia Human Development Report 2001* (UNDP)

Appendix 3: Glossary

abxad – leather storage container for women to keep their valuables in
af-maimiy – language spoken by the Rahanweyne agro-pastoral peoples
af-Somali – language spoken by the nomadic pastoral ethnic Somalis and the national language of Somalia
allabari – traditional collective prayer meeting
alool – stripped thick sticks, tied together to cover the front of the *aqal* where the nomadic pastoralists cook
aqal – Somali pastoralist hut
baarqab – uncastrated male camels (stud camels)
baaq – clan-specific signals
bakhaaro – rented storage building
beel – a group of nomadic families who share the same grazing land in a season
berked – rectangular-shaped cement-lined water storage tanks or reservoirs
biri-ma-geydo – 'spared from the spear': traditional codes of war that confer immunity on certain groups such as women and children
buraanbur – the highest poetic form in women's literature
buul aws/aqal – shelter within family compound used by girls of marriageable age
caws – woven materials used in construction of nomadic home
dabar jabin – military intelligence
dayr – short rainy season

dhaanto – evening entertainment organised by and for unmarried young pastoralist men and women of marriageable age (the term is *iyargud* in the north western regions)
dhabar-garaac – forced marriage involving abduction
dhabadheer – one of the most disastrous droughts of the mid 1970s
dhibaad – gift to the bride from her family
dhigo – main branches used in the frame of the nomadic house
dhiil – milk container
dhiriq – stripped branches tied together to remove animal manure from the den
dhoor – top-knot
dhudhun – longest type of mat woven for the nomadic house
dhumbal – woven walls of the nomadic house (central regions)
digo xaadh – flat piece of wood for cleaning the animal den
diya – compensation or 'blood money' paid collectively as a penalty for a member of one's group having killed a person
doc – house
doobi – temporary milk container
doonid – formal meeting to propose marriage
faqash – corrupt military officers; derogatory term used by opposition in the north west to refer to Siad Barre loyalists, especially members of the armed forces and officials of the regime
faro-xumeyn – sexual or other violence intended to harm women, used euphemistically to describe rape
food – girl's hairstyle post-circumcision
gaadiid – transport camels
gabaati – goodwill payment by man's family to the *diya* group of his wife's father
gablan – barren and unproductive; derogatory term for childless women and men
galool – type of acacia tree, the roots of which are used to construct the frame for the nomadic shelter
gambo – black headscarf worn by pastoral women after marriage
garas – dress
garbasaar – type of cloth
gashaanti – a girl of marriageable age
gu' – long rainy season
gudniin – infibulation
guulwade – Siad Barre's 'victory pioneers' or *guulwadayal* (plural)
guurti – assembly of clan elders
haan – milk container for transporting milk over longer periods
habra wadaag – children whose mothers are sisters
haggaa – long dry season
hakbad – women's savings and credit group (northern Somalia and Somaliland)
hangesh – military police

harar – mats used to cover nomadic house
hayin – older transport camels
heerin – men of marriageable age
hijab – scarf worn by Muslim women to cover their head and shoulders, leaving only their face exposed (Arabic)
ilma abti – cousins linked through parental brother-and-sister relationship
ilma adeer – cousins whose fathers are brothers
inan la yeel – the man moves to stay with in-laws on marriage
iyargud – collective entertainment organised by and for pastoral men and women of marriageable age
jilaal – short dry season
jimini – language of people of Brava
jiriir – bandit (Puntland)
karbaash – protection for transport camels
koofiyed cas – Presidential Guard or Red Berets of Siad Barre
kufsi – rape
kur-bun – wok for coffee beans
laheyste-galmo – sexual hostage
laxoox – thin pancakes
lool – softer branches in frame of nomadic house
ma'alin – teacher
macawis – type of cloth
magan-gelyo – a person another entrusts with their safety
malaq – traditional clan ruler (also known as *sultan*)
mareeg – light tethering rope to hold young livestock for a short period
marriin – clothes
meher – bride price given to the bride herself
mooryaan – southern Somali term for armed gang, often of young men (also spelt *muuryaan* and known as *dey-dey* in the North; *jiriir* in Puntland)
muqmad – preserved meat (known as *oodkac* in south)
qaad – a plant (*catha edulis*) chewed for stimulant properties (also spelt *qat, khat* and *qaat*)
qaalin – newly trained transport camels
qalwo – fence for small livestock
qaraabo qansax – distant relatives
qararaflay – women who trade in household utensils, onions and other goods
qarbed – leather water container
qobtol – protection for transport camels
qoys – single household
qumman – rich women
reer – elder and his family with married sons and daughters living in the same compound
reer abti – mother's family

reer adeer – father's family
saylada dadka – 'meat market'; a term used to refer to Hargeisa Police Station during the repression of the 1980s
shifta – bandit (Kiswahili)
shir – peace meeting
shollongo – traditional savings and credit group (southern Somalia)
siibraar – leather milk container
sultan – traditional clan rulers
sumad – tribal livestock brands
tawfiq – in agreement/common understanding (Arabic)
udub dhexaad – central post supporting nomadic house
u gelid – marriage initiated by a woman
weer – headband, usually white, worn by women as a sign of mourning
xadhig siin – long rope
xeedho – container of meat, ghee and dates used in marriage ceremonies and symbolic of the virgin bride
xidid – in-laws
xig iyo maydhax – sisal and bark fibre used in rope making
xigto – next of kin
xoola goyn – livestock given to a potential groom by his family
xudun xidh – livestock given to a new family after marriage
yarad – marriage payment by a groom's family to the family of the bride
yeesha – ropes made of animal skin used to tie the *aqal* onto a camel's back
zar – spirit possession
zikri – Koranic recitations

Appendix 4: Bibliography

Abdillahi, Mohamed Sheik (1997) *Somaliland NGOs: Challenges and Opportunities* (London: CIIR).

Adam, Hussein M. & Ford, Richard (eds) (1997) *Mending Rips in the Sky: Options for Somali Communities in the 21st Century* (Trenton NJ: Red Sea Press).

Adan, Zeinab (1992) 'Somali Refugee Women in Canada', *INSCAN*, Vol.6, No.2/3.

Africa Watch (1990) *A Government at War With its Own People. Somalia, Testimonies About the Killings and the Conflict in the North* (New York, Washington, London: Africa Watch Committee).

Africa Watch Women's Rights Project (1993) *Seeking Refuge, Finding Terror. The Widespread Rape of Somali Women Refugees in North Eastern Kenya* (New York, Washington, London: Africa Watch Committee).

African Rights (1993) *The Nightmare Continues. Abuses Against Somali Refugees in Kenya* (London: African Rights).

Ahmed, Christine Choi (1995) 'Finely Etched Chattel: The Invention of the Somali Woman', in Ali Jimale Ahmed (ed.) *The Invention of Somalia* (Trenton NJ: Red Sea Press).

Ahmed, Sadia M. (1995) 'The Transformation of Somali Marriage: Fission and Fusion', unpublished MA thesis for the School of Anthropology (London: University College London).

Andrezejewski, B.W. and Sheila (1993) *An Anthology of Somali Poetry* (Indiana: Indiana University Press).

Besteman, Catherine (1995) 'The Invention of *Gosha*: Slavery, Colonialism, and Stigma in Somali History', in Ali Jimale Ahmed (ed.) *The Invention of Somalia* (Trenton NJ: Red Sea Press).

Besteman, C. & Cassanelli, L. (eds) (2000) *The Struggle for Land in Southern Somalia: The War Behind the War* (London: Haan).

Bixi, Adam, J. (2001) 'Building from the Bottom Up: Basic Institutions of Local Governance', in *Rebuilding Somalia: Issues and Possibilities for Puntland*, War Torn Societies Project (WSP) Somali Programme (London: Haan Associates & WSP).

Boyd, Monica (1987) *Immigrant Women in Canada: Profiles and Policies* (Ottawa: Research Division, Immigration Canada and Status of Women Canada).

Bradbury, Mark (1993) *The Somali Conflict. Prospects for Peace*, Oxfam research paper No.9 (Oxford: Oxfam).

—— (1994) 'The Politics of Vulnerability, Development and Conflict: Exploring the Issues with Reference to Somalia and Somaliland', unpublished thesis for the School of Public Policy, University of Birmingham.

—— (1997) *Somaliland Country Report* (London: CIIR).

—— (2002) 'Somalia: The Aftermath of September 11th and the War on Terrorism', unpublished paper for Oxfam GB.

Bradbury, Mark, Dr Adan Y. Abokor & A. Haroon (2003) 'Choosing Politics over Violence: Multi-party Elections in Somaliland', *Review of African Political Economy* (forthcoming).

Brons, Maria H. (2001) *Society, Security, Sovereignty and the State in Somalia. From Statelessness to Statelessness?* (The Netherlands: International Books).

Brons, Maria & Amina M. Warsame (2003) 'Empowerment after Return: Negaad Women in Somaliland', unpublished paper.

Bryden, M. and Steiner, M. (1998) *Somalia Between Peace and War: Somali Women on the Eve of the 21st Century*, African Women for Peace Series (Nairobi: UNIFEM).

Cairns, Alan C. (1992) *Charter vs Federalism: The Dilemma of Constitutional Reform* (Montreal: McGill-Queen's University Press).

Cawl, Faraax (1981) *Ignorance is the Enemy of Love* (London: Zed Press).

CIIR/ICD (1997) 'Somali Conflict and Peace: Perspectives of Somali Women', unpublished report (London: CIIR).

CIIR/ICD (2003) *Multiparty Local Government Elections in Somaliland December 2002* (London: CIIR) www.ciir.org

CIIR/ICD & Amnesty International (1997) *Human Rights in Somaliland: Awareness and Action* (London: CIIR).

Coalition Against Trafficking in Women (1997) *Coalition Report*, Vol.4, No.1.
Dualeh Abdulla, Raqiya Haji (1982) *Sisters in Affliction. Circumcision and Infibulation of Women in Africa* (London: Zed Press).
Ethnocultural Data Base (1993) *Ethnic origins – 1991 Census Update* (Toronto: Policy Services Branch, Ministry of Citizens).
Farah, Ahmed Yusuf (2001) 'Somalia: Modern History and the End of the 1990s', in *Rebuilding Somalia: Issues and Possibilities for Puntland*, War Torn Societies Project (WSP) Somali Programme (London: Haan Associates & WSP)
Farah, Nuruddin (2000) *Yesterday, Tomorrow. Voices from the Somali Diaspora 2000* (London: Cassell).
Giama, Safia (2000) *Caring for our Children. The Somali Tradition* (New York: UNICEF).
Hanafi, Ahmed (1993) 'Family Problems', *INSCAN*, Vol.7 No.2.
Hassan, Dahabo Farah, Amina H. Adan & Amina Mohamoud Warsame (1995) 'Somalia: Poetry as Resistance Against Colonialism and Patriarchy', in Saskia Wieringa (ed.) *Subversive Women: Historical Experiences of Gender and Resistance* (London: Zed Books).
Kapteijns, Lidwien (1994) 'Women in the Crisis of Communal Identity: The Cultural Construction of Gender in Somali History', in I. Ahmed Samatar (ed.) *The Somali Challenge* (Boulder: Westview Press).
Kassim, Mohamed M. (1995) 'Aspects of the Benadir Cultural History: The Case of the Bravan Ulama', in Ali Jimale Ahmed (ed.) *The Invention of Somalia* (Trenton NJ: Red Sea Press).
Lewis, I.M. (1961) *A Pastoral Democracy: A Study of Pastoralism and Politics among the Northern Somali of the Horn of Africa* (Oxford: Oxford University Press).
—— (1962) *Marriage and Family in Northern Somaliland* (Kampala: University of Glasgow and East African Institute of Social research).
—— (1994) *Blood and Bone: The Call of Kinship in Somali Society* (Trenton NJ: Red Sea Press).
—— (2002) *A Modern History of the Somali* (Ohio: James Currey).
McGowan, Sharon (1982) *Immigrant Women in Canada: A Resource Handbook for Action* (Vancouver: Task Force on Immigrant Women).
Meintjes, S., Pillay, A. & Turshen, M. (eds) (2001) *The Aftermath – Women in Post-Conflict Transformation* (London: Zed Books).
Menkhaus, Kenneth (1996) 'From Feast to Famine: Land and the State in Somalia's Lower Jubba Valley', in Catherine Besteman & Lee Cassannelli (eds) *The Struggle for Land in Southern Somalia. The War Behind the War* (Boulder: Westview Press).
Minority Rights (1997) *War: The Impact on Minority and Indigenous Children* (London: MRG).
Mohamed, Hamdi S. (1997) 'The Somali Refugee Women's Experience in Kenyan Refugee Camps and their Plight in Canada', Hussein M.

Adam & Richard Ford (eds) *Mending Rips in the Sky: Options for Somali Communities in the 21st Century* (Trenton NJ: Red Sea Press).

Mohamed, Mohamed Abdi (1997) 'Somali Kinship and Relations Derived From it' in Hussein M. Adam & Richard Ford (eds) *Mending Rips in the Sky: Options for Somali Communities in the 21st Century* (Trenton NJ: Red Sea Press).

Moser, C. and Clark, F. (eds) (2001) *Victims, Perpetrators or Actors? Gender, Armed Conflict and Political Violence* (London: Zed Books).

Mukhtar, Mohamed Haji (1996) 'The Plight of the Agro-pastoral Society of Somalia', *Review of African Political Economy*, No.70: 543–53.

Musse, Fowzia (1993) *Women Victims of Violence. Report on Refugee Camps in Kenya*, United Nations High Commission for Refugees internal document (Nairobi: UNHCR).

Natsios, Andrew S. (1997) 'Humanitarian Relief in Somalia: The Economics of Chaos', in Walter Clarke & Jeffrey Herbst (eds) *Learning from Somalia. The Lessons of Armed Humanitarian Intervention* (Boulder: Westview Press).

Nur, Ibrahim (2002) 'Somalia Case Study', *Gender Sensitive Programme Design and Planning in Conflict-Affected Situations, Annex 5* (London: ACORD, unpublished).

Nyakabwa, Kabahenda, and Caroline Lavoie (1995) 'Sexual Violence Against Women Refugees in the Horn of Africa', *African Woman*, March/September.

Rehn, E. & Sirleaf, E.J. (2002) *Progress of the World's Women 2002 Vol 1, Women, War and Peace: The Independent Experts' Assessment* (New York: UNIFEM).

Sahnoun, Mohamed (1994) *Somalia: The Missed Opportunities* (Washington, DC: US Institute of Peace Press).

Samatar, Ahmed I. (1985) 'Underdevelopment in Somalia: Dictatorship Without Hegemony', *Africa Today*, 32, No.3: 23–40.

Save the Children Fund (1993) *First Steps to Recovery: Somaliland Household Survey* (Hargeisa: SCF).

Simons, Anna (1995) *Networks of Dissolution: Somalia Undone* (Boulder: Westview Press).

Somali Delegation of the International Committee of the Red Cross (1997) *Spared from the Spear. Traditional Somali Behaviour in Warfare* (Nairobi: ICRC/SRCS)

Tompkins, Tamara L. (1995) 'Prosecuting Rape as a War Crime: Speaking the Unspeakable', *Notre Dame Law Review*, Vol.70: 4.

UNDOS (1997) *Studies on Governance 1, Lower Shabelle Region* (Nairobi: UNDOS).

United Nations Children's Fund (1998) *Somalia. Situation of Women and Children Report 1997/8* (Nairobi: UNICEF Somalia).

United Nations Development Programme (2002) *Somalia Human Development Report 2001* (Nairobi: UNDP).

Vetaid (1997) *Pastoralism and Sedentarisation in Waqoyi Galbeed Region, Somaliland*, a report for Oxfam (Edinburgh: Vetaid).
de Waal, Alex (ed.) (2002) *Demilitarizing the Mind: African Agendas for Peace and Security* (New Jersey: Justice Africa/Africa World Press Inc.).
Wandera, Marie (1995) 'The Unheeded Cry. Refugees and Sexual Violence: A Gender Analysis of Sexual Violence and Somali Women Refugees in Kenya' (Norwich: University of East Anglia, unpublished dissertation).
Warsame, Amina M. (2001) *Queens Without Crowns. Somaliland Women's Changing Roles and Peace Building*, Horn of Africa Series 4 (Kenya: Life & Peace Institute/Somaliland Women's Research and Action Group).
—— (1997) 'The Impact of the Civil War on Pastoralists, Especially Women and Children' (The Hague: NOVIB/Institute of Social Studies, unpublished thesis).
—— (1987) 'Moving to the Cities: Somali Women's Quest for Economic Independence', unpublished MA thesis (The Hague: Institute of Social Studies).
Warsame, Faiza (2001) 'The Role of Women in Rebuilding Puntland', *Rebuilding Somalia: Issues and Possibilities for Puntland*, War Torn Societies Project (WSP), Somali Programme (London: Haan Associates & WSP).
Wood, Nancy (1993) 'Immigration: A Reluctant Welcome', *Maclean's*, Vol.105, No.101.

The Catholic Institute for International Relations (CIIR) is an international development agency that works for the eradication of poverty and an end to injustice. We work with people of all faiths and none. In some countries, CIIR is known as International Cooperation for Development (ICD).

Unit 3, Canonbury Yard
190a New North Road
London N1 7BJ

Tel: 020 7354 0883
Fax: 020 7359 0017 (Fax)

www.ciir.org

Index

Compiled by Sue Carlton